Black Box Voting
Ballot Tampering in the 21st Century

By Bev Harris
with David Allen

Edited by Lex Alexander
Cover Art by Brad Guigar

Plan Nine Publishing

Plan Nine Publishing

1237 Elon Place.
High Point, NC 27263
336.454.7766
www.plan9.org

Black Box Voting: Ballot Tampering in the 21st Century is an original publication of Bev Harris and is published by Plan Nine Publishing

Contents © 2003 by Bev Harris
ISBN 1-929462-45-X
First Printing December 2003

www.blackboxvoting.org

Printed in the USA

Dedication

First of all, thank you, Lord.

I dedicate this work to my husband, Sonny, my rock and my mentor, who has tolerated being ignored and bored and galled by this thing every day for a year and without fail, has stood fast with affection and support and encouragement. He must be nuts.

And to my father, who fought and took a hit in Germany, who lived through Hitler and saw first-hand what can happen when a country gets suckered out of democracy. And to my sweet mother, whose ancestors hosted a stop on the Underground Railroad, who gets that disapproving look on her face when people don't do the right thing.

And, to the kids, Megan and CJ and David IV and, of course, Casey, who supplied me with constant encouragement and located some hackers to provide a point of view. And Erika, the nosiest child on Earth, who grew up to become a reporter for a major news outlet, for telling me, "Mom, that is not a story. You have to prove it." And when I did prove it, for saying, "This is good, Mom, but it's B-section. Get some more if you want it on A-1."

Black Box Voting: *Any voting system in which the mechanisms for recording and/or tabulating the vote are hidden from the voter, and/or the mechanisms lacks a tangible record of the vote cast.*

— David Allen

Introduction

When we started digging around on this story, we expected to find the odd body part or two. Little did we know we were digging in a graveyard. Suddenly, the dead bodies were piling up so fast that everyone was saying, "Enough, enough, we can't take any more!"

This book was originally designed to be a handy little activism tool, an easy-to-understand introduction to the concept of electronic voting risks. It was to contain a history, interviews and a discussion of theoretical vote-rigging. But as we were plugging along, researching the subject, it got a little too real — even for us.

C'mon over. No time to waste. We have a democracy to defend.

Bev Harris
David Allen

Table of Contents

1
I Will Vote
And no one's gonna stop me

Anthony Dudly, a mulatto from Lee's Mill, North Carolina, believed that he was undereducated. He had a vision in mind for his children: They would become educated — all of them — and one day they would vote.

His country was struggling to recover from a war that had ripped the South from the North, forcibly rejoined them and led to the Emancipation Proclamation. Now it was trying to decide what to do about voting rights for freed black citizens. Reconstruction Acts ordered voting rights for African-Americans in the South but not the North. The border states wanted nothing to do with black voters.

After the Fifteenth Amendment, guaranteeing black suffrage in all states, was ratified on March 30, 1870, Anthony figured all that remained was to make sure his children got an education.

Anthony's children learned to read and write so well that they looked up the traditional spelling of their own name and changed it to "Dudley," and they also discovered that voting was not as guaranteed as the Constitution promised.

Politicians clashed over the rights of former slaves. Vigilante groups like the Ku Klux Klan found ways to prevent black citizens from voting. Will Dudley, one of Anthony's children, vowed that *his* children would go to college, and by golly, they were going to *vote*.

Will was not an affluent man, but he was a man of conviction, and all nine of his children went to college. Eight of them got their degrees. Will's third child, David, noticed something that caused him to put college life on hold. Around election time in Greensboro, North Carolina, black folks had become so intimidated that they often just locked the door and stayed home on Election Day. Even registering to vote could get you on the "list," and you might get a visit in the middle of the night.

A singular goal took over David's life, and he dropped out of college to drive all over North Carolina, persuading African-Americans to vote.

"We must have the courage to exercise this right," he said. "If we don't vote, we can never truly be a free people." David preached voting and the value of a good education until the day he died.

Jerome Dudley was David's youngest son, and he became the most pissed-off Dudley when it came to voting. It was 1964, nearly 100 years since Anthony had pinned his hopes on the Fifteenth Amendment, and people still were being cheated out of their votes.

The cheating took various forms. Sometimes "challengers" were posted at the voting locations, demanding answers to questions like, "Who was the 29th president of the United States?" before allowing citizens to vote. Sometimes you'd get into the polling place and a poll worker would tell you to step aside and let the "regular Americans" vote.

Jerome became student body president at North Carolina A&T State University, leading demonstrations to integrate schools and fighting for voting rights.

It was in this climate that Jerome's nephew was raised. Sonny Dudley spent his younger years projecting his voice in community theater; when he becomes passionate about a topic, he bellows so dramatically that he shocks everyone.

"I will vote for who I want, and no one's gonna stop me," he announced. He said it loud and said it proud, and then Sonny cast his very first vote, for Eldridge Cleaver.

This is the man I married, now 53 years old, a great, gentle bear of a family man.

We watched the bizarre 2000 presidential election together, and while I ranted about the disenfranchisement of the Florida voters, Sonny just sat there with a quizzical look.

"But look what they are doing!" I said. "These are violations of their right to vote!"

"Oh, they've always done that," he said quietly. "You just notice it because now they're playing games with the white folks, too. How's it feel?"

Not too good.

Two years later, something made me stay up all night.

"I just got curious," I told Sonny. "There's this article by a writer named Lynn Landes that says no one knows who owns the voting-machine companies. I did some research and found out that one of the owners is a Republican senator who is running for office right now. Does that seem right?"

"Heck, no!"

So I wrote it up and and posted it on my Web site, along with corporate papers and financial documents. A few days later I got a certified letter from lawyers for Election Systems and Software (ES&S), demanding that I remove information about ES&S ownership from my Web site.

Well, yikes! Does *this* seem right?

Heck, no, so I sent copies of the ES&S cease-and-desist letter to 3,000 reporters. Then it occurred to me that it might be a good idea to mention it to my husband.

"We can't afford a lawyer, you know," I said. "We might lose the house. Maybe I shouldn't have done that."

"It was Christmas," said Sonny, "and my son David was six months old." He speaks slowly and with great flourish, and it gets me impatient when he goes off on these tangents. "I was so broke that all I had in the refrigerator was a jar of pickles." He added a long pause for effect. "I went out in the back yard and cut a branch off a tree and decorated it." His voice softened. "Now what's the problem?"

He stood up, towering over me.

"My people *died* for the right to vote," he boomed. "I will vote for who I want, and *no one's* gonna stop me."

But I have a question: Can we trust these machines to let us vote for whom we want?

2
Can We Trust These Machines?

In the Alabama 2002 general election, machines made by Election Systems and Software (ES&S) flipped the governor's race. Six thousand three hundred Baldwin County electronic votes mysteriously disappeared after polls had closed and everyone had gone home. Democrat Don Siegelman's victory was handed to Republican Bob Riley, and the recount Siegelman requested was denied. Six months after the election, the vendor still shrugged. "Something happened. I don't have enough intelligence to say exactly what," said Mark Kelley of ES&S. [1]

When I began researching this story in October 2002, the media was reporting that electronic voting machines are fun and speedy, but I looked in vain for articles reporting that they are accurate. I discovered four magic words, "voting machines and glitch," which, when entered into the DJInteractive.com [2] search engine, yielded a shocking result: A staggering pile of miscounts was accumulating. These were reported locally but had never been compiled in a single place, so reporters were missing a disturbing pattern.

I published a compendium of 56 documented cases in which voting machines gotten it wrong.

How do voting machine makers respond to these reports? With shrugs. They indicate that their miscounts are nothing to be concerned about. One of their favorite phrases is: "It didn't change the result."

Except, of course, when it did:

In the 2002 general election, a computer miscount overturned the House District 11 result in Wayne County, North Carolina. Incorrect programming caused machines to skip over several thousand party-line votes, both Republican and Democratic. Fixing the error turned up 5,500 more votes and reversed the election for state representative. [3]

This crushing defeat never happened. Voting machines failed to tally "yes" votes on the 2002 school bond issue in Gretna, Nebraska. This error gave the false impression that the measure had failed miserably, but it actually passed by a 2-to-1 margin. Responsibility for the errors was attributed to ES&S, the Omaha company that had provided the ballots and the machines. [4]

According to the *Chicago Tribune*, "It was like being queen for a day — but only for 12 hours," said Richard Miholic, a losing Republican candidate for alderman who was told that he had won a Lake County, Illinois, primary election. He was among 15 people in four races affected by an ES&S vote-counting foul-up in the Chicago area. [5]

An Orange County, California, election computer made a 100 percent error during the April 1998 school bond referendum. The Registrar of Voters Office initially announced that the bond issue had lost by a wide margin; in fact, it was supported by a majority of the ballots cast. The error was attributed to a programmer's reversing the "yes" and "no" answers in the software used to count the votes. [6]

A computer program that was specially enhanced to speed the November 1993 Kane County, Illinois, election results to a waiting public did just that — unfortunately, it sped the wrong data. Voting totals for a dozen Illinois races were incomplete, and in one case they suggested that a local referendum proposal had lost when it actually had been approved. For some reason, software that had worked earlier without a hitch had waited until election night to omit eight precincts in the tally. [7]

A squeaker — no, a landslide — oops, we reversed the totals — and about those absentee votes, make that 72-19, not 44-47. Software programming errors, sorry. Oh, and reverse that election, we announced the wrong winner. In the 2002 Clay County, Kansas, commissioner primary, voting machines said Jerry Mayo ran a close race but lost, garnering 48 percent of the vote, but a hand recount revealed Mayo had won by a landslide, receiving 76 percent of the vote. [8]

Apparently voting machine miscounts have been taking place for some time. In a 1971 race in Las Vegas, Nevada, machines declared Democrat Arthur Espinoza to be the winner of a seat on the city assembly, but Republican Hal Smith challenged the election when he determined that some votes had not been counted because of a faulty voting machine. After unrecorded votes were tallied, Smith was declared the winner. [9]

The excuses given for these miscounts are just as flawed as the election results themselves. Vendors have learned that reporters and election workers will believe pretty much anything, as long as it sounds high-tech. They blame incorrect vote counts on "a bad chip" or "a faulty memory card," but defective chips and bad memory cards have very different symptoms. They don't function at all, or they spit out nonsensical data.

In the November 2002 general election in Scurry County, Texas, poll workers got suspicious about a landslide victory for two Republican commissioner candidates. Told that a "bad chip" was to blame, they had a new computer chip flown in and also counted the votes by hand — and found out that Democrats actually had won by wide margins, overturning the election. [10]

We usually don't get an explanation for these miscounts. In 1986 the wrong candidate was declared the winner in Georgia. Incumbent Democrat Donn Peevy was running for state senator in District 48. The machines said he lost the election. After an investigation revealed that a Republican elections official had kept uncounted ballots in the trunk of his car, officials also admitted that a computerized voting program had miscounted. Peevy insisted on a recount. According to the *Atlanta Journal-Constitution*: "When the count finished around 1 a.m., they [the elections board] walked into a room and shut the door," recalls Peevy. "When they came out, they said, 'Mr. Peevy, you won.' That was it. They never apologized. They never explained." [11]

In a Seminole Nation election held in Oklahoma in August 1997, electronic voting machines gave the election to the wrong candidates twice. The private company hired to handle the election announced results for tribal chief and assistant chief, then decided that its computer had counted the absentee ballots twice. So the company posted a second set of results. Tribal officials then counted the votes by hand, producing yet a third, and this time official, set of results. A different set of candidates moved on to the runoff election each time. [12]

If you insist on the right to vote for whom you want (and no one's gonna stop you), does it make a difference if misprogramming, rather than a human being, forces you to vote for someone you *don't* want?

News reports often explain miscounts as "software programming errors," with no follow-up and certainly no outrage. Yet incorrect programming is more insidious than Mad Myrtle secretly stuffing the ballot box. At least when we vote on paper ballots, hand counted, we can hold someone accountable. We don't even know the names of our voting machine programmers.

A software programming error gave the election to the wrong candidate in November 1999 in Onondaga County, New York. Bob Faulkner, a political newcomer, went to bed on election night confident he had helped complete a Republican sweep of three open council seats. But after Onondaga County Board of Elections staffers rechecked the totals, Faulkner had lost to Democratic incumbent Elaine Lytel. Just a few hours later, election officials discovered that a software programming error had given too many absentee ballot votes to Lytel. Faulkner took the lead. [13]

Akron, Ohio, discovered its votes got scrambled in its December 1997 election. It was announced that Ed Repp had won the election — no, cancel that, a programming error was discovered — Repp actually lost. (Look! Twins!) Another error in the same election resulted in incorrect vote totals for the Portage County Board election. (Make that triplets.) Turns out the bond referendum results were wrong, too. [14]

In a 1998 Salt Lake City election, 1,413 votes never showed up in the total. A programming error caused a batch of ballots not to count, even though they had been run through the machine like all the others. When the 1,413 missing votes were counted, they reversed the election. [15]

* * * * *

Voting machine vendors claim these things are amazingly accurate. Bob Urosevich, who has headed three different voting machine companies under five different corporate names, said in 1990 that his company's optical-scan machines had an error rate of only "one-thousandth of 1 percent." [16]

At that time, Urosevich was with ES&S (then called American Information Systems). Recently, the same Urosevich (now president of Diebold Election Systems, formerly called Global Election Systems) gave an even more glowing endorsement of his company's touch-screen accuracy.

"Considering the magnitude of these elections, which includes more than 870,000 registered voters within the four Maryland counties, we are very pleased with the results as every single vote was accurately counted," he said. [17]

When Chuck Hagel accepted his position as chairman of American Information Systems, he offered a rousing endorsement: "The AIS system is 99.99 percent accurate," he assured us.[18]

But do these claims hold up?

According to *The Wall Street Journal*, in the 2000 general election an optical-scan machine in Allamakee County, Iowa, was fed 300 ballots and reported 4 million votes. The county auditor tried the machine again but got the same result. Eventually, the machine's manufacturer, ES&S, agreed to have replacement equipment sent. Republicans had hoped that the tiny but heavily Republican county would tip the scales in George W. Bush's favor, but tipping it by almost four million votes attracted national attention.

"We don't have four million voters in the state of Iowa," said Bill Roe Jr., county auditor.

Todd Urosevich of ES&S said, "You are going to have some failures." [19]

November 2003: Boone County, Indiana, officials wanted to know why their MicroVote machines counted 144,000 votes cast when only 5,352 existed.

"I about had a heart attack," said County Clerk Lisa Garofolo, according to the *Indianapolis Star*. "Believe me, there was nobody more shook up than I was." [20]

If you are an elections official, I hope this litany gives you pause. Do you really need this kind of stress?

With computerized voting, the certified and sworn officials step aside and let technicians, and sometimes the county computer guy, tell us the election results. The Boone County information technology director and a few MicroVote techs "fixed the problem." (For voting, I prefer the term "corrected.")

Better than a pregnant chad — these machines can actually give birth.

In the 1996 McLennan County, Texas, Republican primary runoff, one precinct tallied about 800 votes, although only 500 ballots had been ordered. "It's a mystery," declared Elections Administrator Linda Lewis. Like detectives on the Orient Express, officials pointed fingers at one suspected explanation after another. One particular machine may have been the problem, Lewis said. That is, the miscounted votes were scattered throughout the precincts with no one area being miscounted more than another, Lewis also explained. Wait — some ballots may have been counted more than once, almost doubling the number of votes actually cast. Aha! That could explain it. (Er ... excuse me, exactly *which* ballots were counted twice?)

"We don't think it's serious enough to throw out the election," said county Republican Party Chairman M.A. Taylor. Error size: 60 percent. [21]

Here's a scorching little 66 percent error rate: Eight hundred twenty-six votes in one Tucson, Arizona-area precinct simply evaporated, remaining unaccounted for a month after the 1994 general election. No recount appears to have been done, even though two-thirds of voters did not get their votes counted. Election officials said the vanishing votes were the result of a faulty computer program. Apparently, the software programming error and the person who caused it are still at large. [22]

Some voters aren't so sure that *every single vote* was accurately counted during the 2002 general election in Maryland.

According to the *Washington Times*, Kevin West of Upper Marlboro, who voted at the St. Thomas Church in Croom, said, "I pushed a Republican ticket for governor and his name disappeared. Then the Democrat's name got an 'X' put in it." [23]

No one will ever know whether the Maryland machines counted correctly because the new Diebold touch-screen system is unauditable.

Tom Eschberger became a vice president of ES&S not long after he accepted an immunity deal for cooperating with prosecutors in a case against Arkansas Secretary of State Bill McCuen, who pleaded guilty to taking kickbacks and bribes in a scheme related to computerized voting systems. [24]

Eschberger reported that a test conducted on a malfunctioning machine and its software in the 1998 general election in Honolulu, Hawaii, showed the machine worked normally. He said the company did not know that the machine wasn't functioning properly until the Supreme Court ordered a recount, when a second test on the same machine detected that it wasn't counting properly.

"But again, in all fairness, there were 7,000 machines in Venezuela and 500 machines in Dallas that did not have problems," he said. [25]

Really?

Dallas, Texas: A software programming error caused Dallas County, Texas's new, $3.8 million high-tech ballot system to miss 41,015 votes during the November 1998 election. The system refused to count votes from 98 precincts, telling itself they already had been counted. Operators and election officials didn't realize they had a problem until after they'd released "final" totals that omitted one in eight votes.

In one of the nonsensical answers that we see so often from vendors, ES&S assured us that votes were never lost, just uncounted.

The company took responsibility and was trying to find two apparently unrelated software bugs, one that mistakenly indicated precinct votes were in when they weren't, and another that forgot to include 8,400 mail-in ballots in the final tally. Democrats were livid and suspicious, but Tom Eschberger said, "What we had was a speed bump along the way." [26]

Caracas, Venezuela: In May 2000, Venezuela's highest court suspended elections because of problems with the vote tabulation for the national election. Venezuela sent an air force jet to Omaha to fetch experts from ES&S in a last-ditch effort to fix the problem. Dozens of protesters chanted, "Gringos get out!" at ES&S technicians. Venezuelan President Hugo Chavez accused ES&S of trying to destabilize the country's electoral process. Chavez asked for help from the U.S. government because, he said, the U.S. had recommended ES&S. [27]

* * * * *

Some people, when you give them the short but horrifying version of the electronic voting issue, insist on minimizing the problem. You tell them about an election that lost 25 percent of its votes, and they say, "That's just an isolated incident." When you add that another election had a 100 percent error, they call it a "glitch." When you tell them a voting machine was videotaped recording votes for the opposite candidate than the one selected, they say, "There are problems in every election."

No. We are not talking about a few minor glitches. These are real miscounts by voting machines, which took place in real elections. Almost all of them were caused by incorrect programming, whether by accident or by design. And if you run into anyone who thinks we are hallucinating these problems, hand them the footnote section so they can examine sources and look them up themselves.

For the third time in as many elections, Pima County, Arizona, found errors in its tallies. The computers recorded no votes for 24 precincts in the 1998 general election, but voter rolls showed thousands had voted at those polling places. Pima was using Global Election Systems machines, which now are sold under the Diebold company name. [28]

Officials in Broward County, Florida, had said that all the precincts were included in the Nov. 5, 2002, election and that the new, unauditable ES&S touch-screen machines had counted the vote without a major hitch. The next day, the County Elections Office discovered 103,222 votes had not been counted.

Allow me to shed some perspective on this. Do you remember when we got excited about a missing ballot box found in a Dade County, Florida, church day-care center in the 2000 presidential election? [29] One hundred and three thousand uncounted votes represents about 1,000 ballot boxes. Broward Deputy Elections Supervisor Joe Cotter called the mistake "a minor software thing." [30]

If you are a candidate, you know that participating even in a small election means raising or borrowing money, passing out flyers, going door to door and standing in the rain at various events. How do you feel if your vote is not counted accurately?

"I knew something was wrong when I looked up the results in my own precinct and it showed zero votes," said Illinois Democrat Rafael Rivera, according to the *Chicago Tribune*. "I said, 'Wait a minute. I know I voted for myself.'"

The problem cropped up during the Lake County, Illinois, election held April 1, 2003. Clerk Willard Helander blamed the problem on ES&S, the Omaha company in charge of operating Waukegan's optical-scan voting machines. Rivera said he felt as if he were living an episode of *The Twilight Zone*. No votes showed up for him, not even his own.

"It felt like a nightmare," he said. [31]

Is this not alarming? These voting systems have miscounted our votes, flipping elections even when they are not particularly close. Even more alarming: We have no idea how many miscounts go unnoticed.

No legal authority permits privately employed technicians — often temporary workers — who are not sworn and don't work for the elections office, who sometimes are not even residents of the U.S., to determine the results of the election when there are discrepancies. Yet they do.

Ten days after the November 2002 election, Richard Romero, a Bernalillo County, New Mexico, Democrat, noticed that 48,000 people had voted early on unauditable Sequoia touch-screen computers, but only 36,000 votes had been tallied — a 25 percent error. Sequoia vice president Howard Cramer apologized for not mentioning that the same problem had happened before in Clark County, Nevada. A "software patch" was installed (more on that risky procedure later), and Sequoia technicians in Denver *e-mailed* the "correct" results. [32]

Not only did Cramer fail to mention to Bernalillo County that the problem had happened before in Nevada — just four months later, Sequoia salespersons also failed to mention it while making a sales presentation to Santa Clara County, California. A Santa Clara official tried to jog their memory. According to the minutes of this meeting, [33] "Supervisor McHugh asked one of the vendors about a statistic saying there was a 25 percent error rate. ... No one knew where this number came from and Sequoia said it was incorrect."

That meeting was held Feb. 11, 2003. Just 20 days before, in Snohomish County, Washington, at a meeting called because Sequoia optical-scan machines had failed to record 21 percent of the absentee votes,[34] I asked about the 25 percent error in Bernalillo County. The Sequoia representative was well aware of the problem, replying quickly that *that* 25 percent error was caused by something quite different from *this* 21 percent problem. OK. *Nothing to see here — move along.*

* * * * *

Sequoia's failure to disclose a miscount when asked about it during a sales meeting really got me wondering: How often do voting companies lie about known errors when they are making sales presentations?

Not often, it turns out. They don't have to lie — because our election officials *don't ask*! That's right. When deciding to buy voting machines, our representatives don't ask whether the machines count accurately. And only occasionally does anyone bother to ask whether the machines can be tampered with. Here's what I mean:

Marion County, Indiana Voting Technology Task Force, Meeting Minutes July 30, 1999

ES&S, Global Election Systems, MicroVote. Mr. Cockrum asked a series of questions to each vendor.

How do you recommend instruction of voters to become familiar with your system?

How many machines per voter/precinct?

Could your system handle split precincts?

Could your systems handle school board elections?

Does your system allow for party crossover voting?

What is the recount capability?

Is your system tamper proof?

Can your system be leased or does it need to be purchased?

What is the percentage of availability of spare machines?

What are the advantages?

There being no further business before the Voting Technology Task Force, Chairwoman Grant adjourned the meeting.

* * * * *

We know the machines have miscounted elections, but could this happen without being discovered?

In Seattle, a malfunction caused voting-machine computers to lose more than 14,000 votes during the November 1990 election. Individual ballots were counted but not the votes contained on them. The computer program didn't catch the problem, nor did any of the election officials. A Democratic candidate happened to notice the discrepancy after the election was over, and he demanded an investigation.

"It was mechanical or electric malfunction with the card reader," said Bob Bruce, then superintendent of elections for King County. "We'd lost the 14,000 votes. We've got them back now. Hallelujah! The prodigal votes have come back. Now we have to make sure we don't have too many votes." [35]

At least two voting machine miscounts resulted in grand jury investigations. In Polk County, Florida, County Commissioner Marlene Duffy Young lost the election to Bruce Parker in November 1996 but regained the seat after a court-ordered hand recount. After the recount, county commissioners unanimously voted to ask for a grand jury probe. One witness was Todd Urosevich, a vice president with American Information Systems Inc. (now ES&S), the company that had sold the county its ballot-counting equipment. The machines had given the election to Parker, a Republican, but a hand recount revealed that Young, a Democrat, had won. Todd Urosevich said his machines were not responsible for the miscount. [36]

A grand jury was convened in Stanislaus County, California, to determine what caused computerized voting machines to misreport election results in the November 1998 election. The grand jury concluded that an ES&S computerized counting system miscounted the votes for three propositions. A hand recount of the ballots resulted in Measure A, a state proposition, being reversed: ES&S machines had reported that it had lost badly, but it had won. According to Karen Matthews, county clerk recorder and registrar of voters, the problem occurred because of a programming error. [37]

Who, exactly, must pay lawyers and court costs if errors made by a voting machine result in litigation? Is it the taxpayer?

If an elections official ruins an election — loses votes forever, or mishandles the voting so badly that no one can repair the error — we can fire that person. If an elections *machine* ruins an election, shouldn't we fire that voting system?

In Knoxville, Tennessee, a software programming error caused more than 40,000 votes cast during 15 days of early voting for the 1996 general election to be lumped together, instead of separating the vote tally into city and noncity ballots. Voters considered this programming error to be an outrage because it caused one of the ballot items to fail when it was voted on county-wide. [38]

In the October 16, 2001, Rock Hill, South Carolina, city election, voting machines were misprogrammed, skipping hundreds of votes cast. In a number of precincts, the ballot-counting software ignored votes for council members when they should have been included, causing omission of 11 percent of the votes cast for these races. In all, voting irregularities were found in seven of the city's 25 precincts. [39]

At its heart, our body of law is on the side of the voter. Our entire governing system is based on the sanctity of the vote. It is not excusable for votes to be counted improperly because of "programming errors." Almost all states have statutes that say something like this:

"If voting machines are to be used, they must count the vote *properly.*"

If a system is so complicated that programming errors become "inevitable" or "to be expected," the system must not be used. And yet the problems continue.

In Union County, Florida, a programming error caused machines to read 2,642 Democratic and Republican votes as entirely Republican in the September 2002 election. The vendor, ES&S, accepted responsibility for the programming error and paid for a hand recount. Unlike the new touch-screen systems, which eliminate voter-verified paper ballots, Union County retained a paper ballot. Thus, a recount was possible and Democratic votes could be identified. [40]

In Atlanta, Georgia, a software programming error caused some votes for Sharon Cooper, considered a "liberal Republican candidate," not to register in the July 1998 election. Cooper was running against conservative Republican Richard Daniel. According to news reports, the problem required "on-the-spot reprogramming." [41]

How can computerized vote-counting possibly be considered secure from tampering when "on-the-spot reprogramming" can be used to alter vote totals?

In November 2002, a voting machine was caught double-counting votes in South Dakota. The error was blamed on a "flawed chip." ES&S sent a replacement chip; voters demanded that the original chip be impounded and examined. Who was allowed to examine it? Citizens? (No.) Experts that we choose? (No.) ES&S? (That's it.) [42]

But they are tested and tested and tested again.

This is the official rebuttal when you ask whether machines can miscount. More on this testing later, but for now, suffice it to say that the ultimate invalidation of the testing a voting machine endures would be *a machine that can't count!* Election officials and voting machine companies can argue 'til they are blue in the face about the excellence of the certification process, but if the testing works, how did this happen: In Volusia County, Florida, during the 2000 presidential election, the Socialist Workers Party candidate received almost 10,000 votes — about half the number he received nationwide. Four thousand erroneous votes appeared for George W. Bush, and at the same time, presidential candidate Al Gore received *negative* 16,022 votes. [43]

I think we should pause for a moment to digest this last example. In fact, if an electronic voting system, in this case a Diebold optical-scan system, can register *minus* votes in sufficient quantity to cause a candidate for president of the United States to erroneously concede to his opponent, we should examine the situation in more detail, don't you agree? We'll revisit this episode in a later chapter.

* * * * *

Sometimes, machines are given a passing grade even when they fail their testing. Dan Spillane, a senior test engineer for the VoteHere touch-screen voting system, says he flagged more than 250 system-integrity errors, some of which were critical and could affect the way votes were counted — yet this system passed every level of certification without a hitch. Spillane claims he brought his concerns up to all levels of VoteHere management but was ignored. Just before the system went through certification testing, Spillane contends, the company fired him to prevent him from flagging the problems during certification. He filed a lawsuit for wrongful termination, [44] which was settled by VoteHere, with details kept confidential. [45]

According to the *Las Vegas Review-Journal*, a member of the Nevada Policy Research Institute's Advisory Council reports the following: "In July 1996, a public test to certify Clark County's Sequoia Pacific machine for early voting was conducted. During the test, a cartridge malfunctioned; also, the examiner had difficulty casting his vote. He had to vote 51 times rather than the designated 50, an option not afforded the voter should the machine malfunction in an actual election. In spite of these malfunctions, the machine was given certification — the equivalent of declaring it accurate, reliable and secure." (Clark County then trotted right out and bought the machines.) [46]

The testing didn't work here either: In Conroe, Texas, congressional candidate Van Brookshire wasn't worried when he looked at the vote tabulation and saw a zero next to his name for the 2002 primary. After all, he was unopposed in the District 2 primary and he assumed that the Montgomery County Elections Administrator's Office hadn't found it necessary to display his vote. He was surprised to learn the next day that a computer glitch had given all of his votes to U.S. Rep. Kevin Brady, who was unopposed for the nomination for another term in District 8. A retabulation was paid for by ES&S, the company that made the programming mistake. The mistake was undetected despite mandatory testing before and after early voting. [47]

What is supposed to happen in theory doesn't always happen in practice. In Tennessee, a computer snafu in the August 1998 Shelby County election temporarily stopped the vote count after generating wildly inaccurate results and forcing a second count that continued into the morning. State Sen. Roscoe Dixon huddled with other politicos around a single copy of the latest corrected election returns, which quickly became dog-eared and riddled with circles and "X"s.

"This system should have been checked, and it should have been known that the scanner couldn't read the cartridges," Dixon said. [48]

Here's another system they tested right before the election, but it miscounted anyway, flipping the election: Pamela Justice celebrated her re-election to the school board in Dysart, Arizona, in the March 1998 election. But the computer had failed to count 1,019 votes from one precinct. When those votes were added in, Justice lost the election to her opponent, Nancy Harrower.

"We did an accuracy test before election day and the computers worked fine," said Karen Osborne, county elections director. [49]

And if you're not yet convinced that our certification system doesn't work: A computer defect at the Oklahoma County State Election Board left more than a dozen state and county races in limbo during the 1996 general election. A final count was delayed until sometime the next morning while technicians installed new computer hardware.

Despite several trial runs with computers the week prior to the election, the problem didn't surface until 7:05 p.m. — five minutes after the election board attempted to begin its count. "That's what's puzzling about it," County Election Board Secretary Doug Sanderson said. "It's one of those deals where you can test it one minute and it's working fine, and you can test it the next and it's not."

Two hundred and sixty-seven precincts (and two close races) were involved.

"We could count it by hand, but I'm not going to do that," Sanderson said, as reported by the *Daily Oklahoman*. "We're just going to wait here until we can do it electronically, so there will be no question that the election's integrity was upheld." [50] Really.

Sometimes they omit testing key systems: The manufacturer of Baltimore's $6.5 million voting system took responsibility for the computer failures that delayed the November 1999 city election results and vowed to repay the city for overtime and related costs. Phil Foster, regional manager for Sequoia Pacific Voting Equipment Inc., said his company had neglected to update software in a computer that reads the election results. Although it tested some programs, the company did not test that part of the system before the election. Before Sequoia agreed to reimburse the city for the problems — a cost that election officials said could reach $10,000 — Mayor Kurt L. Schmoke had threatened a lawsuit against the company. [51]

After every election, you will hear this happy refrain: "The election went smoothly." More recently, as we have brought concerns to light, this has become: "Though some people expressed concerns about the voting machines, the election went without a hitch."

Here's the hitch: You won't discover miscounts until you do the audit, which does not take place on election night, and errors sometimes aren't identified until several days later, if at all.

Most errors are detected only when voter sign-in sheets are compared with vote tallies. Many of the errors listed in this chapter were found *only* because the number of votes cast did not match the number of voters who had signed in. But suppose 100 votes are cast, 55 for Mary and 45 for John, but the computer says you have 100 votes, 48 for Mary and 52 for John. John wins. How will we know the election was given to the wrong person if no one checks the paper ballots?

The California Institute of Technology and the Massachusetts Institute of Technology mobilized a team of computer scientists, human-factors engineers, mechanical engineers and social scientists to examine voting technology. Here are voting system error rates, as estimated by the Caltech/MIT Voting Technology Project report, issued in July 2001: [52]

Most lost votes — Congressional and gubernatorial races

1. Lever machines **7.6%** — 1.5% for presidential races
2. Touch-screen machines **5.9%** — 2.3% for presidential races
3. Punch card **4.7%** — 2.5% for presidential races
4. Optical scan **3.5%** — 1.5% for presidential races
5. Hand-counting **3.3%** — 1.8% for presidential races

The Caltech/MIT study omits three critical issues: programming errors, tampering and dirty politicking.

If we are going to use computerized systems, we need computer scientists to help us create safe voting systems. Dr. Rebecca Mercuri, now with Harvard University, and Dr. Peter Neumann, from SRI International Computer Science Laboratory, are among the best known computer scientists in the elections field and were the first to really investigate electronic voting systems. They were joined by Dr. Doug Jones, a computer scientist from the University of Iowa who became a member of the Iowa Board of Examiners for Voting Machines in 1994. For many years, these were the voices of reason in the mad dash to electronic voting. New faces have entered the fray within the last two years, but for more than a decade, much of the heavy lifting has been done by these three computer scientists.

They've done a stellar job, but computer scientists usually see this as a programming challenge, rather than an auditing problem or a decision about election procedures, and they tend to concentrate their attentions on touch-screen voting, though some of the most disturbing problems take place on optical-scan systems.

Because we have become over-reliant on input from this one type of expert, we have not adequately evaluated simpler, cheaper solutions, like going back to hand-counted paper ballots (perhaps using a computer as a printer, for legibility and accessibility).

Linda Franz, a voting integrity activist you'll meet later in this book, puts it more tactfully:

"Democracy builds from many pieces. We have an absolute need for accounting expertise, and part of the puzzle is the input of experts on good accounting practices. Computer scientists know the theory of plotting out the need before the design, and in current electronic voting systems, it doesn't look like the vendors have done much of that. How do we convince them that the system needs to be thought out with the input of experts in many fields?"

Current voting systems suffer from a very poor understanding of accounting — and make no mistake about it, counting the vote is a form of accounting. We also need better input from candidates and campaign managers, from historians, from legal and civil rights people, and from the officials who run the elections.

"I often see overgeneralization [believing that expertise in one area translates into wisdom in other domains] with top performers in advanced technical fields," says leadership psychologist Dr. Susan Battley, who troubleshoots for organizations such as JP Morgan Chase and Brookhaven National Laboratory. "In reality, when high achievers overlook fundamental differences in skill requirements, it courts not just failure, but disaster." [53]

We may have such a disaster with current auditing systems. We've been using inappropriate statistical models for auditing, and this model (random spot-checks of a tiny percentage of the ballots) has now become the law in many jurisdictions This can help catch random error, but a more robust procedure is needed to detect fraud.

November 2002, Comal County, Texas: A Texas-sized anomaly on ES&S machines was discovered when the uncanny coincidence came to light that three winning Republican candidates in a row tallied exactly 18,181 votes. It was called weird, but apparently no one thought it was weird enough to audit. [54] Comal County's experience shows why a simple, random, spot-check audit is insufficient.

Suppose you are an auditor but you must follow election audit rules. You are only allowed to spot check, and you can only look at 1 percent of the receipts. You see this:

$18,181 - Utilities
$18,181 - Advertising
$18,181 - Payroll

But you can't do anything about it, because according to the law, you can't audit any more. You have already looked at 1 percent of the receipts. If you try to pull the records on the $18,181 anomaly, party hacks object that you want to "audit and re-audit and then audit some more." A real audit allows you to look at any darned thing you want, even on a hunch, and when you spot an anomaly of any kind, you get to pull all the records.

1950s, Louisiana: Ivory tower, meet raw politics. When automated voting machines were brought into the state as a way to reduce election fraud, then-Gov. Earl Long said, "Gimme five (electoral) commissioners, and I'll make them voting machines sing 'Home Sweet Home.'" [55]

Actually, accountants for Las Vegas casinos have better expertise on fraud-prevention techniques than computer professors. Auditors and forensic accountants are never invited onto voting system task forces or to voting symposiums, nor were they called upon to testify when the Help America Vote Act, which prescribed new voting requirements, was being written. Hint, hint. Nudge.

July 1996, Clark County, Nevada: According to a *Las Vegas Review-Journal* article, a technician removed thousands of files from the tabulation sector of the program during the vote count "to speed up the reading of the count." Reconfiguring a computer program that affects the tabulation of votes is prohibited without prior state verification, but they did it anyway. [56] In a real audit, people don't get to remove part of the bookkeeping system, and in the real world, people don't always follow instructions.

November 2002, Miami, Florida: Fuzzy math in Miami? On November 10, the *Miami Herald* listed the following figures for the total votes cast at the Democrat-friendly Broward County Century Village precinct in the general election:

    1994: 7,515
    1998: 10,947
    2002: 4,179

Yet an accountant called Century Village and was told that its occupancy had remained stable (around 13,000 residents) since the complex had hit capacity in 1998. [57]

A spot-check audit, in this case, will achieve nothing. Because there is usually no provision in the law to allow an audit based on anomalies, all a fraudster had to do was figure out a way to delete a block of votes and cook the sign-in books. Impossible, you say? Here's a five-letter method: b-r-i-b-e.

* * * * *

When a human being handles a voting system, you'll see mistakes, but when a computer handles the voting, you'll see some complete boondoggles.

November 1998, Clearwater, Florida: The voting computer crashed on election night. Republicans who lost complained that the crash could have corrupted files, skewed data or lost votes. Tom McKeon, a county commissioner candidate, said, "There's no guarantee the votes went to the right candidate." Elections Supervisor Dot Ruggles said it was not the first time such a crash had occurred. [58]

March 2000, Shelby County, Tennessee: Computer problems halted the voting at all 19 of Shelby County's early-voting sites during the 2000 Republican presidential primary, forcing officials to use paper ballots (which were supposed to be provided by the voting machine company as a backup but were unavailable when needed). Election officials had to make voters wait in line or tell them to come back later. Because early voting turnout in this election was six times normal, this snafu affected about 13,000 voters. [59]

November 2000, Glenwood Springs, Colorado: At a special city council meeting held just after the election, Mayor Skramstad announced that the Garfield County Clerk and Recorder asked that he read a press release. It stated, "The Garfield County Clerk and Recorder wishes to inform the public that she is continuing to experience difficulty with the ES&S Inc. software utilized for tabulating election results. I will receive a corrected computer chip this evening. On Friday, November 10th … my office will utilize a new chip to count the ballots for Precinct 20 and re-tabulate the results … I anticipate this process will take most of the day. Thank you for your patience during this process. Signed, Mildred Alsdorf." [60]

Question: Did this new chip go through certification? Nope. The only one who knew what was on this chip was some guy in Omaha. What Mildred didn't realize when she accepted that chip was that she had just opened the door for any candidate to file a lawsuit against the county, ultimately paid for by you, the taxpayer, and guaranteed to produce a great deal of stress for Mildred, the County Clerk and Recorder.

November 2000, Allegheny County, Pennsylvania: City Councilwoman Valerie McDonald reported that machines in Pittsburgh's 12th and 13th wards and other predominantly black neighborhoods malfunctioned on Election Day. They began smoking and spitting out jammed and crumpled paper. Poll workers felt the machines had been intentionally programmed incorrectly and had been sabotaged. Whether or not there was sabotage, the spit-and-polish image so carefully crafted in election company press releases didn't seem to apply to the African-American precincts that day. Poll workers in the 12th and 13th wards waited hours for repairs, and voters who couldn't spend the day at the polling place were rendered politically voiceless. [61]

February 2000, Passaic, New Jersey: About 75 percent of the voting machines in the city of Passaic failed to work when the polls opened on Election Day, forcing an undetermined number of voters to use paper ballots during the morning. Independent consultant V. Thomas Mattia, a Philadelphia voting machine supervisor who later examined the machines, concluded the problem was due to sabotage, which led a Democratic candidate to refer the matter to the FBI.

For no discernable reason, Mattia later reversed himself.

"I believe that it was an oversight, and there was no fraud involved," Mattia stated in a letter.

Freeholder James Gallagher, who had referred the matter to the FBI based on Mattia's previous suspicions, said that he was surprised by the reversal and needed more information about why the expert had changed his mind. [62]

November 2002, Tangipahoa Parish, Louisiana: "I can't say every precinct had a problem, but the vast majority did," Tangipahoa Parish Clerk of Court John Dahmer said. He reported that at least 20 percent of the machines in his parish malfunctioned. "One percent might be acceptable, but we're not even close to that," Dahmer said. He said 15 employees worked to combat the malfunctions. [63]

November 2002, Maryland: Vote Republican (read "Democrat") — In Maryland, a software programming error on Diebold touch-screen machines upset a lot of voters when they saw a banner announcing "Democrat" at the top of their screen, no matter whom they voted for. [64]

November 2002, New Jersey: Forty-four of forty-six machines malfunctioned in Cherry Hill, New Jersey: Election workers had to turn away up to 100 early voters when it was discovered that 96 percent of the voting machines couldn't register votes for mayor, despite the machines' having been pretested and certified for use. [65]

November 2002, New Jersey: "What the hell do I do with this?" A bag full of something that looked like rolls of cash register tapes was handed to the Mays Landing County Clerk. A computer irregularity in a New Jersey vote-counting system caused three of five relay stations to fail, leaving a single county clerk holding the bag for a hand count. [66]

November 2002, Ascension Parish, Louisiana: An elections official gnashed his teeth as more than 200 machine malfunctions were called in. The Parish Clerk said his staff was on the road repairing machines from 5 a.m. to 9 p.m. In one case, a machine wasn't repaired until 12:30 a.m. Wednesday. "A mechanic would fix a machine, and before he could get back to the office, it would shut down again," Kermit "Hart" Bourque said. [67]

November 2002, Ohio: A voting machine malfunctioned with 12 of Crawford County's 67 precincts left to count. A backup vote-counting machine was found, but it also could not read the vote. Election workers piled into a car and headed to another county to tally their votes. [68]

November 2002, Pickens County, South Carolina: Pickens County couldn't get totals from two precincts because of computer problems. [69]

November 2002, Georgia: Fulton County election officials said that memory cards from 67 electronic voting machines had been misplaced, so ballots cast on those machines were left out of previously announced vote totals. Fifty-six cards, containing 2,180 ballots, were located, but 11 memory cards still were missing two days after the election. Bibb County and Glynn County each had one card missing after the initial vote count. When DeKalb County election officials went home early Wednesday morning, they were missing 10 cards. [70]

What is a memory card? It's a ballot box. Electronic ballot boxes for the Diebold machines used in Georgia are about the size of a credit card. With the new electronic voting systems, you can pocket a dozen ballot boxes at once, slip one up your sleeve or tote 67 ballot boxes around in your purse.

An interesting (and suspicious) anomaly appeared with these missing electronic ballot boxes. I interviewed a Georgia computer programmer named Roxanne Jekot for this book. When Jekot quizzed Dr. Brit Williams, official voting machine certifier for the state of Georgia, during an August 22, 2003, public meeting, Williams explained that the memory cards were not lost, but had inadvertently been left in the machines.

Really? Something appears to be missing in this explanation. The procedure in Georgia for transmitting electronic votes from Diebold touch-screens is as follows: If you have seven voting machines at a polling place, each one has a memory card which stores its votes. You take all seven cards and, one by one, put them into a single machine, which accumulates them and runs a report. When votes from all seven machines are accumulated, they are transmitted to the county tabulator. A printout of the accumulated results is run, and this is placed in an envelope with the memory cards. The envelope is then sealed, signed and delivered to the county.

Jekot raised this excellent question: If the votes are accumulated from all cards before transmitting to the county, this means all the votes would be transmitted as one batch. So why did 2,180 more votes show up when individual cards were "found" inside the machines?

I also have this question: If the procedure is to accumulate, print the report, place it into an envelope with cards, seal the envelope, sign it and then take it to the county, how is it that different people, at different polling places, forgot to do this 67 times in the same county?

Perhaps we should look into the Georgia election a little more.

* * * * *

November 2002, Nebraska — This example shows, I think, just how far we've deviated from the concept of fair and open election procedures. Paul Rosberg, the Nebraska Party candidate for governor, eagerly took advantage of a Nebraska law that lets candidates watch their votes being counted. He first was invited to watch an optical-scan machine, which had no counter on it, and then was taken into a private room, where he was allowed to watch a computer with a blank screen. So much for public counting of votes. [71]

* * * * *

"Take the rest of the examples out or put them in an appendix — this is just completely overwhelming," said an editor. So I did. All in all, I documented 100 of these examples and could have continued for another 100, had space allowed and our ability to tolerate this outrage permitted. See Appendix A for a continuing compendium.

3
Why We Need Disclosure of Owners

Elections In America – Assume Crooks Are In Control [1]
By Lynn Landes

"Only a few companies dominate the market for computer voting machines. Alarmingly, under U.S. federal law, no background checks are required on these companies or their employees. Felons and foreigners can, and do, own computer voting machine companies.

"Voting machine companies demand that clients sign 'proprietary' contracts to protect their trade secrets, which prohibits a thorough inspection of voting machines by outsiders.

"And, unbelievably, it appears that most election officials don't require paper ballots to back up or audit electronic election results. So far, lawsuits to allow complete access to inspect voting machines, or to require paper ballots so that recounts are possible ... have failed.

"As far as we know, some guy from Russia could be controlling the outcome of computerized elections in the United States."

* * * * *

This is the article that triggered my interest in voting machines. After all, how hard can it be to find out who owns these companies?

Chuck Hagel
Poster Boy for Conflict of Interest

He stunned them with his upsets. Nebraska Republican Chuck Hagel came from behind twice during his run for the U.S. Senate in 1996. Hagel, a clean-cut, crinkly-eyed, earnest-looking millionaire, had achieved an upset win in the primary against Republican Attorney General Don Stenberg, despite the fact that he was not well-known. According to CNN's *All Politics*,[2] "Hagel hoped he could make lightning strike twice" — and he did: Hagel then defeated popular Democratic Gov. Ben Nelson, who had led in the polls since the opening gun.

The *Washington Post* called Hagel's 1996 win "the major Republican upset in the November election."[3] Hagel swept all three congressional districts, becoming the first Republican to win a U.S. Senate seat in Nebraska in 24 years. "He won counties up and down the politically diverse Platte River Valley and topped it off with victories in Omaha and Lincoln," reported the *Hastings Tribune*. [4]

What the media didn't report is that Hagel's job, until two weeks before he announced his run for the Senate, was running the voting machine company whose machines would count his votes. Chuck Hagel had been chairman of American Information Systems ("AIS," now called ES&S) since July 1992.[5] He also took on the position of CEO when cofounder Bob Urosevich left in November 1993.[6]

Hagel owned stock in AIS Investors Inc., a group of investors in the voting machine company. While Hagel was running AIS, the company was building and programming the machines that would later count his votes. In March 1995, Hagel stepped down as chairman of AIS; on March 31, he announced his bid for U.S. Senate.[7]

When Hagel won what *Business Week* described as a "landslide upset,"[8] reporters might have written about the strange business of an upstart senator who ran his own voting machine company. They didn't because they didn't know about it: On Hagel's required personal disclosure documents, he omitted AIS. When asked to describe every position he had held, paid or unpaid, he mentioned his work as a banker and even listed his volunteer positions with the Mid-America chapter of the American Red Cross. What he never disclosed was his salary from or stock holdings in the voting machine company whose machines had counted his votes.[9]

Six years later, when asked about his ownership in ES&S by Lincoln's Channel 8 TV News, Hagel said he had sold that stock. If so, the stock he says he sold was never listed as one that he'd owned.

This is not a gray area. This is lying. Hagel's failure to disclose his financial relationship with the company was not brought to the attention of the public, and this was a material omission. Reporters surely would have inquired about it as they researched stories about his amazing upset victories.

It is therefore understandable that we didn't know about conflicts of interest and voting machine ownership back in 1996. Had we known, perhaps we never would have chosen to herd every precinct in America toward unauditable voting. Certainly, we would have queried ES&S about its ties to Hagel before allowing 56 percent of the U.S. to count votes on its machines. In October 2002, I discovered that he *still* had undisclosed ownership of ES&S through its parent company, the McCarthy Group.

The McCarthy Group is run by Hagel's campaign finance director, Michael R. McCarthy, who is also a director of ES&S. Hagel hid his ties to ES&S by calling his investment of up to $5 million in the ES&S parent company an "excepted investment fund." This is important because senators are required to list the underlying assets for companies they invest in, unless the company is "excepted." To be "excepted," the McCarthy Group must be publicly traded (it is not) and very widely traded (it is not).

Charlie Matulka, Hagel's opponent in 2002 for the U.S. Senate seat, finally got fed up. He called a press conference in the rotunda of the Nebraska Capitol Building on October 23, 2002.

"Why would someone who owns a voting machine company want to run for office?" Matulka asked. "It's like the fox guarding the hen house."

Matulka wrote to Senate Ethics Committee director Victor Baird in October 2002 to request an investigation into Hagel's ownership in and nondisclosure of ES&S. Baird wrote back, in a letter dated November 18, 2002, "Your complaint lacks merit and no further action is appropriate with respect to the matter, which is hereby dismissed."

Neither Baird nor Hagel ever answered Matulka's questions, but when Hagel won by a landslide, Matulka dug his heels in and asked for a recount. He figured he'd lost, but he asked how much he'd need to pay to audit the machine counts. It was the principle of the thing, he said. Matulka received a reply from the Nebraska Secretary of State telling him that Nebraska has no provision in the law allowing a losing candidate to verify vote tallies by counting the paper ballots.

In January 2003, Hagel's campaign finance director, Michael McCarthy, admitted that Hagel had ownership ties to ES&S. When the story was finally told, Hagel's staff tried to claim there was no conflict of interest.

"[Hagel's Chief of Staff, Lou Ann] Linehan said there's nothing ir-regular about a person who used to run a voting-machine firm run-ning for office," wrote Farhad Manjoo of *Salon.com.* " 'Maybe if you're not from Nebraska and you're not familiar with the whole situation you would have questions,' she says. 'But does it look questionable if there's a senator who is a farmer and now he votes on ag issues? Everybody comes from somewhere.' "[10]

Two points, Ms. Linehan: A senator who is a farmer, if he follows the law, *discloses* that he is a farmer on his Federal Election Commis-sion documents. Then, if he votes oddly on a farm bill, people scruti-nize his relationship with farming. Second, the farmer's own cows aren't counting his votes. Anyone with an I.Q. bigger than a cornhusk knows the real reason Hagel hid his involvement with American Infor-mation Systems on his disclosure statements.

Hagel was reelected in November. An article in *The Hotline* quoted a prominent GOPer predicting that Hagel would run for president in 2008. The article then quotes Linehan: "It's abundantly clear that many people think that's a possibility for Senator Hagel." [11]

I called Victor Baird, counsel for the Senate Ethics Committee, be-ginning with an innocuous question: "What is meant by 'widely traded' in the context of an 'excepted investment fund?' "

Baird said that the term refers to very diversified mutual funds. I asked why there were no records of Hagel's ties to the voting com-pany in his disclosure documents. Was he aware of this? Had he re-quested clarification from Hagel? I knew I had struck a nerve. Baird was silent for a long time and then said quietly, "If you want to look into this, you'll need to come in and get hold of the documents."

Something in his tone of voice made me uncomfortable. I did not get the impression that Baird was defending Hagel. I rummaged through my media database and chose a respected Washington publication called *The Hill,* where I talked with reporter Alexander Bolton. He was intrigued, and over the next two weeks we spoke several times. I provided source material and he painstakingly investigated the story.

Unfortunately, when Bolton went to the Senate Public Documents Room to retrieve originals of Hagel's 1995 and 1996 documents, he was told they had been destroyed.

"They said anything over five years old is destroyed by law, and they pulled out the law," said Bolton.

But the records aren't quite gone. Hagel's staff told Bolton they had the documents. I located copies of the documents at OpenSecrets.org, a Web site that keeps a repository for FEC disclosures. In 1997, Baird had asked Hagel to clarify the nature of his investment in McCarthy Group. Hagel had written "none" next to "type of investment." In response to Baird's letter, Hagel filed an amendment characterizing the McCarthy Group as an "excepted investment fund," a designation for widely held, publicly available mutual funds.

According to Bolton, Baird said that the McCarthy Group did not appear to qualify as an "excepted investment fund." [12] Then Baird resigned.

When Baird met with Bolton, he told him that Hagel appeared to have mischaracterized his investment. Then Hagel's staff met with Baird. This took place on Friday, Jan. 25, 2003. Hagel's staff met with Baird again on Monday, Jan. 27. Bolton came in for one final interview Monday afternoon, just prior to submitting his story to *The Hill* for Tuesday's deadline.

Baird had just resigned, it was explained, and Baird's replacement, Robert Walker, met with Bolton instead, urging a new, looser interpretation of Hagel's disclosures — an interpretation that did not mesh with other expert opinions, nor even with our own common sense.

Where was Victor Baird? Could he be interviewed at home? Apparently not. Bolton was told that Baird still worked for the Senate Ethics Committee, just not in a position that could talk to the press.

Could there have been another reason for Baird's resignation? Maybe. Baird had announced in December 2002 that he planned to resign at

the end of February 2003. But he changed his mind and left the position he'd held for 16 years, a month early and in the middle of the day.

In a nutshell:

• Hagel omitted mentioning that he received a salary from American Information Systems in any disclosure document.

• He omitted mentioning that he held the position of chairman in his
1995 and 1996 documents but says he included it in a temporary interim 1995 statement. The instructions say to go back two years. Hagel
also held the CEO position in 1994 but omitted that on all forms.

• He omitted mentioning that he held stock in AIS Investors Inc.
and also did not list any transfers or sale of this stock.

• He apparently transferred his investment into ES&S' parent company, the McCarthy Group, and he disclosed investments of up to $5
million in that. He omitted the itemization of McCarthy Group's underlying assets. Under "type of investment," he originally wrote "none."

• When asked by Baird to clarify what the McCarthy Group was,
he decided to call it an "excepted investment fund."

• Baird failed to go along with Hagel's odd description of the McCarthy
Group as an "excepted" fund.

• Baird was replaced by a new Ethics Committee director who did
support Hagel's interpretations.

Hagel has never been called upon to answer for material omissions
about ownership in AIS Investors Inc., nor for his omissions about the
positions he held with the company.

Bolton told me that something had happened during his investigation
of the Hagel story that had never occurred in all his time covering
Washington politics: Someone had tried to muscle him out of running a
story. Jan Baran, perhaps the most powerful Republican lawyer in
Washington, and Hagel's Chief of Staff, Lou Ann Linehan, walked
into *The Hill* and tried to pressure Bolton into killing his story. He
refused. "Then soften it," they insisted. He refused.

Bolton is an example of what is still healthy about the consolidated
and often conflicted U.S. press. Lincoln's Channel 8 TV News is another example — it was the only news outlet that reported on Matulka's
allegations that Hagel had undisclosed ties with the voting machine
company scheduled to count their votes. The 3,000 editors who ig-

nored faxed photocopies of Hagel's voting machine involvement, and especially the Nebraska press who had every reason to cover the story but chose not to inform anyone about the issue, are an example of what is wrong with the media nowadays.

Here's what Dick Cheney had to say when he learned that Hagel was also being considered for the vice presidential slot in 2000: "Senator Chuck Hagel represents the quality, character and experience that America is searching for in national leadership."

According to an AP wire report, Sen. Chuck Hagel thinks he's capable of being an effective president and says he isn't afraid of the scrutiny that comes with a White House bid.

"Do I want to be president?" Hagel commented, "That's a question that you have to spend some time with. ... I'm probably in a position as well as anybody — with my background, where I've been, things that I've gotten accomplished." [13]

Whether or not Hagel is in a position to run for president, the company he managed is certainly in a position to count most of the votes. According to the ES&S Web site, its machines count 56 percent of the votes in the U.S.

* * * * *

This is not, ultimately, a story about one man named Hagel. It is a story about a rush to unauditable computerized voting using machines manufactured by people who sometimes have vested interests.

4
A Brief History of Vote-Rigging

Election rigging is nothing new. We've been conducting elections for more than a dozen centuries, and at one time or another, every system ever designed has been rigged.*

We're a flawed species. The best in us shows up in our desire to make our government "of the people, by the people and for the people." The worst in us shows up when, no matter what the system, somebody figures out how to cheat.

How to rig paper ballots: Because at first there was little voter privacy, candidates tried to pay people to vote for them. People used to wander around town with their ballots, where the slips of paper got into all kinds of trouble.

Similar problems can crop up with absentee voting. In the 2000 presidential election in Oregon, according to *The Wall Street Journal*, "unidentified people carrying cardboard boxes popped up all over Portland, attempting to collect ballots. One group set up a box at a busy midtown intersection. Outside the Multnomah County election office, a quartet of three women and a man posted themselves in the

---

* I have footnoted my sources, but Douglas W. Jones, a University of Iowa associate professor of computer science, deserves more than a footnote here. We all know that election-tampering is a political reality, but it was not easy to find any authoritative information on specific techniques. A great deal of the information in this chapter was found by perusing Dr. Jones's work. [1]

middle of the last-minute rush of voters. The county elections director says she was incredulous when she spied people gathering ballots. Nobody knows what happened to the ballots after that. [2]

The Australian paper ballot system, which keeps all ballots at the polling place, sets a very high standard: privacy, accuracy and impartiality when properly administered. It's difficult, but not impossible, to rig this system. Here's how you can manipulate this system:

(1) Create a set of rules for which votes "count" and which do not.

(2) Make sure your team is better trained — or more aggressive — than the other team.

(3) Fight against miniscule flaws on ballots for your opponent and defend vigorously the right to count your own candidate's ballots.

According to the 1910 *Encyclopedia Britannica* entry for voting machines, a really well-coached vote-counting team used to be able to exclude as many as 40 percent of the votes. For this reason, some states insist on written standards for counting paper ballots.

Another way to rig paper-ballot elections is to gain unauthorized access to the ballot box. These boxes are supposed to be carefully locked, with an airtight chain of custody. Typically, sealed ballot boxes must be transported with a "chain of custody" form that includes the signatures and times in which they are in the custody of each official. However, chain of custody sometimes mysteriously disengages, and the "seal" is a little twisty-wire that does not take a master burglar to penetrate.

In San Francisco, ballot box lids were found floating in the bay and washing up on ocean beaches for several months after the November 2001 election.

"Beachcombers find them on sand dunes west of Point Reyes. Rowers come upon them bobbing in the bay. The bright red box tops that keep washing up around the Bay Area are floating reminders of a problem in San Francisco, the remnants of ballot boxes that somehow got beyond the control of the city's embattled Department of Elections," reports the *San Francisco Chronicle*. [3]

According to a San Francisco citizens group that publishes reports under the name "First Amendment Defense Trust," the June 1997 vote on the 49ers football stadium was well on its way to losing.

The defeat could not be announced, however, until after the "extremely late delivery of more than 100 ballot boxes which turned out to have an abundance of 'yes' votes."

The delay was attributed to ballots that somehow got wet and had to be dried in a microwave oven, causing great suspicion. When the tardy ballots showed up, so dramatic was the shift to "yes" that the bond, worth $100 million to contractors, was passed by a narrow margin. [4]

The most famous person caught tampering with paper ballots was President Lyndon Johnson, who defeated the popular former Texas governor Coke Stevenson in the 1948 Democratic Senate primary. Johnson trailed Stevenson by 854 votes after the polls closed, but new ballots kept appearing. Various witnesses describe watching men altering the voter rolls and burning the ballots. Finally, when 202 new votes showed up (cast in alphabetical order), Johnson gained an 87-vote margin and was declared the winner.

LBJ's campaign manager at the time, John Connally, was publicly linked to the report of the suspicious and late 202 votes in Box 13 from Jim Wells County. Connally denied any tie to vote fraud. [5]

Lever machines: These are being phased out. They are not particularly accurate, and they are unauditable and cumbersome, but they are not easy to tamper with. One inhibiting factor is their sheer size. It is impossible to tote one of these big metal contraptions around unnoticed, and the job of moving them is so immense that it happens only at election time and requires several beefy guys and a truck. Private access to lever machines is not easy to come by, but it can be done.

To rig a lever machine, you buy off a technician or one of the caretakers who has custody over the machines. Just file a few teeth off the gear that matches the candidate you don't want, causing the machine to randomly skip votes, and you'll improve your own candidate's chances immensely, though not precisely.

Lever machines are not complex and tampering is not invisible, but if no one looks for it, tampering sometimes goes unnoticed for years. At least lever machines cannot be rigged on a national scale. Their problems are confined to small geographic areas.

Punch Cards: One way to rig a punch card system is to add punches to the cards with votes for the undesired candidate. The double-punched cards become "overvotes" and are thrown out.

In the 2000 general election in Duval County, Florida, according to the *Los Angeles Times*, "a remarkable 21,855 ballots were invalidated because voters chose more than one presidential candidate." [7] These overvotes were never examined in the Florida recount, and they came primarily from a handful of black precincts.

Another way to rig punch cards is to find a crooked card printer. Printing companies sometimes get both the punch card order and the printing contract for ballot positioning. If they can print punch card batches that are customized for each area, an unscrupulous card manufacturer can rig the cards. There are two ways to do this, and it is difficult to detect either method without a microscope:

(1) Adjust the die that cuts the card so that perforations make the favored candidate easier to punch out, or the undesired candidate's chads hard to dislodge. It is possible to die-cut the favored candidate so that his chads can be dislodged with a strong puff of air.

(2) Affix an invisible plastic coating to the back of the undesirable candidate's chads. They will not dislodge easily and may even snap back into place after being punched.

Another way to rig the punch card vote would be to tamper with the automated counting system.

*   *   *   *   *

These methods are clever, but computerized methods are more elegant. Using computers, you can manipulate more votes at once.

5
Cyber-Boss Tweed
21st-Century Ballot-Tampering Techniques

With old-style voting systems, for the most part, no special training was needed to realize something was amiss. Not so with rigging computers, but many public officials don't understand this.

"Subverting elections would be extremely unlikely and staggeringly difficult," said Georgia Secretary of State Cathy Cox when interviewed about Georgia's touch-screen voting system. "It would take a conspiracy beyond belief of all these different poll workers. ... I don't see how this could happen in the real world." [1]

My premise, though, is this: An insider, someone with access, can plant malicious computer code without getting caught. Just as we know that banks will have robbers, that blackjack tables will have card-counters and that embezzlers will slip in amongst the bean-counters, so we should expect to find a few ethically challenged individuals among the honorable programmers and technicians who work with our voting machines.

Certainly, human nature did not change just because we entered the age of computers. Every other kind of voting system has been tampered with. Sooner or later, someone's going to try to steal votes on these things.

What kind of cheaters are we looking for?

Candidates may not be the most likely people to cheat. Few candidates are likely to possess the combination of motive and cash to rig their own elections. I believe that vested interests behind the candidate are more likely suspects, and the candidate need not even know.

Zealots are a bigger danger, especially if they happen to be connected to people with giant wallets. "True believers" may feel that the end justifies any means. Some are very wealthy, and some congregate in radical groups in which they can pool their cash and push their agenda. Zealots of any kind may believe they are "helping" the rest of us by imposing their candidates on us. You do not need to hand a zealot a bribe, and the candidate they select never even needs to know his election was rigged.

Gambling interests may not be squeamish about pulling strings. Gambling rights have turned into a brawl, with some tough players who are seeking riverboat gambling rights, the right to compete with Native American casinos and just plain liberalized and legalized gambling in communities all over the world.

Hackers, more accurately called "crackers," get their kicks by compromising legitimate software systems. These people may not need bribe money or a cause; like climbing a mountain, they just want to see if they can do it.

Profiteers can make billions by putting the right candidate into office. Electronic voting systems give a small number of people access to a great number of votes. If you control the counting software, ballot tampering on a massive scale is possible. We should expect this to attract the all-star players.

In the old days, a city boss might want a particular candidate to win, perhaps throw a few construction contracts his way, take a kickback. But high-volume tampering provides a motive for a much different clientele.

Defense contractors stand to make billions with the right candidate. Oil companies benefit from new pipelines all over the world, if they select candidates likely to vote for open exploration and geopolitically strategic development. Highway contractors garner hundreds of millions on freeway and bridge projects. Global financiers gain power and profit when international trade policies are set up to favor their interests. Pharmaceutical companies want legislative protection for pricing policies and product patenting and protection from international competition. Investment holding companies stand to gain control over privatized retirement and pension funds.

So much to spend, so few techies to corrupt. Where to begin?

Well, for starters, you could send your own compromised programmer into a voting machine company toting a resume. But suppose I am a political operative for a wealthy and powerful, but crooked, corporation, and I just want to buy off an employee. How would I find and contact an employee, and how would I know whom to approach?

I set out to answer that question. I figured that if a middle-aged woman like me who has never done a "covert op" in her life, working on the Internet, could find the people who program our voting machines, then certainly a corporation like Multinational Profiteers LLC must already know who they are.

I discovered that you can locate software engineers who once worked for voting machine companies by looking at online resumes and job-search sites. The resumes often have home phone numbers. You can call them up, say you are writing an article and ask them how a machine can be rigged. And they will tell you. I know this because I did it.

You will find software engineers who currently work for voting machine companies by finding any example of the company e-mail. For example, ES&S employees have e-mail addresses that end in "essvotc.com." If you enter "essvote" in a search engine, you'll find people who submitted information to high-school reunion sites and programmers who post comments on forums, join listservs, create personal Web pages and post their wedding plans on the Internet. One guy even listed his hobbies and his favorite vacation spots.

I located eight dozen voting-company employees this way. I also found the home phone number for someone in human resources at ES&S, who in turn has access to contact information, including the home phone number, for every single employee. This took three hours.

How would you choose someone to approach?

For $80 you can run a background check. That will give you a person's Social Security number, which opens up more information. You can also run a credit check. Doing this, you find out if the programmer has a gambling problem, has gotten into credit-card debt, is over her head in student loans, has had run-ins with the law, likes fancy cars, is overcommitted on a mortgage. Additional searches reveal political affiliations and even lead you to people who are disgruntled or believe they will soon be fired.

How to compromise an Internet voting system

Some cities, like Manatowoc, Wisconsin, and Liverpool, England, are eager to vote by Internet. Among computer professionals, however, Internet voting advocates are difficult to find. Here's why:

Companies like VoteHere claim that encryption techniques are a key to Internet voting security, but encryption won't protect our vote from software programming errors.

Rigging an Internet election is as simple as "DoS"-ing a server. Denial of Service attacks can knock out servers in targeted areas, and no amount of encryption will help. (Let's take the technospeak out: Suppose you connect to the Internet using America Online, but on election day, for some reason, your AOL access numbers don't work. Can you vote on the Internet?)

A company that specializes in Internet voting, election.com, ran a January 2003 contest in Toronto, Canada, which was disrupted by a malicious attempt to shut down the computer system.

"Earl Hurd of election.com said he believes someone used a 'denial of service' program to disrupt the voting — paralysing the central computer by bombarding it with a stream of data," CBC News reported. " 'We had one log-in attempt that corrupted the ability of everybody to get access to our servers,' he said ... When asked if a second ballot might be delayed by another act of computer vandalism, election.com conceded that the culprit might strike again.

" 'Unless he died in the last few minutes because of the evil thoughts in my brain, he or she is still out there,' Hurd said." [2]

Even the most elaborate encryption can't solve a power outage. If some clown with a backhoe pulls the phone cables up out of the ground, how will you vote? If an ice storm takes out power in the city, will your modem work? If you forget to pay your cable bill and they turn it off on Election Day, what will you do?

If you can vote from the privacy of your home, you can sell that vote as well. Proof of how you voted would be as close as your printer.

And while we're talking about privacy, what if you neglect to put in the latest Microsoft patch? You know, the one that says, "*A security issue has been identified that could allow an attacker to compromise a computer running Windows XP and gain control over it.*"

Heck, if there is as much "spyware" out there as my spam claims, Internet voting would mean big trouble. From what I can tell, a lot of people don't trust the privacy of their computer even when they are not doing something mission-critical, like casting a vote. Even if scientists make a safe system, how do we get everyone to trust it?

You might find other people voting for you. Read up on identity theft, which is getting worse every year. [3]

Dirty tricks will proliferate. Your elderly Aunt Martha may get convincing messages that send her to bogus voting sites which dispose of her vote. Come to think about it, beloved Aunt Martha is eighty-three years old. Learning to vote on the Internet might stress her out, and why should she have to?

Do you want to vote with your spouse looking over your shoulder? Many of us connect to the Internet at work: Do you really want to cast your vote next to your union leader or your boss?

And what about "technical difficulties?" You cast your vote and your computer screen turns blue and a message appears:

Iexplorer.exe has caused a general protection fault in vote.exe. Your system may be unstable. Save all your work, close all windows and reboot your system.

Oookay. Did your vote go through? How will you know?

If it didn't, will you be able to vote again? If you do and the same thing happens, then what? Where will we find enough people to staff the tech support desks on Election day? Will we farm the job out to a service company in Bombay? And if so, how secure is that?

People are out there pushing Internet voting, but this concept is flawed and cannot be repaired. Any money we would save closing down the polls would be lost trying to make the system secure and reliable, and new laws would have to be passed to deal with each problem that arises. People and agencies would have to be appointed to enforce those laws. Election law would come to resemble the tax code in complexity.

Bottom line? Voting for your favorite movie online may be cool, but it's no way to run the Republic.

* * * * *

How to compromise an optical-scan system

Optical-scan systems involve filling in an oval or drawing an arrow on a paper ballot, which then is fed into a scanner. People think these systems can't be rigged because they have a paper ballot, but there are anecdotal reports of optical-scan systems flipping elections as far back as 1980.

An election official I spoke with from California reported that in her county, Jimmy Carter soundly defeated Ronald Reagan during the 1980 presidential election. However, the computer tally from the optical scanner reversed the results, giving Carter's votes to Reagan and vice versa. By doing a hand audit using the paper ballots, they were able to straighten out the results, but when she requested that the state of California do more audits to see how widespread the problem was, she was ignored.

Most people believe that optical-scan machines are tamper-proof because they provide a paper ballot. But election officials generally don't use the ballots to check the machine count, and in some states it's against the law to do so. If you don't audit properly, optical-scan machines are no safer than paperless touch screens.

Some people think that all we need to do is vote absentee and the touch-screen problem is solved. Unfortunately, it will not be solved until we actually look at those ballots. When you vote absentee, your ballot is usually run through an optical-scan machine. Hack either the scanner or the main accumulation and you take the election away, while ballots sit forlornly in a box that no one is allowed to open.

The official results come from the county, not the polling place, so if you adjust the optical-scan data before it gets into the county accumulator, you've just rigged the election. No one's going to look at those paper ballots, but if they do a spot check, see below. I'll show you how a crooked programmer can create a safety net for spot checks.

The greatest danger is during the transfer of the vote from the polling place to a central counting facility (which is one reason we should be counting votes at the polling place). Optical-scan votes are vulnerable when transferred by modem or by *cell phone*, as happened in Marin County, California, during the gubernatorial recall election on Oct. 7, 2003. [4]

Another way to compromise an optical-scan system is to attack the program that accumulates the votes from the polling place.

One way to do this would be to enable a double set of books. If the software keeps a duplicate set of records and uses the first set for the totals, and the second set for the real numbers, you can rig the totals but keep the detail intact in case of spot checks.

Anyone with access to the central count machine can hack an election, and this access may be available through either telephone lines or Internet connections, allowing complete strangers to tamper. One way to deter this tampering, or detect it, is to audit the paper ballots against the totals.

* * * * *

More ways to compromise an electronic voting system

Hiding functions in software programs is called putting in "back doors." Visit any computer forum on the Internet, and you'll find that programmers can think up back doors faster than anyone can figure out how to test for them. I spoke with sources who had worked for voting-machine companies and who came up with one method after the next. Here are some of their ideas:

Create a program that checks the computer's date and time function, activating when the election is scheduled to begin, doing its work, and then self-destructing when the election is over. It is possible to write hit-and-run code that changes the *original votes*, then destroys itself. It can pass testing because it activates only on election day.

Create a dummy ballot using a special configuration of "votes" that launches a program when put through the machine. Quite diabolical, actually: You rig the election by casting a vote! You could extend this to all machines using the same software by embedding the program in the "ender card," which is run through some systems to close the election.

Create a replacement set of votes, embed them on a chip, and arrange for someone with access to substitute the chip after the election. Chip replacement took place in the 2002 general election in Scurry County, Texas. Another chip replacement was done in 2002, also by ES&S, in South Dakota, where technicians discovered a machine double-counting Republican votes.

Overwrite the approved program with new commands by install-ing upgrades or "patches" that have not been examined. I asked Paul Miller, an official from the Washington State Secretary of State's election division, about procedures for updates. He told me that tracking and examining program updates is "not an issue." *But any time a program is changed, it can change things you don't see.*

Include a layer of software that is insulated from certification test-ing. Diebold voting machines use Microsoft Windows, but when ex-amining the code, no one looked at the Windows files. By embedding malicious programs in the Microsoft operating system instead of the voting software, a hacker can skip right through certification. Some Diebold machines run old versions of Microsoft operating systems, such as Windows 95 and Windows 98, which arc not recommended, even by Microsoft, for use in security-sensitive applications.

Work with an unscrupulous vendor for your components. Manu-facturers are not required to disclose who their vendors are. Some com-panies reportedly use components from Russia or the Philippines. Others share components from vendors in the USA who are not scrutinized by independent testing authorities.

Find a video-game programmer to tamper with the video driver. Because so many people create video games, the source codes are fairly readily available. A good game programmer can make the screen do one thing while the innards do something else.

Exchange files with support techs by putting them on a server. Anyone who gains access to the server can replace one with another — for example, replacing the central counting program with a file of the same name that contains a variation of the program.

Add a field into the program that attaches a multiplier to each vote, based on party affiliation, rounding one party slightly up and the other slightly down, using a decimal so that when votes are printed one by one (which is almost never done), they round off and print correctly, but when tallied, the total is shaved. For example: "Affiliation = Demo-crat; multiplier = 0.95 ... Affiliation = Republican; multiplier = 1.05." This will create totals that correlate with demographics.

Buy a tech and plant him as a poll worker in a key precinct where your competitor's machines are used. Have him go through the train-ing and then have him flub the election by preventing machines from booting up on time, or causing them to crash and then blaming it on the manufacturer. If things really get messed up, have him call the press and grant interviews.

Using wireless technology embedded in the voting machine, monitor the election results on a remote basis as the contest proceeds and send your adjustment in when the election nears its end.

Put a back door into the compiler used for the source code (a compiler is used to "compile" software code from a high-level programming language into faster machine language). The source code can be clean, but no one looks at the compiler, and with this method, the digital signature (a method for detecting changes in software after certification) will remain intact.

Switch the card used to start up the machine. For some models, this overwrites the voting program with a new one. In Palm Beach County, Florida, in a March 2003 election, some precincts reported problems with electronic cards used to activate touch-screen machines, but according to the news reports, "backup cards worked." [5]

Compromise the binary code, below the level of the source code, which will not be detectable even with a line-by-line examination of the source code and won't be solved by using a digital signature.

By the way, people who have worked around touch screens know that rubbing them can screw them up big time. And almost everyone who works on computers knows that strong magnets and magnetic storage don't mix.

Accidentally put a few bugs in the software. Software engineering is like writing music or creating a painting. It is inspired, sometimes in the middle of the night, and in the wee hours things slip past the best of them. Sometimes engineers just don't catch bugs in the code. Or perhaps, a programmer plays with bugs for a hobby...

Bugs in the Code

Voting-machine source code apparently has turned into the digital equivalent of "The Blob," with such massive code, around a million lines long, that no one really catches all the bugs.

With such bulbous source code, who would notice a few *malicious* lines that can be explained away? Just a bug. A glitch. Remember, it's easy and fun to vote on these machines.

Following are examples of actual voting-machine software bugs.

Found on Internet voting source code, called votation

// really no idea on how to resolve rollback failure... :(perhaps praying :) //

Found these comments in Diebold source code files:

- Fix bug in VIBS causing Straight Party races not to work properly.
- Fix problem with race stats results not being sent correctly.
- Fixed bug in BallotDLG when ballot with the votes appears after touching Start button or anywhere else on the screen couple of times.
- Revert improvement in detection of invalid smart cards
- Fixed minor bug when internal keyboard did not work properly.
- Fix problem with transfer sending wrong precinct id
- Fix problem with not closing election after setting for election.
- Fixed problem that caused an error when view ballot results.
- Fixed problem in FileUtil that did not correctly determine if path was empty.
- Fixed problem in PollBook for Closed Primary Elections.
- Work around problem reporting zero totals when runing [sic] on Win95 units and Win98 units upgraded from Win95
- Fix bug with starting PollBook when main and def. Directories do not match.
- Fix bug uploading candidate totals
- Fixed problem in Poll Book where it fails to clear totals.
- Fixed bug that did not accumulate write-in votes.
- Handle failure of some files during upload.
- Fix bug in validating ResultFile
- Ballot station remembers opened election (again)
- Truly fixed the bug in LanSelView
- Enter a start condition. This macro really ought to take a parameter, but we do it the disgusting crufty way forced on us by the ()-less definition of BEGIN.

* * * * *

Do the bugs ever make it into the software used in elections? Absolutely. That's why "patches" (after-the-fact program modifications) are put on the machines.

6
Who's Beholden to Whom?

Everyone thinks we got into this mess because of irregularities ex-posed during the Florida recount in November 2000. I disagree.

If you go back to Chapter 2 and delete all the Florida 2000 prob-lems, you're still left with 97 out of 100 examples. This problem is not limited to Florida or the 2000 election, and it cannot be blamed on hanging chads or a butterfly ballot. The root cause of this problem is money.

Vendors and lobbyists leveraged the Florida fiasco to persuade well-meaning legislators to enact a sweeping election reform bill, the Help America Vote Act (HAVA), creating a gold rush to purchase new vot-ing systems under tight deadlines, using federal money. Vendors did not disclose to lawmakers that their optical-scan systems and touch screens had a history of glitches, bugs and miscounts, and because their computer code was kept secret and proprietary, even U.S. sena-tors and representatives could not know about security flaws or learn just how broken the "certification and testing" system really is.

But I'm getting ahead of myself.

In later chapters, I'll take you inside one of our secret electronic voting systems, and you'll see just how little confidence they should inspire. By rights, we should demand an immediate moratorium on electronic voting, returning to paper ballots, hand-counted if necessary, until we solve underlying problems, such as certification that doesn't work and failure to audit properly.

The Election Center, a private entity that receives little federal oversight and is cozy with vendors,[1] provides training for county clerks and auditors.

The county election officials who purchase these systems are persuaded by a nonstop barrage of talking points, sales presentations and "training programs" provided by vendors and that strange little entity called The Election Center. They have been told to buy now or lose government funds and get fined. Most county officials are honest folks who have not been given the option to buy safer, more secure systems. They may not even know such systems exist.

Not all county officials are well behaved, however. According to one of our sources, who made sales presentations for a voting-machine vendor mentioned in this book, it is all too common for county buyers to hint at gifts ("That's a nice laptop ...") and, sometimes, place an empty envelope on the desk, hoping it will be filled.

County officials must abide by what the regulators say, but the regulators keep getting hired by the vendors.

VoteHere hired former Washington state Secretary of State Ralph Munro, who helped to usher in his protegé, Washington's current secretary of state (and avid voting-machine advocate), Sam Reed. [2]

Former California Secretary of State Bill Jones is now a paid consultant for Sequoia Voting Systems. [3] Former Florida Secretary of State Sandra Mortham was hired by ES&S. She promptly got into hot water for being a lobbyist for both the state's counties and the company that sold them their touch-screen voting machines. [4]

Lou Dedier, the California official responsible for recommending which voting systems to buy, took a job with ES&S. [5] Diebold employs Deborah Seiler, a former assistant to California Secretary of State March Fong Eu. [6]

The three finalists for Ohio's 2003 voting-machine recommendations happened to be the companies that hired the most lobbyists. Diebold lobbyists Mitchell Given and Jonathan Hughes formerly worked for Ohio Attorney General Jim Petro, and six ES&S lobbyists showered Ohio county elections officials with gifts. [7]

While we're on the subject of cashing in, take a look at the commissions these companies pay. Sequoia paid $441,000 in a single year to John Krizka for selling voting machines to four Florida counties. Krizka sued, claiming Sequoia had stiffed him for $1.8 million. [8]

Amid these commissions, hope-filled envelopes, job offers and former bosses-turned-regulatees, some election officials don't seem to welcome input from scientists like Dr. David Dill, the Stanford computer professor who wrote, " ... Some of the equipment being purchased, while superficially attractive to both voters and election officials, poses unacceptable risks to election integrity — risks of which election officials and the general public are largely unaware."

Dill urged a more prudent voting system, and his "Resolution on Electronic Voting" [9] garnered 1,212 endorsements by technologists. No comparable group of computer scientists — in fact, no technology group at all — has embraced paperless voting.

It's not just the quantity of computer experts who endorsed this demand for a voter-verifiable audit ballot that is impressive, but the quality of their expertise. They include renowned experts such as Eugene Spafford, professor of computer sciences and CERIAS director at Purdue University, and Ronald L. Rivest, from the Massachusetts Institute of Technology; Peter Neumann, principal scientist for SRI International, who has studied computerized voting security for nearly two decades; Arnold B. Urken, from Stevens Institute of Technology, who founded the first national certification and testing lab for computerized voting machines; and Dr. Rebecca Mercuri, one of the most famous analysts of voting-machine technology.

But that's not all. Add Douglas W. Jones, associate professor and former chairman of the Iowa Board of Examiners for Voting Machines and Electronic Voting Systems, from the University of Iowa; Charles Van Loan, professor and chairman of the Department of Computer Science at Cornell University; and Martyn Thomas, professor in software engineering at Oxford University.

One thousand, two hundred twelve *for* providing a voter-verified, tamper-resistant paper ballot, *zero* computer scientists *against*. And these are not just academics. They include industry experts from Sun Microsystems Inc., Bell Laboratories and Lucent Technologies, and General Motors.

You may wonder why I'm going on about this, and it is for this reason: After being presented with the urgent concerns of so many learned professionals, and after being offered the voter-verified paper ballot feature at no extra charge, Santa Clara County, California, purchased unauditable touch-screen voting machines anyway.

"*They've created this whole UFO effect*," said Jesse Durazo,[10] registrar of voters, who is not versed in computer science.

Durazo was not persuaded by 1,212 of the nation's top computer scientists, choosing instead to follow advice from vendors.

A look at the regulators

State certification procedures rely on a procedure called the "Logic and Accuracy" (L&A) test. The L&A test is called a "black-box" test, whereas examining the source code is called "white-box" testing.

According to Arnold B. Urken, who founded Election Technology Laboratories, the first voting-machine testing lab, white-box testing — eyes-on examination of the source code — should be mandatory if certification is to mean anything. Urken told me that he refused to certify ES&S (then called AIS) because the company would not allow him to examine its source code.

In an L&A test, you run test ballots through the machine. If the machine counts correctly, it passes the test. Some touch screens use an automated program to simulate someone casting test votes.

You can practice with all the test ballots you want, but tampering with a program in such a way that it will pass the L&A test is as simple as hatching an egg. An "Easter egg" is a tiny code embedded into the program which launches a function when triggered. When the egg receives a signal, it hatches — and the signal can be as simple as receiving a vote containing a special combination of choices.

Dr. Britain Williams, the official voting-machine examiner for the state of Georgia, described testing procedures that sound impressive.

"The law gives the Secretary of State the authority to say what systems are certified and what are not. What I do is an evaluation of the system. The FEC [Federal Election Commission] publishes standards for voting systems. We have national labs that examine for compliance with the FEC, and if they are in compliance, certification is issued by NASED [the National Association of State Election Directors]. Once that's done, it's brought into the state, and I evaluate them as to whether or not the system is in compliance with Georgia rules and regulations. Then the Secretary of State takes that report, in combination with the others, and certifies it." [11]

He described a procedure in which teams of people with a test script checked out each machine, testing the printer, the card reader, the serial port, the screen calibration.

I went to the ES&S Web page, which said that its voting machines were tested by Wyle Laboratories. David Elliott, Washington state's elections director, said that Wyle is a very reputable firm that tests aircraft systems. [12]

Sounds pretty good. Except that in Georgia, where Dr. Brit Williams oversees the testing, and Washington state, where State Elections Director and former NASED board member David Elliott is in charge, they have been using software *that was never certified at all*.

Diebold's principal engineer, Ken Clark, wrote a memo on January 14, 2002, describing his intent to avoid putting his newly modified software through California's certification process by fudging a version number. He wrote, "What good are rules if you can't bend them now and again?" [13]

Ahem.

But suppose for a moment that they actually do test the stuff. How bulletproof is this testing?

Both David Elliott (Washington state) and Brit Williams (Georgia) said that Wyle Laboratories tests their voting machines. But it turns out that Wyle decided to stop testing voting machine software in 1996, citing bloated code that was more than 900,000 lines long. I called Edward W. Smith at Wyle Labs, who confirmed this. Wyle only tests hardware and firmware. Can you drop it off a truck? How does it stand up to being left in the rain? Good things to know, but some of us also want to know that someone has examined the source code to make sure no one tampered with it.

Wyle says they don't test the software, but in a way, they do. Wyle tests the programs that go inside the optical-scan and the touch-screen machines. Because these programs are stored in read-only memory (ROM) or programmable ROM (PROM) chips, or flash memory, Wyle calls the programs "firmware." Basically, this is just industry jargon for software that doesn't reside on a hard drive.

After the program is certified, it must not be changed without re-examination, so you can imagine my surprise when I ran into these comments, written into the source-code files for Diebold Election Systems by its programmers:

"Remove SCWinApi module till pass WYLE certification."

And because the version sent to Wyle for certification is supposed to be the *official* version, and the voting machines are supposed to use *only* the officially-certified version, you might wonder at this comment:

"Merge WYLE branch into the stable branch." [14]

Why are we removing things before we send them to Wyle, and why are we merging the officially certified version back into something else? Just wondering.

A lab called Ciber, Inc. tests the voting-system software. Another lab, SysTest, is also authorized to certify software, but all the major companies seem to be certified by Ciber. The software that sits on the county server and accumulates the votes as they come in from the polling places is tested by Ciber.

I thought the certification process would involve, say, an expert in voting putting on a white lab coat, brushing away the voting-machine employees and independently, painstakingly, testing the accuracy and integrity of the software. After all, our voting system is at stake. Surely, Ciber holds the key to our confidence. I decided to give them a call but found out that the public is not allowed to ask Ciber any questions. Here are the instructions at NASED's Web site:

"The ITAs DO NOT and WILL NOT respond to outside inquiries about the testing process for voting systems, nor will they answer questions related to a specific manufacturer or a specific voting system from the public, the news media or jurisdictions. All such inquiries are to be directed to The Election Center..." [15]

What government agency is the Election Center connected with? None: The Election Center is a private, nonprofit entity set up during the late 1980s. Who set it up? Some people in Washington, D.C., whose names are not published. Who provided its seed money? No one seems to know. Who runs the Election Center now? A man named R. Doug

Lewis, who was not elected by anyone.

What are the credentials of R. Doug Lewis? With some persistence, I located a bio for Doug Lewis,[16] but all it said was that he was an assistant to the president in the White House (doesn't say which president); that he ran campaigns for various important politicians (doesn't name any of them); that he headed the Democratic Party for the states of Texas and Kansas (doesn't say what years); and that he consulted for the petrochemical industry (doesn't say what company). With a little more digging, I found that he "managed affairs" for former Texas governor John Connally.

The Election Center works with the National Association of Secretaries of State (NASS), the National Association of State Election Directors (NASED) and the International Association of Clerks, Recorders, Election Officials and Treasurers (IACREOT).

When election officials want to know if these voting machines can be trusted, they ask R. Doug Lewis. I'm sure R. Doug Lewis is a terrific guy. (The feeling apparently isn't mutual; he hangs up on me when I call him.) But what I do want to know is this: What specific credentials qualify him for the critical work of overseeing the security of voting systems in the United States? Who appointed him?

I called The Election Center to ask about certification and was told that the only person who could answer my questions was R. Doug Lewis.

Harris: "Mr. Lewis, I understand that your organization is the one that, basically, certifies the certifiers of the voting machines, is that correct?"

Lewis: "Yes."

(This turns out not to be true; perhaps he misunderstood my question. The NASED ITA Technical Sub-Committee of the Voting Systems Board is a small group of people who select the certification agencies. This group does seem to work closely with R. Doug Lewis, but I am unclear as to who's in charge of whom.)

Harris: "Do you have anything in writing that shows that a line-by-line examination of source code was performed by either Ciber or Wyle?"

Lewis: "No. But that's what they do. They go line by line. They're not trying to rewrite it."

Harris: "Where can I get something in writing that says they look at the code line by line?"

Lewis: "I don't know where you'd find that."

Harris: " ... Let me be more precise. Are you saying that Wyle and Ciber do a line-by-line check on the code, and the way it interacts with the system, to make sure that no one could have put any malicious code into the voting-machine software?"

Lewis: "Oh. That's what you're talking about. I don't know if they do a line-by-line check to see if there's a problem."

Harris: "Who can I speak with at Ciber and Wyle?"

Lewis: "I don't think anyone there could answer your questions."

Harris: "Who do you speak with at those labs?"

Lewis: (muttered) "Shawn S....... at Wyle — No, Shawn S....... is at Ciber ... "

Harris: "I couldn't quite catch the name of the person at Ciber. Did you say Shawn S....... what was that last name?"

Lewis: (muttered) "Shawn Sou....."

Harris: "I'm sorry, I couldn't understand you. What is that name again?"

Lewis: (muttered) "Shawn South....."

Harris: "How do you spell that?"

Lewis: (muttered very fast) "Southw...."

Harris: "I'm sorry, you'll have to slow down. How do you spell that?"

Lewis: (quietly) "S-o-u-t-h-w-[ard?]" (I was never able to understand him. The correct spelling of the name is Shawn Southworth.)

Harris: "I have one more question: Prior to taking over The Election Center, you owned a business that sold used computer parts, which ended up going out of business. Shortly after that you took over The Election Center. Did you have any other experience at all that qualified you to handle issues like the security of national elections?"

Lewis: "Oh, no, no, no. I'm not going to go there with you."

Harris: "I have newspaper articles published shortly after your computer reselling company went out of business that refer to you as an expert in election systems. What else did you do that qualified you to take over your current position?"

Lewis: "My background is that I owned a computer hardware and software business. I've never claimed to be an expert. That's the reason we have laboratories, nationally recognized laboratories."

Lewis's used-computer reselling business was called Micro Trade Mart, which appears in the Texas franchise-tax database this way:

Micro Trade Mart Inc.
Director: R. Doug Lewis
President: R. Doug Lewis

This corporation is not in good standing as it has not satisfied all state tax requirements. Lewis ran Micro Trade Mart from 1986 through June 1993. He became Executive Director of The Election Center in 1994.

I don't know why R. Doug Lewis, after holding the position of "Assistant to the President in the White House," spent eight years selling used computers. All I really want to know is: What qualifies him to certify voting-machine certifiers, and why must everyone, including the media, talk *only* to R. Doug Lewis when they want to find out how our voting machines are tested?

* * * * *

When Wyle's division in Huntsville, Alabama, stopped testing this software in 1996, that certification process went to Nichols Research, also of Huntsville, Alabama.

Shawn Southworth tested the voting-machine software for Nichols Research. But Nichols Research quit doing it, and voting-software examination went to PSInet, of Huntsville, Alabama. Shawn Southworth tested the voting machine software for PSInet. PSInet ran into financial difficulties. Voting-software certification was taken over by Metamore, in Huntsville, Alabama, where Shawn Southworth handled it. Metamore no longer does software certification for voting machines. Now it is done by Ciber, of Huntsville, Alabama. Shawn Southworth is in charge of it.

I called to talk to Shawn Southworth, but his assistant told me that she was supposed to refer all questions back to The Election Center. The only person at The Election Center who is authorized to answer questions about certification procedures is R. Doug Lewis.

I looked up Shawn Southworth on the Web. I found pictures of his motorcycles, and I found pictures of him at the beach. Though I'm sure he is eminently qualified (but we're not allowed to ask his credentials), no one has yet convinced me that Shawn Southworth should be entrusted with the sanctity of the vote-counting for all of America.

And now for the rudest question of all:

Why should we trust anyone? Why can't we just audit the accuracy of these machines, using paper ballots and practical procedures?

7
Why Vote?

Does anyone really care about voting anymore? Only about half of the eligible U.S. voters even bother to vote in federal elections. The percentage ranges from around 49 percent (1996) to 63 percent (1960). In the 2000 U.S. national election, only 51.3 percent of eligible voters chose to go to the polls. [1]

Now, if you live in a country like Australia, where the law requires that you vote, you might find our lackadaisical voting behavior here in the U.S. to be shocking. Perhaps we should be taken to the woodshed for our frequent failure to vote, but — although it's certainly true that we are a bit cavalier about exercising our voting rights — have you ever heard of anyone who doesn't want the *right* to vote?

When the United States was formed, our founders had a clear idea what government should and should not be. The purpose of the government was to provide for the common good. As Benjamin Franklin wrote, "*In free governments the rulers are the servants and the people their superiors and sovereigns.*"

Our founders intended that the ultimate power in our society should rest in the people themselves. They set it up so that we should exercise those powers either directly or through representatives.

"Government is instituted for the common good; for the protection, safety, prosperity, and happiness of the people; and not for profit, honor, or private interest of any one man, family, or class of men; therefore, the people alone have an incontestable, unalienable, and indefeasible right to institute government; and to reform, alter, or totally change the same, when their protection, safety, prosperity, and happiness require it."

— John Adams, Article VII, Massachusetts Constitution

"There is only one force in the nation that can be depended upon to keep the government pure and the governors honest, and that is the people themselves. They alone, if well informed, are capable of preventing the corruption of power, and of restoring the nation to its rightful course if it should go astray. They alone are the safest depository of the ultimate powers of government."

— Thomas Jefferson

If we, collectively, are the source of authority for our government, we must have a way to communicate our instructions. We must be able to select the representatives we think can best implement our will; we need to be able to change them, reorganize them if need be, and decide how they will conduct our business.

Most importantly, we must reach some approximate agreement about what we want, and that is done by placing people, initiatives and referenda on the ballot and casting our votes on them.

We are a nation of laws, but if our laws conflict with our collective will, there will be little incentive to follow them. It is only because our representatives were chosen by our own voice that we agree to abide by the laws they vote upon, on our behalf.

Because our representatives must return to us from time to time, asking for permission to represent us again, we have a way to encourage them to behave the way we want them to.

"Nothing so strongly impels a man to regard the interest of his constituents, as the certainty of returning to the general mass of the people, from whence he was taken, where he must participate in their burdens."

— George Mason, speech, Virginia Ratifying Convention,
June 17, 1788

Trust is the element that keeps us from taking to the streets every time we disagree with something our government does. As long as we feel our representatives are deciding most things, and the very important things, the way we would ask them to, we are content. If we elected them in an election that all agreed was fair, but they make an egregious choice, one that many of us feel we cannot live with, our governmental system sanctions our protest. We reserve such behavior for unusual circumstances, knowing that when the next election rolls around, we can always vote them out.

Perceived lack of integrity in the voting system is guaranteed to produce shouts of indignation, but because *most* elections are perceived to be fair, we can still show some patience with the situation.

If, however, we come to perceive that most elections cannot be trusted, we've got a huge problem. Suddenly, these people don't have our permission to do anything. Why should we follow laws that they passed if we don't believe they were fairly elected? Why should we accept anything they do? Why should we follow the law if *they* didn't? Why should we cooperate with our government at all?

> "That love of order and obedience to the laws, which so remarkably characterize the citizens of the United States, are sure pledges of internal tranquility; and the elective franchise, if guarded as the ark of our safety, will peaceably dissipate all combinations to subvert a Constitution, dictated by the wisdom, and resting on the will of the people."
>
> — Thomas Jefferson to Benjamin Waring, 1801

Take away trust in the voting system, and all bets are off. This is what the architects of the new, unauditable voting systems have never understood: The vote is the underpinning for our authorization of every law, every government expenditure, every tax, every elected person. But if we don't *trust* the voting system, we will never accept that those votes represent our voice, and that kind of thing can cause a whole society to quit cooperating.

> "I like to see the people awake and alert. The good sense of the people will soon lead them back if they have erred in a moment of surprise."
>
> — Thomas Jefferson to John Adams, 1786

* * * * *

Democracy is for suckers?

Americans prefer to feel good. They want to believe that elections are fair, that machines count right and that people don't cheat. And yet, there are scholars even within our own country who might advocate, if not subverting the system, at least lying to the voters.

According to the late University of Chicago professor Leo Strauss, all city states are based on fraud. He believed that ordinary people can't handle this truth. [2] "[Strauss] argued that Platonic truth is too hard for people to bear," writes political columnist William Pfaff. " ... Hence it has become necessary to tell lies to people about the nature of political reality. An elite recognizes the truth, however, and keeps it to itself. ... The ostensibly hidden truth is that expediency works." [3]

Such a philosophy, when applied by radicals, might lead to considerable disarray in our society. In fact, when writers like Pfaff and Seymour Hersh exposed the Straussian studies of Deputy Defense Secretary Paul Wolfowitz, Abram Shulsky of the Pentagon's Office of Special Plans, and writer William Kristol, a great hue and cry arose. Some of the writings of Strauss appear sinister indeed. Have his followers put our democracy at risk?

Strauss is complex, and to select only those writings that can form a rationale for evildoing and then apply them to anyone who studied under him is a bit disingenuous. Besides, many other philosophers provide fodder for those who will do wrong.

But I bring up Strauss, and the powerful men in public office who studied under Strauss and his protegés, to show you that simply wanting to feel good about our political systems, wanting to trust and have faith, is not always wise. While you are feeling comfortably safe, someone may very well be out there rationalizing the elitism and greed that can eliminate your freedom. Whatever your opinions on current political figures, our founding fathers would tell you to expect and prepare for usurpation of power by people who care not a fig about your comfort. It is not inconceivable that at some point, someone in power will believe that his agenda is more important than your vote.

It's just a matter of time, our founders said, before you'll need to rein in your leaders. Thomas Jefferson, especially, foresaw many of the dangers we face today and exhorted us toward constant vigilance:

"Unless the mass retains sufficient control over those entrusted with the powers of their government, these will be perverted to their own oppression, and to the perpetuation of wealth and power in the individuals and their families selected for the trust."

—Thomas Jefferson to M. van der Kemp, 1812

"No other depositories of power [but the people themselves] have ever yet been found, which did not end in converting to their own profit the earnings of those committed to their charge."

— Thomas Jefferson to Samuel Kercheval, 1816

"If once [the people] become inattentive to the public affairs, you and I, and Congress and Assemblies, Judges and Governors, shall all become wolves. It seems to be the law of our general nature, in spite of individual exceptions."

— Thomas Jefferson to Edward Carrington, 1787

"[We] should look forward to a time, and that not a distant one, when corruption in this as in the country from which we derive our origin will have seized the heads of government and be spread by them through the body of the people; when they will purchase the voices of the people and make them pay the price. Human nature is the same on every side of the Atlantic and will be alike influenced by the same causes."

— Thomas Jefferson: Notes on Virginia Q.XIII, 1782

"How long we can hold our ground, I do not know. We are not incorruptible; on the contrary, corruption is making sensible though silent progress."

— Thomas Jefferson, 1799

Maybe you have never written a letter to your legislator. Perhaps you think that no matter what you do, they'll just do what they want anyway. But can you live with yourself if you do nothing? And what legacy will you leave your children? Later chapters focus on practical activism; this section is about your responsibility to engage.

Our founders did not promise to be the caretakers for their gift of democracy to us. They told us that if we don't feed it, our democracy will die. They warned us that it would get sick sometimes and explained that it was up to us to administer the right medicine.

If things are not going right, let your elected officials know. If you have to, remind them that they'll soon need to return to you for a vote. What good is your voice if you don't use it? If you believe that government has taken the wrong course, educate your legislators, and if they won't listen, throw them out and elect someone who promises a revision of the course. If you conclude, after reading this book, that your vote might not be counted correctly, then you have decisions to make.

Why vote? Is your country what you want, or is it becoming something else? Do you feel your vote is in danger? What would the founders of this country ask you to do? Will you choose to engage?

> "The liberties of our country, the freedom of our civil Constitution, are worth defending at all hazards; and it is our duty to defend them against all attacks. We have received them as a fair inheritance from our worthy ancestors: they purchased them for us with toil and danger and expense of treasure and blood, and transmitted them to us with care and diligence. It will bring an everlasting mark of infamy on the present generation, enlightened as it is, if we should suffer them to be wrested from us by violence without a struggle, or to be cheated out of them by the artifices of false and designing men."
>
> — Samuel Adams

> "Governments are instituted among men, deriving their just powers from the consent of the governed."
>
> — Declaration of Independence

8
Company Histories
(What you won't find on the company Web sites)

If anything should remain part of the public commons, it is voting. Yet as we have progressed through a series of new voting methods, control of our voting systems, and even our understanding of how they work, has come under new ownership.

> "It's a shell game, with money, companies and corporate brands switching in a blur of buy-outs and bogus fronts. It's a sinkhole, where mobbed-up operators, paid-off public servants, crazed Christian fascists, CIA shadow-jobbers, war-pimping arms dealers — and presidential family members — lie down together in the slime. It's a hacker's dream, with pork-funded, half-finished, secretly-programmed computer systems installed without basic security standards by politically-partisan private firms, and protected by law from public scrutiny." [1]

The previous quote, printed in a Russian publication, leads an article which mixes inaccuracies with disturbing truths. Should we assume crooks are in control? Is it a shell game?

Whatever it is, it has certainly deviated from community-based counting of votes by the local citizenry.

We began buying voting machines in the 1890s, choosing clunky mechanical-lever machines, in part to reduce the shenanigans going on with manipulating paper-ballot counts. By the 1960s, we had become enamored of the poke-a-hole method (punch cards). In the early 1980s, we saw the advent of fill-in-the-oval ballots, run through a scanner for tabulation (optical-scan systems). In the mid-1990s, we decided to try computers that mark votes using touch screens or dial-a-vote devices (direct recording electronic, or DRE, systems). Then we began experimenting with Internet voting.

We first relinquished control to local election workers, who managed lever machines and punch-card voting. With the advent of optical-scan systems, local election workers gradually gave up control to private, for-profit corporations and their programmers and technicians.

In a frenzy of mergers and acquisitions during the 1980s, local election-services companies sold control of our voting systems to a handful of corporations. During the 1990s, these corporations engaged in a pattern of setting up alliances and swapping key personnel that has given just a few people, some of whom have vested interests, far too much access to and influence over our voting systems.

This is not a computer-programming problem. It is a procedural matter, and part of the procedure must involve keeping human beings, as many of us as possible, in control of our own voting system. Any computerized voting system that requires us to trust a few computer scientists and some corporate executives constitutes flawed public policy. It doesn't matter whether they come up with perfect cryptographic techniques or invent smart cards so clever they can recognize us by sight. The real problem is that we've created a voting system controlled by someone else.

During the 1980s, mom-and-pop companies sold election supplies. That changed when the dominant player in the elections industry, Business Records Corp. (BRC), embarked on an acquisitions blitz. You'd almost think they wanted to corner the elections industry.

Business Records Corp. (BRC)

Business Records Corp. was a subsidiary of a Dallas, Texas, company named Cronus Industries Inc.,[2] which was owned by a consortium of wealthy Texas power brokers.

July 1984: BRC acquired Data Management Associates of Colorado Springs, Colorado, a closely-held concern that supplied county

governments with computer software and services, and acquired David
G. Carney Co., a closely-held San Antonio firm that marketed records-
keeping services. Then it purchased the assets of C. Edwin Hultman
Co., a closely-held Pittsburgh company that provided county-govern-
ment information services. [3]

November 1984: BRC acquired Western Data Services Inc., a firm
that provided on-line computer services to several hundred county and
municipal governments, school districts and other governmental agencies
in Texas. [4]

November 1984: BRC acquired Contract Microfilm Services and
Business Images Inc. [5]

February 1985: BRC acquired Roberts & Son Inc. of Birmingham,
Alabama, a firm which provided voting equipment and election ma-
terials to county governments. [6]

April 1985: BRC acquired Frank Thornber Co., a Chicago firm
specializing in election-related services, equipment and supplies. [7]

November 1985: BRC acquired Dayton Legal Blank Co. [8]

December 1985: Cronus Industries Inc., the parent company of BRC,
completed the purchase of Computer Election Systems Inc. of Berkeley,
California. At that time, Computer Election Systems was the nation's
largest manufacturer of election machines and related equipment. It
provided election computer programs and equipment to more than 1,000
county and municipal jurisdictions. [9]

January 1986: BRC acquired Integrated Micro Systems Inc. of Rock-
ford, Illinois. [10]

March 1986: BRC merged with Computer Concepts & Services Inc.
of St. Cloud, Minnesota. [11] During the same month, it acquired Sun
Belt Press Inc. of Birmingham, Alabama and merged it into Roberts
& Son, one of the election- and voting-equipment companies acquired
by BRC in February 1985. It also bought the government operations
of Minneapolis-based Miller/Davis Company. The government portion of Miller/Davis provided legal forms, election supplies and office supplies to local governments in Minnesota. [12]

Business Records Corp. dominated the U.S. elections industry until 1997, when it was purchased by Election Systems and Software.

Election Systems and Software (ES&S)

Founded in Omaha, Nebraska, under the name "Data Mark Systems" by brothers Todd and Bob Urosevich, the company soon changed its name to American Information Systems (AIS). The Uroseviches obtained financing from William and Robert Ahmanson, whose family piled up a fortune in the savings-and-loan and insurance industries. [13]

Howard Ahmanson Jr., a younger cousin of the AIS financiers, has parlayed his fortune into extremist right-wing politics, pushing the agenda of the Christian Reconstructionist movement, which openly advocates a theocratic takeover of American democracy. [14]

William and Robert Ahmanson appeared to be more moderate than Howard Jr. and invested money in theater and public broadcasting. In 1987, they sold their direct shares in the voting-machine company to the Omaha World-Herald (which took a 45 percent stake in the company) and the McCarthy Group (35 percent). [15]

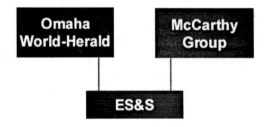

And here the fun begins — watch the bouncing ball ...

It turns out that the Omaha World-Herald has also been an owner of the McCarthy Group. [16]

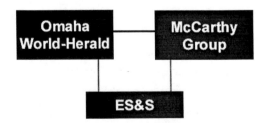

The Omaha World-Herald was owned by Peter Kiewit, the head of Peter Kiewit Sons' Inc., until his death. [17]

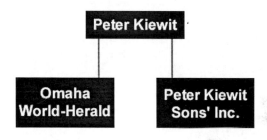

Before he died, Peter Kiewit set up the Peter Kiewit Foundation, requiring that at all times the foundation have a director from Peter Kiewit Sons' Inc. as a trustee.

Kiewit arranged for the Omaha World-Herald stock to be purchased by its employees and the Peter Kiewit Foundation, which holds a special class of stock, giving it veto power over any sale proposal. The largest single stockholder in the World-Herald Company is the Peter Kiewit Foundation. [18]

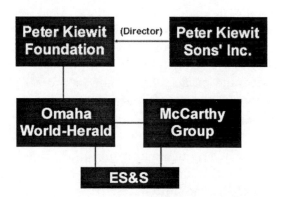

Tracing ES&S ownership thus leads us to the World-Herald and then to the Peter Kiewit Foundation.

It also leads to the McCarthy Group, which is headed by Michael McCarthy. He came to Omaha to sell Peter Kiewit's ranch when he died. [36] Michael McCarthy assumed Peter Kiewit Jr.'s position as a director of Peter Kiewit Sons' Inc. in 2001. [19]

The McCarthy Group shows up as one of the investments of a World-Herald subsidiary, in turn leading back to the World-Herald and the Peter Kiewit Foundation. Dizzy yet?

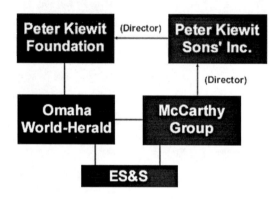

I became interested in Kiewit because if anything is less appropriate than Chuck Hagel's ties to ES&S, it would be a Kiewit relationship of any kind to any voting-system vendor. So who is Kiewit?

Peter Kiewit Sons' Inc. and its subsidiaries have been tied to a string of bid-rigging cases in as many as 11 states and two countries.

In an antitrust case that involved charges of bid-rigging in New Orleans, Kiewit pleaded no contest and paid $100,000 in fines and $300,000 in a civil settlement. In South Dakota, a Kiewit subsidiary pleaded guilty to bid-rigging on road contracts and paid a fine of $350,000. In Kansas, a Kiewit subsidiary was found guilty of bid-rigging and mail fraud on a federal highway project. The firm was fined $900,000 and a company official was sentenced to a year in jail. A Kiewit subsidiary paid $1.8 million for bid-rigging on a state highway project in Nebraska, and a Kiewit vice president was jailed. [20]

The Army Corps of Engineers at one point decided to bar Kiewit from bidding on all federal projects but later changed its mind. Kiewit builds munitions plants and military airstrips.

Does Kiewit have a political agenda? Absolutely. Kiewit's Jerry Pfeffer has spoken before Congress to ask for more privatization:

"Kiewit, based in Omaha, built more lane-miles of the Interstate Highway System than any other contractor," he said. "…We're active in toll roads, airports and water facilities …" [21]

Pfeffer, advocating privatization of the highway system, has stated glibly that "American motorists will gladly pay market prices to avoid congestion."

He goes on to suggest to Congress that Kiewit should get special tax treatment. Kiewit also owns CalEnergy Corp., has been involved with Level 3 Communications and is a quiet giant in telecommunications; underneath its highways, Kiewit lays fiber-optic cable and has been outfitting our roads with video surveillance cameras since 1993.

When the state of Oklahoma forbade Kiewit to bid anymore, Kiewit set up a different company called Gilbert Southern Corp. According to *The Sunday Oklahoman,* "Gilbert Southern Corp. recently submitted a sworn affidavit to the transportation department saying it had no parent company, affiliate firms or subsidiaries." [22]

But Kiewit owned Gilbert Southern Corp. lock, stock and barrel. When the state of Oklahoma found out, it yanked the contracts.

In another obfuscation, Peter Kiewit & Sons took contracts in Washington state under the guise of a minority-owned firm. The government thought it was giving contracts to a company owned by African-American women; actually, it was a bunch of white guys in Nebraska. Kiewit paid more than $700,000 in fines while denying liability or wrongdoing. [23]

Kiewit's corporate papers indicate that investigations and litigation are normal, saying there are "numerous" lawsuits. This is a handy thing to know: Apparently you can skip disclosure of pending litigation if there's a lot of it.

This example illustrates why voting-machine vendors should be required to provide full disclosure on owners, parent companies, stockholders and key personnel. Kiewit has connections with both ES&S parent companies and has a track record of hiding ownership when it wants to, it has a powerful profit motive for getting the people it wants into office and it has broken the law in the past to achieve its goals.

We should require enough disclosure so that we can at least ask informed questions next time we buy voting machines.

* * * * *

In 1997, the company that had called itself American Information Systems bought elections-industry giant BRC and changed its name to Election Systems and Software. The Securities and Exchange Commission objected on antitrust grounds, and an odd little deal was cooked up in which the assets of BRC were shared between two voting companies: ES&S and Sequoia.

Sequoia Voting Systems

Sequoia Voting Systems has nearly jockeyed its way into position to grab voting-machine dominance away from ES&S and Diebold.

We are told to trust Sequoia's voting systems, along with the people who sell and service them. Well, come with me for a moment and let's do a little reenactment. After this, you, the jury, can decide for yourself how much trust you want to offer Sequoia.

You be Philip Foster, Sequoia's southern regional sales manager and the project manager who oversaw the first touch-screen election in Riverside County, California. I'll be your brother-in-law, David Philpot of Birmingham, Alabama.

I am going to hand you a manila envelope stuffed with $20,000 or $40,000 of kickback cash.[24] These envelopes are sealed, and I won't tell you what is in them. I instruct you to travel to Louisiana and place them in a drawer belonging to Louisiana state elections chief Jerry Fowler. You do so. And then you do it again. Five times.

If we are to trust Sequoia Voting Systems, we must believe that Phil Foster had no idea what was in those envelopes. Foster said in an interview that he did nothing wrong. He continued to work for Sequoia after these allegations were revealed.

Peter Cosgrove, Sequoia's chief executive officer at the time, decided that the allegations against Foster (two counts of conspiracy to commit money laundering and one count of conspiracy to commit malfeasance in office) were "without merit," so he continued to employ him.

"As a company, we believe the allegations against him are without merit," said Cosgrove, "and we believe the statements against him were made by convicted felons." [25]

Well that much is true. Both Foster's brother-in-law, David Philpot, and Louisiana's elections chief, Jerry Fowler, pleaded guilty. Fowler went to federal prison. Another participant in the scam, which reportedly cost

Louisiana taxpayers $8 million, was New Jersey's Pasquale Ricci, who pleaded guilty to conspiracy to commit money laundering. [26]

When the charges against Foster were thrown out, the prosecutor appealed. State District Judge Bonnie Jackson upheld the dismissal of charges, ruling that prosecutors had failed to show the charges resulted from evidence collected separately from Foster's grand-jury testimony. Because he had been immunized, prosecutors could not use Foster's own statements against him. [27]

"My investigation of the charges reveals he hasn't done a thing in the world wrong," Foster's Baton Rouge lawyer, Karl Koch, is reported to have said.

OK. Let us assume that Foster really had no idea what was in those envelopes. Forty thousand dollars is a minimum of four hundred $100 bills, a pile two inches thick. We are trusting these guys with our vote. Do we really want someone around our voting machines who is so naive that he doesn't understand the implications of sticking manila envelopes stuffed with two-inch-thick wads of something shaped like money into desk drawers belonging to election officials?

Of the big four voting vendors, Sequoia currently has the tidiest corporate ownership but the most recent indictment of an employee and the most prolific habit of hiring its own regulators.

Besides hiring former California Secretary of State Bill Jones, Sequoia hired Kathryn Ferguson, the elections official who helped purchase Sequoia machines for Clark County, Nevada, and Santa Clara County, California, as Vice President, Corporate Communications. In October 2003 she moved to Hart Intercivic. [28]

Michael Frontera, former executive director of the Denver Election Commission, went to work for Sequoia after awarding it $6.6 million in contracts from his own department. [29]

Alfie Charles, former spokesman for Secretary of State Bill Jones, is now spokesman for Sequoia Voting Systems. [30]

At the time of the bribery scandal, Sequoia Voting Systems was owned by Jefferson Smurfit Group, a company based in Ireland. In May 2002, Sequoia was purchased by Great Britain's De La Rue plc, and Phil Foster's loyal and trusting boss, Peter Cosgrove, was retained and promoted.

De La Rue is considered a blue-chip company. Its fortunes are heavily affected by politics, and it has at least one politically active investor.

It is the world's biggest commercial money printer. De La Rue was one of the first British companies to profit from the war in Iraq, earning a quick windfall when it received the assignment to print the new Iraqi bank notes. During the first Bush administration, De La Rue was called in toward the tail end of Sandinista rule in Nicaragua to create new money. [31]

De La Rue is also involved in Britain's national lottery, through its investment in Camelot Group plc. In this capacity, it enraged British citizens when they learned that Camelot had assigned its executives a 40 percent pay hike while reducing the funds allocated to good works. [32]

De La Rue would very much like to take Diebold's position, and not just in election systems. The firm also sells ATMs and smart cards and lists Diebold Inc. as one of its competitors. [33]

In July 2003, the U.S. Department of Justice launched an investigation into a U.S. division of De La Rue, alleging that it had engaged in an illegal price-fixing scheme in relation to the supply of holograms for Visa banking cards, violating U.S. antitrust laws. In a statement, De La Rue said the "individual implicated" in the price-fixing allegation had "left the business in October 1999." [34]

One of the most aggressive investors in De La Rue stock is the hugely wealthy Australian Lowy family, who by March 2003 had picked up 5.5 million shares (just over 3%) through their private investment vehicle, LFG Holdings. Frank Lowy is Australia's second-richest man.

He is highly political, particularly with pro-Israel issues, and has come under fire for his company's payments to Lord Levy, British Prime Minister Tony Blair's "special envoy to the Middle East," which the Aussie billionaire authorized directly. At first, his payments raised suspicions of a "cash for access" intrigue at the highest level of British politics, but as the size of the payments (£250,000) became apparent, the Australian media began raising questions of "cash for foreign policy." [35]

The Lowy family contributes heavily to the Democratic Party. [36]

* * * * *

On August 4, 2003, Sequoia Voting Systems quietly announced a partnership with VoteHere Inc. for electronic ballot verification on its touch-screen machines. [37] It is amazing how much money the elections industry is willing to spend just to avoid giving us ballots we can read and use for audits. The VoteHere system provides a receipt with a code number on it, not a human-readable ballot. You get to check your single vote using a secret code.

If you believe this constitutes public counting of the vote then please meet me under the bridge at midnight and enter your special password into my PalmPilot, and I'll slip you a brown paper bag with some stock tips in it. Count on 'em. Trust me.

Instead of allowing the vote to be counted in the open, viewed by citizens, the VoteHere solution requires us to give control of our elections to a handful of cryptographers with defense-industry ties.

VoteHere Inc.

Like a Timex watch, this company takes a licking but keeps on ticking. Launched by a cryptographer named Jim Adler during the height of the dot-com boom, VoteHere hoped to usher us into the brave new world of Internet voting.

Adler picked up funding from Compaq Computer and Cisco Systems and Northwest Venture Associates, $15 million by November 2000. [38] He also did an honorable thing: He made his company's source code available for review.

Adler's Internet voting system did not fare well in a simple review titled "Vote early, vote often and VoteHere," a master's thesis by Philip E. Varner. After defining threats to the publicly available VoteHere system in such areas as completeness, privacy, verifiability, fairness and reliability, and creating an attack tree, Varner identified several weaknesses in the VoteHere system and concluded it was not ready for use. [39]

Undaunted, the entrepreneurial Adler charged ahead with a plan to have us try voting on totable Compaq iPAQ hardware using VoteHere software and on-line polling sites connected to the Internet. [40]

But his Internet plans did not materialize, and Adler also stopped making his source code available for public review. VoteHere persuaded places like Swindon, England, and the city of Suwanee, Georgia, to try the system and conducted an on-line advisory election for the Conservative Party in Sweden. But by 2003, it had few sales to show for six years of work and $15 million in outside investments.

I have seen no more sources of funding for VoteHere, nor much in the way of sales revenues, but one thing I did find was a board of directors spiked with power brokers from the defense industries.

For a long time, VoteHere's chairman was Admiral Bill Owens, a member of the Defense Policy Board and Vice Chairman of Scientific Applications International Corp. (SAIC), which did the Diebold review for the state of Maryland. Robert Gates, former CIA director and head of the George Bush School of Business at Texas A&M, was another director.

In 2003, VoteHere decided instead to go after the innards of other vendors' touch screens, perhaps hoping to become the Good Housekeeping Seal of Approval for electronic voting machines. VoteHere is now marketing itself as a verification system in lieu of paper ballots.

I have always been a proponent of hybrid systems, combining voter-verified paper ballots with computers. Systems like VoteHere, though, make me wonder if we aren't safer to go back to straight hand-counted paper ballots. Every time we propose a solution to solve a problem with computerized voting systems, a new salesman pops up with a different cure, new techno-jargon, a fresh sales pitch and friends in high places and starts lobbying our public officials. By the time we figure out the latest spin, it could be too late.

* * * * *

VoteHere had its eye on a Pentagon project called SERVE, designed to convert our armed forces over to Internet voting. Despite its clout, VoteHere did not win the contract. Instead, the contract was awarded to election.com and Hart Intercivic.

election.com

This company is no longer in existence, at least in its original form. I am including it so that you can see just how slipshod our government procurement system, which originally awarded the SERVE contract to election.com, really is.

According to its Web site, election.com was a global election software and services company which provided election services like voter registration and Internet voting.

Newsday's Mark Harrington discovered that election.com had sold controlling ownership to an unnamed group of Saudi investors who, he reported, paid $1.2 million to acquire 20 million preferred shares, for 51.6 percent of the voting power. The investment group was identified as Osan Ltd. [41]

I spoke with Amy Parker, press contact for election.com, in February 2003.

Harris: "Is the Newsday article, which states that 51.6% of election.com is owned by Osan Ltd., accurate?"

Parker: "No, that is not true."

Harris: "Is Osan Ltd. involved?"

Parker: "Osan Ltd. became the largest shareholder of election.com in December 2002 — that's an accurate statement — and after December 2002 Osan held 36.2% of all outstanding shares."

Harris: "Is Osan based in the United States, or where?"

Parker: "In the Cayman Islands."

Harris: "So when *Newsday* said they have controlling interest ... "

Parker: "After December 2002, Osan held 36.2% of all outstanding shares. And that's equal to 58.2% of the voting power."

OK. So Osan actually owned *more* controlling interest than reported by Newsday. Why would we want our military votes counted by a Saudi-owned company?

At least, if it's approved by the Pentagon, one would assume that it's a pretty solid operation. But for some reason, election.com pulled the names of its directors off the Internet. There are ways to find pages that have been removed, so I did and began contacting directors. I soon received an e-mail from one of the directors which said simply: "You should call me."

I did, and he spoke with me at some length but only after getting my agreement not to reveal which director he was when I printed this interview.

Harris: "I notice they've taken the names off the Web. Are you still involved?"

Director: "No."

Harris: "Tell me about your experience with election.com."

Director: It looked like a hot company, [was] featured in *Red Herring* as one of the companies most going to affect the world and all that. ... What happened is that Joe — they had a CEO named Joe, Joe something ... "

Harris: "Joe Mohen?"

Director: "That's it. He ended up loving publicity too much. They put those machines in on the Democratic Convention, a giant waste of money, over a million, so Joe could get on TV. When they wanted to start going that way I got concerned. If they were getting into public elections, the market wasn't as huge [as elections in the private market, such as stockholder votes and union elections].

"Of course, the reason I got into it was we wanted to run a business, we wanted to become profitable. ... So the 2000 election in Florida happens, and they change their philosophy and want to do public elections. I said, 'This isn't going to work.'

"Finally we get Joe to resign as CEO and we got the Number 2 guy [Charles Smith] to resign also. By this time we were about out of money." (He explained that they brought in a new CEO, who pumped in new money and got some contracts in Australia, but it wasn't long before they ran out of money again.)

Director: "Then, the guy we fired [Charles Smith] comes back with this Arab money. They wanted the board as well as the company. For $5 million, they bought the whole damn thing. At the time the Arab money came in, I made the motion to go ahead and dismiss our butts."

Harris: "What about Charles Smith? I hear he's the guy who represents the Arabs."

Director: "Charles Smith is the guy who we fired. He is sort of an Arab himself; I don't know why he has the name Smith." [According to his bio, Smith previously worked with Procter & Gamble in Saudi Arabia and with PepsiCo in Cairo.]

Harris: "Who else is in the group of investors?"

Director: "Nobody knows who this group is."

Harris: "How Saudi is Osan Ltd.?"

Director: "Oh, it's all Saudi as far as I know. What do you know about the thing?"

Harris: "Just what I read in *Newsday*."

According to the *Newsday* article, Defense Department spokesman Glenn Flood, when asked how the department screens the background of contractors, said: "We don't look into that [country of origin] part of it. ... It's the process we're interested in, not the company, unless they screw up."

Penelope Bonsall, director of election administration for the Federal Election Commission, told *Newsday* that tracking issues like election.com's change of control doesn't fall under the purview of any federal agency.

I decided to ask Amy Parker more about the Pentagon deal, but the conversation got derailed:

Harris: "With regard to the military contract, what will election.com be doing and what will Hart Intercivic do?"

Parker: "We're not the prime contractor on that project."

Harris: "Election.com is not the main contractor?"

Parker: "No."

Harris: "Who is, then?"

Parker: "That's Accenture."

Harris: "I spoke with Hart Intercivic, who has explained to me that Accenture does not make voting systems. What they do is procurement. They procured the contract and then subcontracted it to election.com and Hart Intercivic, is that true?"

Parker: "Yes."

Harris: "Accenture holds shares in Election.com also, doesn't it?"

Parker: "No."

Harris: "No?"

Parker: "Accenture, we have a formal strategic marketing alliance and as part of that they took an equity position."

Harris: "So Accenture holds shares in election.com, then."

Parker: "Yes."

* * * * *

On July 2, 2003, election.com announced that it had sold its assets to Accenture, turning the military SERVE project over to an Arthur Andersen spin-off and Hart Intercivic.

Hart Intercivic

You might get the impression that Hart Intercivic, a voting-system vendor based in Austin, Texas, is a cozy little family-owned operation, giving us real faces that we can hold accountable and trust with our vote. Not quite.

The chairman of Hart Intercivic is David Hart, whose family developed Hart Graphics, at one time the largest privately-held commercial printer in Texas.[42] Internet growth and the ease of putting documentation on disks and CD-ROMs reversed the company's fortunes.

"We began to see, in the later part of the '90s, a crack in the strategy," David Hart said. "The presses weren't staying busy." In looking for other work to fill the void, "we just ran into a wall. We were singularly unsuccessful." [43]

And it was here that the comfortable, family-owned company turned into a venture-capital- and government-privatization-driven election vendor. Hart Intercivic sells the eSlate, a dial-a-vote variation on the touch-screen concept that uses a wheel instead of a poke with a finger to register your vote.

The finances and managerial control of Hart Graphics were at one time closely controlled by the family, but Hart took a different approach to its election business. They lined up three rounds of venture capital and formed an alliance with a gigantic social-services privatizer.

For initial funding, Hart went to Triton Ventures, a wholly-owned subsidiary of Triton Energy, a firm that primarily exploits oil fields in Colombia. Triton, in turn, is a subsidiary of Amerada Hess. [44]

The $3.5 million awarded by Triton in 1999 didn't last long, but the Help America Vote Act, with its massive allocation of federal money, hovered just over the horizon. In October 2000, Hart picked up $32.5 million more from five sources. [45] In 2002, it raised another $7.5 million. [46]

RES Partners, which invested in Hart's second and third rounds, is an entity that represents Richard Salwen, retired Dell Computer Corporation vice president, general counsel and corporate secretary, who had also worked with Perot Systems and EDS. Salwen is a heavy contributor to George W. Bush and the Republican Party. [47]

Hart's most politically charged investor is an arm of Hicks, Muse, Tate & Furst, which was founded and is chaired by Tom Hicks. Hicks bought the Texas Rangers in 1999, making George W. Bush a millionaire 15 times over. Tom Hicks and his investment company are invested in Hart Intercivic through Stratford Capital. They are also heavily invested in Clear Channel Communications, the controversial radio-raider that muscled a thousand U.S. radio outlets into a more conservative message. [48]

In Orange County, California, and in the state of Ohio, Hart Intercivic entered into a joint enterprise called Maximus/Hart-InterCivic/DFM Associates, led by Maximus Inc.

Maximus Inc. is a gigantic privatizer of social services. It cuts deals with state governments to handle child-support collections, implement welfare-to-work and oversee managed care and HMO programs.

A Wisconsin legislative audit report found that Maximus spent more than $400,000 of state money on unauthorized expenses and found $1.6 million that Maximus couldn't properly document. These unauthorized expenses included a party for staff members at a posh Lake Geneva resort; $23,637 for "fanny packs" to promote the company, with the bills sent to the state; and entertainment of staff and clients by actress Melba Moore. Maximus settled for $1 million. [49]

Maximus jumped into the smart-card business and soon afterward entered the elections industry through an alliance with Hart Intercivic.

* * * * *

All this alliance-building and venture capital-seeking and political shoulder-rubbing is very nice for the big boys in Texas. However, it fundamentally changes the way we run our democracy. Do we really need to bring in Maximus, Hart Intercivic, DFM Associates, Triton oil, CapStreet Group, Dell Computers, Texas Growth Fund and the owner of the Texas Rangers just to count a vote?

The voting-machine industry has created such a Byzantine path to computerized voting that it cannot possibly be cheaper or more efficient than voting in a much-simplified way.

What do we really know about the certifier, Wyle Laboratories?

Texas billionaires Sam and Charles Wyly were the ninth-biggest contributors to George W. Bush in 2000, and Sam Wyly bankrolled the dirty tricks that wiped out John McCain's lead during the South Carolina primary. I wondered if the Wyly brothers are involved in Wyle (pronounced Wyly). I found many Wyly companies, and at least two companies called Wyly E. Coyote, but never found a link between Texas Bush-pal Wyly brothers and Wyle Laboratories.

I did find a link between Wyle Laboratories and prominent, right-wing, monied interests: William E. Simon, who, along with Richard Mellon Scaife and the Coors family, has been one of the primary supporters of the Heritage Foundation and its derivatives.

And I did find conflict of interest. You would expect that a company that certifies our voting machines would not have its owners running for office. You would also expect that no one who owns the certification company would be under criminal investigation. You'd be disappointed.

Shortly after Wyle Laboratories split off from Wyle Electronics in 1994, controlling interest was acquired by William E. Simon & Sons, a firm owned by a former Secretary of the Treasury, William E. Simon, and his son, Bill Simon, a candidate for governor of California in 2002.

Just before the election, in August 2002, William E. Simon & Sons was convicted of fraud and ordered to pay $78 million in damages. In what is surely record time for our glacial judicial system, the conviction was overturned in September 2002. The reason? William E. Simon & Sons had partnered up with someone who was a criminal and no one could tell who was the guiltiest. [50]

Recently, Wyle Laboratory shares held by William E. Simon & Sons were bought out. Now Wyle Laboratories is a wholly owned subsidiary of LTS Holdings, Inc., an entity I can find no information about, controlled by individuals whose names arc not available.

* * * * *

Diebold Election Systems

By now, Diebold Inc., the owner of what is now arguably the largest voting-machine company in the U.S., has become famous for its vested interests and an idiotic written statement made by its CEO.

Diebold director W. H. Timken has raised over $100,000 for the 2004 campaign of George W. Bush, earning the designation "Pioneer." Bush supporters qualify as Pioneers if they raise at least $100,000, and Rangers if they raise $200,000. [51]

On June 30, 2003, Diebold CEO Walton O'Dell organized a fundraising party for Vice President Dick Cheney, raising $600,000 and many of our antennas. [52]

Julie Carr-Smyth, of *The Plain Dealer*, discovered in August 2003 that O'Dell had traveled to Crawford, Texas, for a Pioneers and Rangers meeting attended by George W. Bush. Then Smyth learned of a letter, written by O'Dell shortly after returning from the Bush ranch and sent to 100 of his wealthy and politically inclined friends, which said:

"I am committed to helping Ohio deliver its electoral votes to the president next year." [53]

Admitting that such candor was a mistake, O'Dell later told Smyth, "I don't have a political adviser or a screener or a letter reviewer or any of that stuff." [54]

O'Dell described Diebold "a model of integrity and reporting and clarity and disclosure and consistency" and said he hoped his company would not suffer because of his personal mistake. A model of integrity and — clarity? Disclosure, perhaps, if you count embarrassing leaks and the sharp hissing sound of security flying out the window.

Wally O'Dell's statement was ill-advised, if not downright arrogant. But while Wally O'Dell can write about delivering the vote, Diebold's programmers may be in a position to actually do so. Where do they come from?

Diebold Election Systems was formed when Diebold Inc. of Canton, Ohio, acquired a Canadian company called Global Election Systems Inc., headquartered in Vancouver, British Columbia. [55] In some ways, nothing changed. The manufacturing body of the elections company continued to be in McKinney, Texas, under the same management, and the programming brain continued to be in Vancouver, Canada, with the same programmers.

Two of these programmers, Talbot Iredale and Guy Lancaster, have been designing and programming voting machines for Diebold Election Systems Inc. and its predecessors since 1988. Iredale and Lancaster developed the ES-2000 optical-scan voting system currently used in 37 states. [56]

These two men worked for North American Professional Technologies (NAPT), a subsidiary of Macrotrends International Ventures Inc. Their assignment was to develop a computerized voting system.

Macrotrends and NAPT were marketed by Norton Cooper. Cooper had been jailed for defrauding the Canadian government in 1974.[57] This did not keep him out of trouble; he became a stock promoter who sold so much stock in flawed companies though Macrotrends that Jaye Scholl, a writer for *Barron's*, portrayed him as a "hazard" and cautioned the well-heeled to avoid him at the golf course.[58] In 1989, members of the Vancouver Stock Exchange (VSE) ordered Macrotrends to cease any doings with Cooper [59] because his deals went south too often and *Forbes* had written an article describing the VSE as "The Scam Capital of the World," causing an erosion of confidence in the entire trading exchange.

Charles Hong Lee, a director of both Macrotrends and NAPT, was a childhood friend of Cooper's. In 1989 Lee was ordered to pay $555,380 in restitution when Lee was sued, together with Norton Cooper, by investors in a Macrotrends venture called Image West Entertainment. Cooper settled, but Lee failed to answer the complaint and also failed to list the lawsuit on his personal disclosure form with immigration officials. In 1994, Lee and his partner, Michael K. Graye, allegedly bilked 43 Chinese immigrants, mostly small businessmen, out of $614,547 more in fees than was authorized by the agreement. The unauthorized fees were paid to United Pacific Management Ltd., controlled by Graye and Lee. [60]

In 1991, NAPT and Macrotrends were reorganized, and the name was changed to Global Election Systems. At this time, Michael K. Graye became a director, a position he held for two years. Earlier, Graye had misappropriated $18 million from four corporations, but the law had not yet caught up with him. In 1996, Graye was arrested on charges of tax fraud, conspiracy to commit tax fraud, and money laundering, stemming from activities from 1987 through 1991 with four other companies. For Graye to make bail, a Hong Kong-based shell company called Nexus Ventures Ltd. obtained $300,000 from unwitting investors in Eron Mortgage. Before Graye's sentence could be pronounced in Canada, he was indicted in the U.S. on stock-fraud charges for his involvement with Vinex Wines Inc., a company he and Charles Hong Lee ran. Graye spent four years in prison on the charges related to Vinex Wines and was returned to Canada in May 2000; in April 2003 he admitted that he had misappropriated $18 million and committed tax fraud, and he was sent back to jail. [61]

These founding partners, along with Clinton Rickards (sometimes listed as C. H. Richards), set up Macrotrends, NAPT, and then Global Election Systems. During these early years, Iredale and Lancaster nurtured the ES-2000 voting system into existence. The company appears to have washed its hands of Cooper, Lee and Graye, and under Clinton Rickards' management achieved more respectability and, for a time, became solvent. Then it hired more criminals, became insolvent again, and was purchased by Diebold.

Musical chairs-style management followed. Howard Van Pelt came on board about the time that Graye left; Bob Urosevich, who had co-founded ES&S, left the reins to that company in Chuck Hagel's hands in 1993 and later founded a company called I-Mark Systems. Todd Urosevich, his brother, continued as a vice president of ES&S. I-Mark was acquired by Global Election Systems in 1997. Van Pelt took a position with Advanced Voting Solutions, taking with him his Global Elections sidekick, Larry Ensminger.

By 2001, Global Election Systems had grown steadily but had accumulated a pile of debt. The company was purchased by Diebold Inc. effective January 31, 2002, and, six weeks later, landed the biggest voting-machine order in history.

9
The First Public Look – Ever –
into a secret voting system

Author and historian Thom Hartmann writes:[1]

*"You'd think in an open democracy that the government —
answerable to all its citizens rather than a handful of corporate
officers and stockholders — would program, repair, and control
the voting machines. You'd think the computers that handle our
cherished ballots would be open and their software and programming available for public scrutiny. ...*

You'd be wrong.

*If America still is a democratic republic, then We, The People
still own our government. And the way our ownership and management of our common government (and its assets) is asserted
is through the vote. ...*

*Many citizens believe, however, that turning the programming
and maintenance of voting over to private, for-profit corporations, answerable only to their owners, officers, and stockholders, puts democracy itself at peril."*

Historians will remind us of a concept called "the public commons."
Public ownership and public funding of things that are essential to
everyone means we get public scrutiny and a say in how things are run.

When you privatize a thing like the vote, strange things happen.

For example, you can't ask any questions.

Jim March, a California Republican, filed a public-records request[2] in Alameda County, California, to ask about the voting machines it had entrusted with his vote. The county's reply: [3]

"Please be advised that the county will not provide the information you requested ... The County will not allow access or disclose any information regarding the Diebold election system as any information relating to that system is exempted from the PRA (Public Records Act) ... The system provided by Diebold Election Systems Inc. ("DESI") is a proprietary system that is recognized as such in the contract between the County and DESI...

"The County contends that the official information privilege in section 1040 of the Evidence Code is applicable because the information requested was acquired by the County in confidence and the County is required to maintain its confidentiality. Any copying or disclosing of such information would violate the license agreements..."

When I called ES&S to ask the names of its owners, the company simply declined to take my call.

When former Boca Raton, Florida, mayor Emil Danciu requested that Dr. Rebecca Mercuri, perhaps the best-known expert on electronic voting in America, be allowed to examine the inner workings of Palm Beach County's Sequoia machines, the judge denied the request, ruling that neither Mercuri nor anyone else would be allowed to see the code to render an opinion.[4]

When best-selling author William Rivers Pitt interviewed Dr. David Dill, a professor of computer science at Stanford University, about his experience with voting machines, Pitt got an earful about secrecy:

"It is frustrating because claims are made about these systems, how they are designed, how they work, that, frankly, I don't believe," says Dill. "In some cases, I don't believe it because the claims they are making are impossible. I am limited in my ability to refute these impossible claims because all the data is hidden behind a veil of secrecy." [5]

When members of the California Task Force on Electronic Voting asked how the machines were tested, Wyle and Ciber declined to answer.

"We wanted to know what these ITAs do," said Dill. "So we invited them to speak to us. ... They refused to come visit us. They were also too busy to join us in a phone conference. Finally, out of frustration, I wrote up 10 or 15 questions and sent it to them via the Secretary of State's office. They didn't feel like answering those questions, either."

"What testing do the manufacturers do?" asks Dill. "If you go to their Web pages, it says, 'If you'd like to know something about us, please go to hell' in the nicest possible way."

You can't examine a machine or even look at a manual. David Allen, one of the many computer techs who helped coach me through the writing of this book, also helped to publish this book.

"These things are so secret we're supposed to just guess whether we can trust them," he said. "We've got to get our hands on a technical manual somehow."

I promised him, somewhat doubtfully, that I'd try calling some programmers to see if I could find one to cooperate. I was most interested in ES&S — at that time, I hadn't done much work at all on Diebold Election Systems. I entered "@essvote.com" into the Google search engine, looking for e-mails that might give me names I could contact, and found a few dozen employees who work for ES&S.

I postponed calling them. What would I say? So I stalled by convincing myself that I should find as many names as possible. I got some from Sequoia. I entered "Global Election Systems" and found some old documents with e-mails ending in "gesn.com."

On page 15 of Google, looking for anything with "gesn" in it, I found a Web page. (You can still find this page at www.archive.org

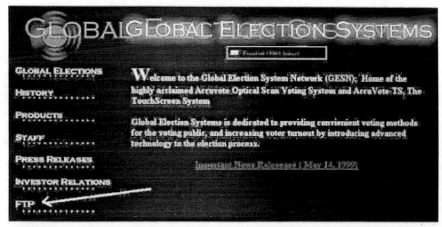

Old Global Election Systems Web page: GESN.com

for GESN.com. The FTP link still appears.)

I clicked "press releases" to see what kind of claims this company was making. Then I clicked all the links. I clicked the link called "FTP" and it took me to a page full of files.

I called David Allen. "What am I looking at?"

He took one look at the page and snorted incredulously. "Incredible stupidity."

"Click 'Pub,' " he suggested. We did. What follows is the first detailed look — ever — into a secret voting system.

(Noun or verb?)

What do you do when you find 40,000 secret files on an unprotected file transfer site on the Internet? Probably just look and go away. But what if you have pledged allegiance to the United States, and to the republic for which it stands?

What if you knew that the devil went down to Georgia on November 5, 2002, and handed that state an election with six upsets, tossing triple-amputee war veteran Max Cleland out of the U.S. Senate in favor of a candidate who ran ads calling Cleland unpatriotic?

Suppose you knew that in Georgia, the first Republican governor in 134 years had been elected despite being behind in every poll, and that African American candidates fared poorly even in their own districts?

If you learned that a $54 million order had been placed by the state of Georgia for 22,000 new voting machines, the biggest single voting machine purchase ever, and that these machines had been installed just prior to an election — and then you saw a folder called "rob-georgia," looked inside, and found instructions to replace the files in the new Georgia voting system with something unknown, what would you do?

I don't know about you, but I'm a 52-year old grandma and I never expected to have to make a choice like this. I wanted someone else to take care of it. *We need investigators like Woodward and Bernstein*, I thought, so I called the *Washington Post*. Of course, Carl Bernstein isn't there anymore, but I left a spicy message on Bob Woodward's voicemail. Never heard from anyone. I learned that *Washington Post* reporter Dan Keating was doing a story on voting machines, so I called him.

"So, will you call Diebold and find out what 'rob-georgia' is?" I asked.

"No."

"Why not?"

"Because I don't think 'rob-georgia' could possibly mean rob Georgia," he said.

I left a somewhat more agitated message on Bob Woodward's voicemail and submitted my experience to a Web site called *Media Whores Online*.

These files might contain evidence. These files might go away. I called people in various places around the world and urged them to go look at rob-georgia. I thought long and hard. And then I downloaded the files, all 40,000 of them. It took 44 hours nonstop. I gave them to someone I trust, who put them in a safe deposit box, and there they sit to this day.

Why in the world would an ATM manufacturer like Diebold leave sensitive files hanging out there on an unprotected Internet site? I made a few phone calls, which confirmed that Diebold *knew* the site was unprotected, and learned that the site had been there for years.

I kept asking if anyone knew who Rob was. Everyone told me there was no employee named Rob in Georgia.

Perhaps rob was a verb?

"rob-georgia" is a compressed folder with three more folders, containing 3,794 more files, inside it. It contains uncertified program modifications, a way to slip any damn thing you want into a voting machine. Here's what it looks like:

Why did they replace voting-machine stuff? *Did* they replace voting-machine files? As I Googled around with various "Georgia, voting machine, Diebold" search words, here's what popped out:

> **16 Sep 2002** *Memo from Chris Riggall (press secretary for Georgia Secretary of State Cathy Cox):*
>
> "Diebold programmers developed a patch which was applied to the units deployed in Hall and Marion counties, and we were pleased that not one freeze was reported among the tens of thousands of votes cast there. Unfortunately, <u>we simply did not have the time to apply the patch to the demo units, but that is now occurring to all units in all counties</u> and the last increment of shipments from Diebold had this fix loaded before leaving the factory."[6]

A program modification was needed because the touch screens were freezing up, crashing the machines. Makes sense. The problem must be a big one to justify modifying the program on all 22,000 voting machines in Georgia. But wait a minute — this is in the Media Backgrounder put out by the Georgia Secretary of State Press Office. [7]

> "Before being considered for acquisition in Georgia ... software is examined for reliability and hardware is subjected to a variety of 'torture tests.' The state testing examines both hardware and software for accuracy and reliability, and mock elections are conducted on the equipment, witnessed by county election officials."

The document names Wyle Laboratories and Ciber, Inc., citing their "extensive experience in NASA-related testing." So how did these NASA-testing labs miss something so obvious that all 22,000 voting machines required a modification to keep them from crashing?

Here is what Diebold wrote to certifier Wyle Laboratories in its latest touch-screen certification documents:

> "It is Diebold Election Systems, Inc. policy that the only acceptable level of conformance is Zero Defects."[8]

Okay, we all know that "zero defects" is one of those terms that sounds good and doesn't happen. But we ought to at least hold Diebold to this promise:

> "The manufacturing test location, test date, and inspector initials will be recorded on a label on every voting machine."

Whose initials, from the factory, are on the Georgia machines? Anyone's?

In its RFP soliciting purchase by the state of Georgia, Diebold submitted the following in its "Schedule for Deployment": [9]

> "Prior to our GEMS' hardware installation at each Georgia county, the hardware will be staged in McKinney, Texas for software integration and testing."

As part of the installation process, Diebold promised that all software and drivers (small programs which "drive" specific pieces of hardware such as printers, touch screens or modems) would be loaded prior to being shipped to Georgia. And according to the Georgia Secretary of State Media Backgrounder:

> "Before leaving the factory, each touch screen terminal receives a diagnostic test."

If each touch screen was tested before leaving the factory, why did every single machine need modifications, in order not to crash, *after* they reached Georgia?

The machines were shipped to Georgia in June 2002. And once they arrived, we are told, there was more testing:

"Upon arrival at Diebold's central warehouse in Atlanta, each unit was put through a diagnostic sequence to test a variety of functions, including the card reader, serial port, printer, the internal clock and the calibration of the touch screen itself. These tests were audited by experts from Kennesaw State University's Center for Election Systems."

The following statement, on Georgia Secretary of State letterhead, remains posted on the state's Web site as of the writing of this book.

"After shipment to each of Georgia's 159 counties, county acceptance testing (which consists of the same types of diagnostic procedures) was performed by KSU staff on each voting terminal."

Was this testing rigorous? Yes, rigorous, they promised. According to the Media Backgrounder:

"Georgia's multi-tiered election equipment testing program [is] among the most rigorous in the nation."

Could someone take a moment to do the math with me? If this testing is "rigorous," might we expect them to invest, say, 10 minutes per machine?

The testing just described adds up to every touch-screen unit being tested three times before it gets to the "logic and accuracy" test. You can check the footnotes for my math; by my calculations, all this testing would take 17 people working 40 hours per week for four months doing nothing but rigorous testing.[10]

Do you believe they did all the testing they claim to have done? Call me a skeptic, but I want to see the payroll records on that.

What does all that modifying at the last minute do to security? Wait — don't program modifications need to be recertified? How many people had to get access to these machines to do this? Was this legal?

And what exactly was in rob-georgia.zip?

* * * * *

With so many unanswered questions, I decided to ask the public officials responsible for voting systems in the state of Georgia about these program modifications. Here are excerpts from a February 11, 2003, interview with Michael Barnes, Assistant Director of Elections for the state of Georgia:[11]

Harris: "I want to ask you about the program update that was done on all the machines shortly before the election."

Barnes: "All right."

Harris: "Was that patch certified?"

Barnes: "Yes."

Harris: "By whom?"

Barnes: "Before we put anything on our equipment we run through state certification labs, and then, in addition to that, we forwarded the patch to Wyle labs in Huntsville. ... Wyle said it did not affect the certification elements. So it did not need to be certified."

Harris: "Where's the written report from Wyle on that? Can I have a copy?"

Barnes: "I'd have to look for it. I don't know if there was ever a written report by Wyle. It might have been by phone. Also, in Georgia we test independently at Kennesaw University — a state university."

Harris: "Can I see that report?"

Barnes: "You'd have to talk to Dr. Williams, and he's out of town ... Dr. Williams is on the National Association of State Election Directors (NASED) certification, and I think he's also at Kennesaw University. He does the certification for the state of Georgia."

Harris: "Was this new patch tested with a Logic and Accuracy test, or was it tested by looking at the code line by line?"

Barnes: "Logic and Accuracy, and also they verify that our version is identical and also any software is tested through Ciber and Wyle."

Harris: "But Wyle decided not to test the patch, you say. Was this patch put on all the machines or just some of the machines?"

Barnes: "All the machines."

Harris: "So every machine in Georgia got this program update."

Barnes: "Yes, every one of the machines used on election day in November. If it had been sent out to counties prior already, Diebold and their technicians went out and manually touched every machine. Some of the machines were still at the manufacturer; they did the patches on those."

Harris: "How long did it take to do patches on — what was it, around 22,000 machines?"

Barnes: "It took about a month to go back out and touch the systems."

Harris: "Can you tell me about the procedure used to install the patches?"

Barnes: "The actual installation was a matter of putting in a new memory card. ... They take the PCMCIA card, install it, and in the booting-up process the upgrade is installed."

A memory card is like a floppy disk but shaped like a credit card. Sometimes they call it a PCMCIA card.

OK, let's regroup. So far, we have thousands of defective voting systems that somehow made it through Wyle's hardware testing, Ciber's software testing, Diebold's factory testing, rigorous testing on arrival at the Georgia warehouse and more testing when delivered to each of Georgia's 159 counties. But the machines didn't work.

Then we have a set of file replacements called "rob-georgia," and a Georgia state elections official telling us they replaced files on all 22,000 machines in Georgia. In an act of computer science clairvoyance, it was determined by telephone that nothing was on the modifications that anyone needed to look at. We know from a memo dated September 16 that there were plans to install program modifications; we know that the Georgia general election was held November 5, 2003, and we've been told that it took about a month to go out and "touch" every machine.

What we have here is a group of Georgia election officials running around the state replacing the computer commands in the voting system *right before the election* without anyone examining what the new commands actually do. Who ordered this? Let's find out where the buck stops.

Harris: "Where did the actual cards come from?"

Barnes: "Diebold gave a physical card — one card that activates each machine. There were about 20 teams of technicians. They line the machines up, install the card, turn on, boot up, take that card out, move on, then test the machine."

Harris: "Were people driving around the state putting the patches on the machines?"

Barnes: "Yes."

The order came from Diebold and was implemented by Georgia election officials and Diebold employees.

Harris: "What comment do you have on the unprotected FTP site?"

Barnes: "That FTP site did not affect us in any way, shape or form because we did not do any file transferring from it. None of the servers ever connected so no one could have transferred files from it. No files were transferred relating to state elections."

When someone issues that many denials in a single answer, it makes me wonder if the truth lies somewhere in the opposite direction.

Harris: "How do you know that no one pulled files from the FTP site?"

Barnes: "One voting machine calls the servers and uploads the info. We don't allow the counties to hook up their servers to a network line."

Harris: "I notice that one of the things the network builder put on the [county] machines was a modem."

Barnes: "The only time you use the modem is on election night. That is the only time the unit was used, was election night when they plug it into the phone."

Harris: "Having the screens freeze up is a pretty severe error — how did 5 percent of the machines get out of the factory with that? How did they get through Wyle testing labs?"

Barnes: "All I know is that the machines were repaired."

Harris: "How do you know that the software in the machines is what was certified at the labs?"

Barnes: "There is a build date and a version number that you can verify. Kennesaw University did an extensive audit of the signature feature — Dr. Williams and his team went out and tested every machine afterwards to make sure nothing was installed on them that shouldn't have been."

Harris: "They tested every one of 22,000 machines?"

Barnes: "They did a random sampling."

So the FTP site, which contained 40,000 files, placed there over a period of six years, was never used and no one transferred files from it, no one could transfer files from it, no files were transferred. And the modems which James Rellinger (the contractor who installed the Georgia servers for 159 counties) was instructed to put into every county voting system were never used except for once.

(When questioned on August 22, 2003, Dr. Britain Williams claimed that most counties did not use these modems *at all*. "Some counties don't have phone lines; some don't even have bathrooms," he told a group of people that included computer programmer Roxanne Jekot and *Atlanta Journal-Constitution* reporter Jim Galloway.)

On February 12, 2003, I interviewed Dr. Williams, Kennesaw Election Center, an organization funded by the Georgia Secretary of State.[12]

Harris: "I have questions regarding your certification of the machines used in Georgia during the last election."

Dr. Williams: "For the state of Georgia — I don't do certification. The law gives the Secretary of State the authority to say what systems are certified and what are not. What I do is an evaluation of the system."

Harris: "What was your involvement in certifying the program patch that was put on? Did you actually certify the patch, or did you determine that it was not necessary?"

Dr. Williams: "Part of our testing program is when these machines are delivered, we look at the machines and see that they comply. And in the process of doing that — representatives of Kennesaw University did this — we found about 4-5 percent of the machines were rejected, not all because of screen freezes, but that was one of the problems."

Harris: "It was the screen freezes that caused them to issue a program patch?"

Dr. Williams: "Yes. The vendor [Diebold] created a patch addressing the screen freezing. It made it better but didn't completely alleviate the problem."

Harris: "Did you do a line-by-line examination of the original source code?"

Dr. Williams: "For the original — no. We don't look at the source code anyway; that's something done by the federal ITAs."

Harris: "Did you do a line-by-line examination of the patch?"

Dr. Williams: "The patch was to the operating system, not to the program *per se*."

Harris: "It only changed Windows files? Do you know that it didn't change anything in the other program? Did you examine that?"

Dr. Williams: "We were assured by the vendor that the patch did not impact any of the things that we had previously tested on the machine."

(The evaluator was assured by the vendor? Who's in charge of whom?)

Harris: "Did anyone look at what was contained in the replacement files?"

Dr. Williams: "We don't look at source code on the operating system anyway. On our level we don't look at the source code; that's the federal certification labs that do that."

Harris: "Did you issue a written report to the Secretary of State indicating that it was not necessary to look at the patch?"

Dr. Williams: "It was informal — not a report — we were in the heat of trying to get an election off the ground. A lot was done by e-mails."

So Barnes points to the ITAs but admits they never examined the program modifications, and then he points to Williams, who in turn points to the ITAs and then points to the vendor. No one writes a report about any of this. Dr. Williams implies that this program replacement was put on when they took delivery, but that was in June. The program modifications were done in October.

Harris: "What month did you install that program patch?"

Dr. Williams: "When we took delivery, we were seeing that the patch was on there."

Harris: "I have a memo from the Secretary of State's office that is dated in August [Sept. 16, actually], and it says that due to a problem with the screens freezing, a patch was going to be put on all the machines in Georgia. ... Apparently, someone had already taken delivery on these machines and they had already been shipped out around the state before the patch was applied, is that right?"

Dr. Williams: "The patches were done while we were doing acceptance testing. One of the things we looked for during acceptance testing was to make sure the patch was put in."

Harris: "But as I understand it, a team of people went around the state putting these patches on."

Dr. Williams: "By the time they put the patches in, the majority of the machines had been delivered. Actually, it was going on at the same time. When they started putting the patches in around the state, we tested the machines where they did that [put the patches in] at the factory."

Harris: "When I spoke with Michael Barnes, he said that you tested all the machines, or a random sampling of the machines, after the patch was put on."

Dr. Williams: "We had five or six teams of people with a test script that they ran on each machine — "

Harris: "The test script did what?"

Dr. Williams: "The test script was generic. It was in two parts. One part tested the functionality of the machine. It was a hardware diagnostic; it primarily tested that the printer worked, that the serial port worked, that the card reader worked, tested the date and time in the machine, and to an extent checked calibration of the machine. Then if it passed all of those, it tested the election. We loaded a small sample election in, the same as the one used during certification testing, and we ran a pattern of votes on there."

This is nice, but he's telling me about testing printers and things. Barnes had told me that "Dr. Williams and his team went out and tested every machine afterwards to make sure nothing was installed on them that shouldn't have been." I wanted to know if anything had been put in the software that might affect our votes.

Harris: "Can you tell me about the digital signature?" [A digital signature is used to show that no changes in the software were done.]

Dr. Williams: "That's part of the test that involves looking at the software — putting the patch on wouldn't change the digital signature."

Harris: "But if you put in a program patch, wouldn't that show that a change has been made?"

Dr. Williams: "No, because the patch was only in the Windows portion — there was no digital signature check on the operating system ... "

I'm sorry to subject you to this excruciating interview, and I apologize for throwing terms like "digital signature" around. I had heard that this "checksum" or "digital signature" was a way to determine that no unauthorized code was put into our voting system, so I was trying to find out how it worked — or if they used it at all.

But Dr. Williams, the official voting machine examiner for Maryland, Virginia and Georgia, was indicating that he did not check things if they involved the Windows operating system. That would open up a security hole the size of British Columbia. All you'd have to do is mess with Windows, upload your handiwork into the Georgia voting system, and you'd have direct access to a million votes at once.

Dr. Williams was interested in the non-Windows code and the ITA labs; I wanted to know about the Windows modifications and the other security problems associated with sticking program modifications on voting machines using PCMCIA cards.

Dr. Williams: "They write the source code and the source code is submitted to the federal lab. When it passes the lab they freeze the source code; at that point it's archived. Any change after that is subject to re-testing."

That's nice, but he just said they changed the frozen source code without out retesting it. But wait — why stop at replacing the Windows operating system — maybe the whole program could be replaced by substituting unauthorized cards during this process of "patching" the voting software.

Harris: "What was the security around the creation of the cards used to implement the patch?"

Dr. Williams: "That's a real good question. Like I say, we were in the heat of the election. Some of the things we did, we probably compromised security a little bit. Let me emphasize, we've gone back since the election and done extensive testing on all this."

Harris: "Based on your knowledge of what that patch did, would it have been needed for all the machines of same make, model and program? Including machines sold to Maryland and Kansas that were built and shipped around the same time?"

Dr. Williams: "Yeah, but now the key phrase is 'with the same system.' Maryland ran a similar version with a different version of Windows and did not have this problem."

Harris: "So the program was certified by the federal labs even when it ran on different versions of the operating system?"

Dr. Williams: "Yes, they don't go into the operating system."

Maybe the federal labs don't, and Williams said that he didn't, but someone was going into the operating system: Talbot Iredale, senior vice president of research and development for Diebold Election Systems, one of the two original programmers hired during the Vancouver Maneuver era, modified the Windows CE operating system used in Georgia.[13] One man. One million votes.

Talbot Iredale could be as honest as a church pastor — actually, one of the pastors at my church once ran off with $16,000 — but even if Iredale has absolute integrity, allowing one person unchecked access to a million votes at once has got to be the biggest security breach in the history of the U.S. electoral system. (Now if one man got his own uncertified software into Diebold's optical-scan system, that would be bigger: In 2002, those machines counted about seven million votes.[14] More on that later.)

Harris: "There was an unprotected FTP site which contained software and hardware specifications, some source code and lots of files. One file on that site was called "rob-georgia," and this file contained files with instructions to 'replace GEMS files with these' and 'replace Windows files with these and run program.' Does this concern you?"

Dr. Williams: "I'm not familiar with that FTP site."

Harris: "Is there a utility which reports the signature? Who checks this, and how close to Election Day?"

Dr. Williams: "We do that when we do acceptance testing. That would be before election testing."

Harris: "What way would there be to make sure nothing had changed between the time that you took delivery and the election?"

Dr. Williams: "Well there wouldn't — there's no way that you can be absolutely sure that nothing has changed."

Harris: "Wouldn't it help to check that digital signature, or checksum, or whatever, right before the election?"

Dr. Williams: "Well, that is outside of the scope of what some of the people there can do. I can't think of any way anyone could come in and replace those files before the election — "

Harris: "Since no one at the state level looks at the source code, if the federal lab doesn't examine the source code line by line, we have a problem, wouldn't you agree?"

Dr. Williams: "Yes. But wait a minute — I feel you are going to write a conspiracy article."

Harris: "What I'm looking at is the security of the system itself — specifically, what procedures are in place to make sure an insider cannot insert malicious code into the system."

Dr. Williams: "There are external procedures involved that prevent that."

Harris: "This is exactly what I want to know. If you know what procedures would prevent that, could you explain them to me?"

Dr. Williams: "We have the source code. How can they prevent us from reviewing it? I have copies of source code that I've certified."

Harris: "But you said you do not examine the source code."

Dr. Williams: "Yes, but the ITA did it. The ITA, when they finish certifying the system, I get it from the ITA — someone would have to tamper with the source code before it goes to the ITA and the ITA would have to not catch it."

Of course, both Williams and Barnes just told us that the ITA never examined the modifications made to 22,000 machines in Georgia. Let's consider a few points here:

Tiny programs can be added to any program modification. The file "Setup.exe" launches many of these, some of which are ".dll" files, which stands for "dynamic link library." These are small files that hide inside executable programs and can launch various functions (whatever the programmer tells them to do). They can be set up to delay their launch until a triggering event occurs. There is nothing wrong with .dll files, but there is something very wrong with putting new .dll files into a voting machine if no one has examined them.

ClockFix.zip

□ ClockFix.zip

NK.bin   BIN File 7/16/2002 8:48 PM

(Hey! What's this? I found it on the Diebold FTP site.)

Other files, such as "nk.bin," also contain executables that can literally rewrite the way the system works. The nk.bin file is sort of like a mini-Windows operating system. If a programmer from Diebold modifies the nk.bin file and these modified files are put on the voting machine without being examined, the truth is, we have no idea what that machine is doing.

Any time you do a program modification, you can introduce a small trojan horse or virus that can corrupt the election.

The rob-georgia.zip folder includes a file called "setup.exe" that was never examined by certifiers. It contains many .dll files. The "clockfix" zip file is an nk.bin file. Someone should have looked at these.

Now, about the Windows operating system: In order to use "COTS" software (Commercial Off-The-Shelf) without having certifiers examine it, the commercial software must be used "as is," with no modifications. If the patches that Barnes and Williams referred to were Windows patches, the moment Diebold modified them they became subject to certification. They did not come from Microsoft. They came directly from Diebold. Therefore, they were not "as is, off the shelf." Someone should have looked at these, too.

The rob-georgia.zip file includes one folder containing replacements for the Windows operating system and two folders with replacement files that are *not* for Windows. You don't need to be a computer scientist to see this: Just look at the file names, which instruct the user to alter the GEMS program. GEMS is not part of the Windows operating system. Someone should have looked at these.

Someone should have looked at all these files, but no one did. In fact, no one has any idea what was on those Georgia voting machines on Nov. 5, 2002. Georgia certified an illegal election. Now what?

* * * * *

As word spread about voting system files found on an open FTP site, it became a favorite topic of conversation on Internet discussion forums.

*"This could make Watergate look like a game of tiddlywinks...
Get a good seat. This could be quite a long ride!"*

— *"TruthIsAll"*

Public examination of the files is the best thing that could have happened. It's the only way we can engage in an informed debate about voting machines. I'm glad we got a look inside, but what we found should divest you once and for all of the idea that we can "trust" secret voting systems created by for-profit corporations.

The Diebold FTP site contained computer files for systems marketed by Diebold Election Systems and, before that, Global Election Systems. These voting systems were used in real elections.

There is no reason to believe that other manufacturers, such as ES&S and Sequoia, are any better than Diebold — in fact, one of the founders of the original ES&S system, Bob Urosevich, also oversaw development of original software now used by Diebold Election Systems.

Because voting systems (except AccuPoll,[15] which is open-source) are kept secret, I am focusing on Diebold only because we can't find out anything about the other vendors' systems.

We do know that ES&S filed a patent infringement lawsuit against Global Election Systems at one time, [16] indicating that some part of the system was alleged to be identical. Also, Chapter 2 shows that Diebold, Sequoia and ES&S have all miscounted elections many times.

Some advocates confuse what happened with Diebold's unprotected FTP site with "open source." Very reputable programs, such as the Linux operating system, have been developed through open source, letting the whole world examine the system and suggest improvements. What Diebold did, though, is quite different.

If you never obtain public feedback to improve your software, what you have is horrific security, not an open-source system. People have by now examined the Diebold files, but it's still not open source because no one has the slightest idea what Diebold has done to correct the flaws, if anything.

If the Diebold system had allowed everyone with expertise to critique the software during development and then showed how it corrected the flaws, that would be open source. Such a procedure would no doubt arrive at a very simple and secure program with a voter-verified paper ballot to back it up, like Australia's open-source voting system.

Instead, Diebold allowed only a small handful of programmers to look at its software. Then they put all the software (along with passwords and encryption keys) on an open Web site and left it there for six years, where crackers could download it and people interested in elections could find it, but respectable experts and citizens' groups were not told of its existence or allowed to examine anything.

Putting that kind of material on an unprotected Web site was "a major security stuff-up by anyone's reckoning."[17] That's how Thomas

C. Greene of *The Register* describes what Diebold did, and he's right. Diebold's entire secret election system was available to any hacker with a laptop.

Our certification system is fundamentally broken. The system is secret, relies on a few cronies and is accountable to no one. Worse, the certifiers have clearly given a passing grade to software so flawed that it miscounts, loses votes and invites people to come in the back door to make illicit changes. But even this inadequate certification system would be better than what we discovered is really happening:

Diebold has used software directly off its FTP site without submitting it for certification at all. Quite literally, this software went from a programmer's desk directly into our voting machines.

* * * * *

If you want to tamper with an election through electronic voting machines, you want to play with:

Ballot configuration — Switch the position of candidates. A vote for one candidate goes to the other.

Vote recording — Record votes electronically for the wrong candidate, or stuff the electronic ballot box.

Vote tallying — Incorrectly add up the votes, or substitute a bogus vote tally for the real one, or change the vote tally while it is being counted.

You'd want to find out as much as you could about procedures. No problem — the Diebold open FTP site contained the "Ballot Station User Manual," the "Poll Worker Training Guide" and at least two versions of the "GEMS User Manual," along with the "Voter Card Programming Manual" and hardware configuration manuals for the AccuVote touch-screen system.

It would be helpful to play with elections in the comfort of your own home. Not a problem — full installation versions of the Diebold voting programs were on the Web site.

BallotStation.exe (vote recording and precinct tallying for the touch-screen machines)

GEMS.exe (county-level tallying of all the precincts, found in the GEMS folders)

VCProgrammer.exe (programs to sign in and validate voter cards)

Just about every version of the Diebold programs ever certified, and hundreds that were never certified, were available.

It might be helpful also to know what kind of testing the voting system goes through, especially the details on the "Logic and Accuracy" testing done right before and after the election. After all, you'd want to make sure that whatever hacking you do doesn't get caught. Testing procedures, sample testing results and instructions on how to do the testing were also on the Diebold FTP site.

You'd want to see some typical ballot configurations — or, better yet, get the data files created for actual elections. That way you'd know the positioning of the candidates on the ballot, and you could even get the candidate I.D. number used by the computers to assign votes. You could do test runs using real election files.

No problem: On the FTP site were files designated for counties in California, Maryland, Arizona, Kentucky, Colorado, Texas, Georgia, North Carolina, Kansas and Virginia. Some files, like one for San Luis Obispo County, California, were date-stamped on an election day (curiously, five hours before the polls closed).

By now you may have heard about a report by Johns Hopkins and Rice University scientists, which used these files. What you may not realize is that these scientists studied less than 5 percent of the information on the FTP site. They studied the source code of one of the voting-system components, the touch screen. The FTP files also included source code for many other components of the voting system, and compiled files, databases and technical documentation and drawings. The site also contained information on how to set up remote access, and passwords.

Guessing many of the passwords is easy because files are named for Diebold employees, and many passwords are simply the name of the location using the software.

x110700-pimageneral.zip	password = pima
norfolk election.zip	password = norfolk
docs.zip	password = voter
ChrisBellis.zip	password = bellisc
Wyle.zip	password = wyle99
JuanR.zip	password = juan

The supervisor password for voting machines at the polling place was "1111." When I saw this in the manual, it reminded me of buying a new briefcase. It comes with a "default" combination, but of course you change the combination as soon as you start using the briefcase.

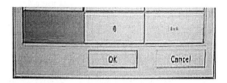

1. Insert the Manager card into the card reader.
2. Enter the password 1,1,1,1,and touch "OK".
3. Remove card when instructed.
4. When the screen below appears, press the "End Election" button.

For some reason, Diebold's voting machines were less secure than your briefcase. That's because programmers hard-wired the password into the source code. That way, no one could change the password, and anyone inside the polling place (the janitor, a crooked politician) could pretend to be a supervisor by entering "1111."

In case you need a fancy password, the files called "passwd" might come in handy. I don't know if anyone found a use for the Diebold programmer passwords, but these were sitting there.

```
passwd
    ken:Cx4JrK4Q4uebk
    guy:APHmbSVeB5WQ6
    tri:GwbsAUF5T1Q9Q
    whitman:KnSetwE/DYtWM
    nel:f1S7xcsCmmxBU
    mike:X5oEayCP1CxN.
    tomg:h8skrG2aFiuqg
    bill:6bFseyII9RxVY
    guest:cZm8UJv9sgzyc
```

```
passwd~
    ken:Cx4JrK4Q4uebk
    tri:UEGNh.UaiLRQk
    dmitry:dyNCBK1jMDVDU
    whitman:g8PfNAeGd9Ao6
    kponti:b/t1xLF5aVUVE
    denisel:b/t1xLF5aVUVE
    ataa:b/t1xLF5aVUVE
    josh:ZHwPOhd5is3JE
```

At the county election supervisor's office, the results from all the polling places are tabulated using a program called GEMS, and the password, "GEMSUSER," was in the user manual. The election supervisor can change "GEMSUSER," but later I'll show you how a 10-year-old could change it right back.

Enter your user logon name and password (i.e. GEMSUSER).
At this point Windows will start.

*The password for the
GEMS program is
"GEMSUSER"*

Setting System Date and Time

After Windows starts, at the bottom right corner of the screen is the system

{

*Supervisor access at the polling
place is granted by the password
1111. Instead of allowing supervisors
to control the password, it is written
into the source code and printed in
the manuals.*

```
//{{AFX_DATA_INIT(CSmartCardEmuDlg)
m_ByAccLevel = '0';
m_ID = _T("01234567890");
m_Level1 = 1;
m_Level2 = -1;
m_Level3 = -1;
m_Party = -1;
m_PIN = _T("1111");
m_Type = VOTER_CARD;
//}}AFX_DATA_INIT
```

}

```
== ADMIN_CARD)) {
                st = VC_NOACCESS;
        } else {
                CVoterInfo writeVoterInfo;
                writeVoterInfo.m_CardType = VOTER_CARD;
                writeVoterInfo.m_Version = VCI_VERSION1;
                writeVoterInfo.m_ElectionKey = pVCardInfo->m_ElectionId;
                writeVoterInfo.m_VCenter = CVCenter(pVCardInfo->m_VCenterId);
                writeVoterInfo.m_DLVersion = pVCardInfo->m_DLVersion;
                writeVoterInfo.m_Reportunit = CDistrict(pVCardInfo->m_PrecinctId);
                writeVoterInfo.m_Baseunit = CBaseunit(pVCardInfo->m_PortionId);
                writeVoterInfo.m_CounterGroup = CCounterGroup(pVCardInfo->m_GroupId);
                writeVoterInfo.m_VGroup1 = CVGroup(pVCardInfo->m_VGroup1Id);
                writeVoterInfo.m_VGroup2 = CVGroup(pVCardInfo->m_VGroup2Id);
                strcpy(writeVoterInfo.m_PIN, "1111");
                strcpy(writeVoterInfo.m_Description, "");
                writeVoterInfo.m_Flags1 = (UCHAR)((pVCardInfo->m_Flags & 0x07) |
NEWTYPE_CARD);
                writeVoterInfo.m_Flags2 = (USHORT)(pVCardInfo->m_Flags >> 4);
                writeVoterInfo.m_VoterSN = pVCardInfo->m_VoterId;

                if (m_CardReader.Write(writeVoterInfo) != SMC_OK)
                        st = VC_FAILEDWRITE;
                else
                        st = VC_OKAY;
        }
    }
    if (m_CardReader.IsOpen()) {
```

A cracker who wants to pretend he is the county elections supervisor might start by installing one of the GEMS vote-tallying programs on his home computer. There were over 100 versions of this program on the FTP site, many of which were never certified but were used in elections anyway.

GEMS is on the central computer at the county elections office. This is the software that creates the ballots before the election, and it also accumulates the incoming votes from the polling place and creates election reports. The same GEMS program handles both touch screens and optical-scan machines. There were many vote databases tagged to cities and counties, so a cracker could practice tampering with real software and real votes.

Any computer that has Windows seems to work, but meticulous people would follow the instructions left on the FTP site and put the GEMS program on a Dell PC with Windows NT 2k installed. Diebold support techs have also helped counties set up GEMS on Windows XP and Windows 2000.

So many versions of the GEMS program, so little time. A good version to start with would be GEMS 1.17.17 — according to NASED documents, that was an officially certified version of GEMS during the general election in November 2002.

A folder called "Pima Upgrade" might be a good choice for a hacker living in Tucson, and the new 1.18 series was also available. An even newer program, version 1.19, was put on the FTP site on January 26, 2003, just three days before it was taken down.

Suppose you wanted to simulate an actual touch-screen voting machine. You need to activate those with a smart card, and the average desktop computer isn't set up for that. Put the word "votercard" into a text search on the Diebold files, and this pops up in a file called "votercard.cpp,v":

```
v3-10-19:1.5
v3-10-18:1.5
b1-1-3-votercard-hack:1.5.0.4
v3-10-17:1.5
v3-10-16:1.5
v3-10-15:1.5
```

Now, if I'm a cracker and I get the "Votercard.cpp,v" file off the Diebold Web site, and I'm running a computer that really isn't a voting machine but want to figure out how it works, here it is: a neat little program that can cancel out the card reader entirely. Diebold handed me the road map and helped me find it by naming it "votercard-hack." A moderately skilled programmer will know how to paste it into the latest touch- screen source code, recompile, install, and start playing around.

The suffix "cpp" stands for "C++," and these files are source code. "Source code" contains the commands given to the computer that tell it how to execute the program. Many people are surprised to learn that source-code files consist of English-like programming commands that people can read. After software engineers write the program, it is compiled to make it machine-readable.

The cvs.tar file that Diebold left on its Web site was a source code "tree" for the program used to cast votes on touch screens. The tree contains the history of Dicbold's software development process, going all the way back to Bob Urosevich's original company, I-Mark Systems, through Global Election Systems, and including 2002 programming under Diebold Election Systems.

Leaving other people's pants unzipped

It's bad enough when you leave your own sensitive stuff on the Web. But Diebold exposed other people's confidential information, also. Diebold left 15,900 of Microsoft's proprietary Windows CE source-code files on its public Web site, ready to assemble like a set of Legos.

The Microsoft Windows CE Platform Builder is a set of development tools for building a Windows CE operating system into customized gadgets. You are supposed to have a license to use it, and, according to Bill Cullinan of Venturcom Inc., a Waltham, Massachusetts-based Windows CE distributor and developer, the kit is not free.

"The Platform Builder development kit for the new Windows CE .NET runs about $995," he told me. "Earlier, the cost was up over $2,000."

Any cracker in the world could access the pricey Microsoft developer's platforms through the Diebold FTP site.

Despite a notice that says, "You may not copy the [Hewlett Packard] Software onto any public network," copies of Hewlett Packard software were on the public FTP site hosted by Diebold.

A document marked "Intel Confidential" pertaining to microprocessor development for personal PCs was on the FTP site, along with the Merlin PPC Sourcekit for personal PCs and the Intel Cotulla development kit and board support packages for Microsoft Windows CE .NET and PocketPC 2002.

So Diebold expects us to trust them with our vote, yet they are quite cavalier with other people's intellectual property and, as we will see in the next section, with people's personal information.

On the Diebold FTP site: Private info on 310,000 Texans

Identity thieves can work anonymously from anywhere in the world and, armed with your Social Security number and a few other details, can quite literally ruin your life. And all they need is your name, address and birthday to get your Social Security number. [18]

During the writing of this chapter, I tried to take a more complete inventory of what was on that site and was surprised to find personal information for 310,000 Texans.

In this file were birthdays. First, middle and last names. Street addresses. Apartment numbers. School districts. Political affiliations. Voting habits. I assume they will say it was some kind of voter registration file, but it sure has a lot of information. Each kind of information (name, zip code, etc.) is called a "field," and this file had 167 fields, which included data from about three dozen elections, logged in over several years by many different people. Ninety-five thousand people from Plano are in this file, and a couple hundred thousand more from Richardson, McKinney, Wylie, Dallas and surrounding areas.

People have a right to privacy, even in the Internet age. Any woman who has an abusive ex-boyfriend will tell you that she doesn't want her apartment number published on a Web site. Child custody cases can get nasty. Thieves who find a database like the one left in the open by Diebold may try to sell the information.

Because of this file I know that Bob L. of Plano is a Republican and likes to do absentee voting, and that he and his wife are the same age. But does Bob know that Diebold hung his undies out the window for all to see?

Someone will explain to me that you can buy voter registration files for a nominal fee. But that doesn't mean you can buy those lists and stick them on the Internet, and what was Diebold doing with this information anyway?

I wondered if any reporters had their personal information posted. Yep — two reporters for the *Dallas Morning News*, the publisher for the *Plano Star-Courier* and the managing editor of the *Herald & Times Newspapers*.

And does Bob Urosevich, the president of Diebold Election Systems, know that his wife and daughter had their private information on that FTP site?

What do Diebold and the other guardians of our vote have to say about this?

"We protect the Bill of Rights, the Constitution and the Declaration of Independence. We protect the Hope Diamond. Now, we protect the most sacred treasure we have, our secret ballot."[19]

— Diebold CEO Wally O'Dell

"Sometimes our customers use the FTP site to transfer their own files. It has been up quite some years. People go there from counties, cities, sometimes there is stuff there for state certification boards, federal certification, a lot of test material gets passed around."[20]

— Guy Lancaster
Diebold contractor

"...the current group of computer 'wizards' who are so shrilly attacking ... are no longer behaving like constructive critics but rather as irresponsible alarmists and it's getting a little old."

— Dan Burk
Registrar of Voters
Washoe County, NV
(from Diebold Web site)

"They're talking about what they could do if they had access to the [computer program] code. ... But they're not going to get access to that code. Even if they did, we'd detect it." [21]

— Dr. Britain Williams

"For 144 years, Diebold has been synonymous with security, and we take security very seriously in all of our products and services."

— Diebold Web site

"It is all fine and well to upload results over the Internet, but we don't exactly have a lot of experience in Internet security in this company, and government computers are crackers favorite targets."

Barry Herron
Diebold Regional Manager
Diebold internal E-mail - 2/3/99

Joe Richardson, official spokesman for Diebold, in response to a question from the author: "Our ongoing investigation has found no merit to the insinuations of security breaches in our election solutions."

Harris: "So if there were 20,000 files including hardware, software specs, testing protocols, source code, you do not feel that is a security breach?"

Richardson [shuffling papers]: "Our ongoing investigation has found no merit to the insinuations of security breaches in our election solutions." [22]

"The scientists are undermining people's confidence in democracy. None of the critics is giving any credence to the extensive system of checks and balances that we employ internally."

Mischelle Townsend, Registrar of Voters
Riverside County, CA
Associated Press 8/17/03

Townsend's county uses Sequoia machines. She made this statement in August 2003; in September, Sequoia's secret voting software was found on an unprotected Web site. It had been sitting there for a year and a half.

10
Who's Minding the Store?
A free press? Public officials? Anyone?

"Our citizens may be deceived for awhile, and have been deceived; but as long as the presses can be protected, we may trust to them for light."[1]

—Thomas Jefferson to Archibald Stuart. 1799.

* * * * *

Has the free press been reined in by corporate interests? Certainly not, I would have told you a year ago. You just have to make sure that you give them something newsworthy. Journalists are seekers of the truth, a balanced truth — this I still believe.

Managing editors understand that our government will become corrupt without critics, and that an honest and fearless press is the only method available to our citizenry to get at the truth — a year ago, I believed that they had such an understanding. But having seen the reluctance of some of our most important editors to consider issues of vested interests and electronic ballot fraud, I have to say that mainstream press support for investigative reporting barely has a pulse.

More insidious than failure to cover important stories as soon as they come out is this: Some members of the press now use their own failure to cover an issue as proof that the issue has no merit.

"If what you say is true, why hasn't it been in *The New York Times*?"

Well I don't know. You'll have to ask *The New York Times* — in the meantime, I have a tape recording I'd like you to take a look at, a document you should see, some internal memos that someone should examine.

> "The press [is] the only tocsin of a nation. [When it] is completely silenced ... all means of a general effort [are] taken away."[2]

> —Thomas Jefferson to Thomas Cooper
> November 29, 1802

Our press is far from "completely silenced," but its voice in matters of great importance has become, at the very least, muffled.

Investigative reporter Greg Palast did an important investigation into the illegal purge of more than 50,000 citizens, who were not felons, from the Florida voter rolls.[3] If your name was Bob Andersen of Miami, and Robert Anderson of Dallas was convicted of a felony, there was a nasty possibility that you might not be allowed to vote in Florida.

Explosive stuff. Proven stuff. Stuff that should be on the CNN news crawler, especially since these wronged voters, even after the case was proven, did *not* get their right to vote back in November 2002. These facts were documented, confessed-to, photocopied and validated in a court of law, but unfortunately, they were not covered at all by most news outlets.

One reason: Early on, some reporters called the office of Governor Jeb Bush and asked whether Florida had purged voters whose rights had been restored in other states, and Jeb's office told them it wasn't so. That was a lie, and documents proved it to be a lie, and an important part of the news story was, in fact, the uttering of that lie, but here's what happened: Reporters decided not to report the story at all, justifying their decision not to cover it by pointing to the lie, without checking to see if it was the truth. After all, it was a statement from the office of the governor.

That is *not* what our founding fathers had in mind when they envisioned the critical role that a free press must play to protect democracy.

> "No government ought to be without censors ... and where the press is free, no one ever will ... it would be undignified and criminal to pamper the former [the government] and persecute the latter [its critics]." [4]

> —Thomas Jefferson

But in today's media age, a Nebraska senator can have his votes counted by a company that he chaired and still partially owns, but even while he is actively running for office, the Nebraska press will not inform Nebraska citizens of the conflict of interest (the lone exception: Lincoln TV *Channel 8 News*).

Atlanta Journal-Constitution reporter Jim Galloway told me he felt that it was more important to write about a state flag controversy than to inform Georgia voters that an illegal program modification had been made to 22,000 voting machines right before an election. [5]

CNN, Fox News, MSNBC, ABC, CBS and NBC were unable to tear themselves away from promising us weapons of mass destruction in Iraq (a story that turned out to be false) in order to spend five minutes asking a single question about the integrity of our voting system, even after a Stanford computer-science professor and more than one thousand computer-security experts insisted that it could not be trusted.

When Diebold, with machines in 37 states, left its voting system out on the Web for six years (free for the hacking), not a single editor from *The Wall Street Journal* or *USA Today* or *Newsweek* magazine bothered to assign anyone to look at the files so they could form an opinion as to the importance of this security gaffe.

It wasn't because they didn't know. I sent more than 100,000 bulletins directly to the appropriate editors and producers, in which I offered documents, cited sources and listed phone numbers of many experts to call. Everyone got the material — investigative, political, government, high-tech, national-news journalists — many have been receiving regular updates since October 2002. Not only has most of the press done a poor job (or at least a delayed one) of informing American citizens about this issue, most reporters didn't even look at the documents to assess the credibility of this story.

So much for the mainstream news media minding the store. If you want to know where the free press is nowadays, here it is:

Alastair Thompson was a reporter for many years before starting his Internet news site, *Scoop Media* (www.scoop.co.nz) — which was launched out of a garden shed in Wellington, New Zealand, and won the New Zealand Internet Awards for "Best Online Writing" and "Best Content." Yeah, I know: It's just New Zealand and only the Internet.

Thompson didn't wait for *The New York Times*. He covered the story of the insecure Diebold FTP site on February 10, 2003, just 18 days after the site was discovered. [6]

On February 13, I sent the "rob-georgia" story about last-minute program modifications on Georgia voting machines. *Scoop Media* covered it, but not the *Atlanta Journal-Constitution* (where it happened) — even though I provided phone numbers so reporters could call election officials themselves to confirm the story. [7]

Since the story broke, some good work has been done. Van Smith of *The Baltimore City Paper* published a detailed statistical analysis of anomalies in the November 2002 Georgia election,[9] even though he was working for a local paper in Baltimore. He realized it was important: Maryland was planning to buy the same machines.

Salon.com has been writing about concerns with electronic voting for some time now, and Salon's tech writer, Farhad Manjoo,[10] continues to write accurate and groundbreaking investigative stories.

Rachel Konrad of The Associated Press has been covering this issue fearlessly since February 2003.

Kim Zetter of *WiredNews.com* wrote a series of articles about electronic voting.[12]

Julie Carr-Smyth of *The Plain Dealer* in Cleveland broke the news about Diebold CEO Wally O'Dell's promise to "deliver the votes" for Bush in 2004.[13]

Erika D. Smith of the *Akron Beacon Journal* reported that Diebold's Mark Radke said that the new Diebold TSx machines will substitute wireless communication of votes for land-line modems. Radke all but admitted the system could be hacked when he made a startling (and cavalier) admission:

"But even if that burst of election data were intercepted, all the hacker would get are unofficial results." [14]

(Um, Mr. Radke? Hacking can put data in as well as take data out.)

If you want to find the free press nowadays, look to these folks, who prove we do have one, though it may not be quite where you've been looking for it. And if you really want to locate the free press, don a pair of hip boots and get one of those caver's hats with a light on it, wade into the Internet, shove the crud aside and you'll find some of the best investigative reporting ever.

Given the abundance of leads, the wealth of information on this topic and its importance, this issue has largely been ignored. Is the paucity of news coverage because reporters have just now learned of the vulnerabilities of electronic voting? Is it because electronic voting is new?

Not exactly. The first major article about electronic voting appeared in *The New Yorker* fifteen years ago, by investigative reporter Ronnie Dugger. [15] He wrote of many of the same concerns you are reading about in this book, but no one paid attention.

Though not covered in the mainstream press until late 2003, word of the Diebold FTP site spread through the Internet as soon as New Zealand's *Scoop Media* broke the news in February. And this, you see, is why true freedom of the press is so important: It informs the citizenry and galvanizes us to engage in the scrutiny that is our duty. Thank goodness for the Internet, for without it this story would never have been fully exposed.

Despite a virtual blackout by major media outlets for nearly a year, ordinary people like you, many of whom had never done any activism in their lives, decided to get involved in this issue.

* * * * *

Efforts by just a handful of people have gotten us to this point, where problems with voting machines are at last reaching public consciousness. Drs. Rebecca Mercuri and Peter Neumann have put forth truly Herculean efforts, toiling nearly in the dark for fourteen years, while newspapers often chose to print press releases about how much "fun" it is to vote on machines instead of examining the more difficult subject matter brought to light by these computer scientists.

When news of the 22,000 illicit patches in Georgia broke, a small contingent of Georgians decided to do something about it. I'm going to refer to them simply as "Georgia activists" because they have asked me not to call them out by name. Citizens in Georgia soon discovered that asking questions about our voting system is like trying to walk up the down escalator.

One of the Georgia activists hunted up the law pertaining to putting modifications on the voting system:

"11. Any modification to the hardware, firmware, or software of an existing system which has completed Qualification, Certification, or Acceptance testing in accordance with these Rules will invalidate the State certification <u>unless</u> <u>it</u> can be shown that the change does not affect the overall flow of program control or the manner in which the ballots are interpreted and the vote data are processed, and the change falls into one or more of the following classifications:

(i)   It is made for the purpose of correcting a defect, and test documentation is provided which verifies that the installation of the hardware change or corrected code does not result in any consequence other than the elimination of the defect.

(ii)   It is made for the purpose of enhancing the utility of the system or adding additional audit or report generating capability.

(iii)   It is made for the purpose of enabling interaction with other general purpose or approved equipment or computer programs and databases, and procedural and test documentation is provided which verifies that such interaction does not involve or adversely affect vote counting and data storage.

(iv)   It is made for the purpose of enabling operation on a different processor or of utilizing additional or different peripheral devices, and the software is unaltered in structure and function.

(From RULES OF OFFICE OF THE SECRETARY OF STATE ELECTION DIVISION, CHAPTER 590-8-1: CERTIFICATION OF VOTING SYSTEMS[16])

When you change software to correct for a problem, the procedure is to assign a bug number. You test it. You document everything. You append a new number to the end of the release. Then it has to be approved. And according to Georgia law, it must be certified. Writing up a fix, sticking it on the Internet, and then running around putting it on voting machines is not how it's done.

Georgia citizens have a right to be incensed. The state violated the law, and Georgia taxpayers now realize that their votes may have been thrown out the window.

The Carter Center, under the auspices of former President Jimmy Carter, seeks to prevent and resolve conflicts, protect freedom and enhance democracy. One of the Georgia activists approached them, but the Carter Center told her that, according to its charter, it can only monitor elections *outside* the United States.

A Georgia computer programmer contacted Lieutenant Governor Mark Taylor's office, who told her to send information. So she sent information about the FTP site, rob-georgia, the Georgia law and the unexamined program modifications. After that, they quit taking her calls.

Georgia legislators were not enthusiastic about discussing computer-security issues and usually were willing to give up no more than three minutes in the hallway, between sessions, to listen to concerns.

Several attempts were made to meet with Secretary of State Cathy Cox, but citizens were only allowed to speak with Assistant Director of Elections Michael Barnes, who was not helpful. They met with Tom Murphy, a former Speaker of the House in the Georgia state legislature.

"He knows where all the bones are buried," confided a self-appointed helper named Chris Hagin, who said he was an ambassador under President Clinton. Tom Murphy called upon Cox to meet with the activists, but she didn't; instead, Barnes told them on March 6 that Cox would be booked up "until July."

What about the American Civil Liberties Union? Activists met with ACLU attorney C. Knowles, but he told them he couldn't take on electronic voting machines because he had fought against the punch cards. ACLU attorney Laughlin McDonald, Director of the Voting Rights Project, was unconvinced.

"Where's the harm?" he said. ("Harm" is a legal requirement needed for some types of lawsuits.)

Concern among citizens continued to grow. In New York, author Mark Crispin Miller asked what he could do to help. One of Miller's contacts, Denis Wright, lives in Georgia and began joining the agitation to have someone — anyone — look into irregularities with Georgia's voting system.

Wright filed a formal request to produce Georgia documents, which yielded this odd response to his simple query about the certification documents — you know, the ones that prove that we should just trust our votes to proprietary secrecy:

From Denis Wright to Kara Sinkule, March 19, 2003:
"Hi Kara. Hope you are doing well. I need some more help, please. I am hoping that I can get hard copies of the following documents, per the Freedom of Information Act: (1) According to state law, any changes in the voting machine software (GEMS and Windows) require documentation in writing. I would like to get copies of any such documentation. (2) A copy of the actual certification letter from the lab (certifying the version of the soft-

ware which was used on election day) as well as any related memos, letters, etc...

* * * * *

From Clifford Tatum, Assistant Director of Legal Affairs, Election Division
To Denis Wright, March 25, 2003; Open Records Request
"Our office has received your request under the Georgia Open Records Act, O.C.G.A. § 50-18-70 regarding electronic voting information... In response to your first category, we have determined that no records exist regarding a change to software used by the voting system. In response to your second category, we have determined that no records exist in the Secretary of State's office regarding a certification letter from the lab certifying the version of software used on Election Day. Please be advised that any records of this type may have been submitted to the Georgia Technology Authority (GTA) in response to the Request for Proposal that was issued by GTA. Accordingly, a request for this type of information should be submitted to Gary Powell with GTA for response. By copy of this letter, I am advising Mr. Powell of your potential request ..."

What have we learned so far?

Uncertified program modifications can allow a single programmer to penetrate election security for millions of votes, a critical breach of electoral integrity.

Georgia requires certification and reports for program modifications, according to the Rules of Office of the Secretary of State Election Division Chapter 590-8-1, Certification of Voting Systems, No. 11.[16]

Diebold knew Georgia required recertification for modifications, according to a Diebold internal document titled "Certification Requirement Summary." [17]

Assistant Director of Elections Michael Barnes; Chris Riggall, press secretary for Cathy Cox; Kara Sinkule, press secretary for Cathy Cox; and Dr. Britain Williams, chair of the NASED Voting Systems Board Technical Committee all admit that modifications were made to Georgia voting machines.

Michael Barnes and Dr. Britain Williams admit that the program modifications were not certified. Clifford Tatum admits there is no documentation for the program modifications. [18]

Dr. Britain Williams later reversed himself and claimed that uncertified patches were impossible in Georgia. On April 23, 2003, Dr. Williams wrote:

> "... This comment ["A patch to Windows can slip through without scrutiny."] assumes that the State of Georgia allows changes and/or upgrades to the Microsoft operating system. This is not the case.

> "The vendor, Diebold, submits to the ITA a specific version of the operating system and a specific version of the election software. This specific version of the operating system and the election software undergoes ITA testing and State Certification testing. The State Certification is for this specific version of the Microsoft operating system and the Diebold election system. After State Certification any change to either the Microsoft operating system or the Diebold election system voids the State Certification.

> "If a change to either the Microsoft operating system or the Diebold election system becomes desirable or necessary, this change voids the State Certification. The revised system must then go back through the entire ITA Qualification and State Certification." [19]

Michael Barnes and Dr. Britain Williams say no one downloaded anything from the FTP site. [20]

Diebold officials decided that modifications were not done at all. In an interview with *Salon.com*, Joseph Richardson, a spokesman for Diebold, denied that a patch had been applied to the Georgia machines, saying, "We have analyzed that situation and have no indication of that happening at all." [21] I was so incredulous when I read this that I decided to call him to see if he was misquoted:

Harris: "Did you say, when interviewed by *Salon.com*, in reference to whether patches were put on machines in Georgia, 'We have analyzed that situation and have no indication of that happening at all'?"

Richardson: "Well, that is what I said at the time; however, we have continued to investigate the matter and ... (very, very long pause) Yes that is what I said to *Salon.com*."

Harris: "Do you stand by that now?"

Richardson: "We have continued to look into the matter."

Harris: "As you have continued to investigate this, do you have any new information as to whether patches were put on in Georgia?"

Richardson: "No."

Harris: "Has anyone thought to just call them up and ask? The Secretary of State's office?"

Richardson: "I can't say."

Harris: "What was the rob-georgia file? Who is responsible for it?"

Richardson: "I'm not privy to that information."

Harris: "Who would be able to answer that question?"

Richardson: "I can't tell you. [22]

* * * * *

Blessed are the whistle blowers. They may save this democracy yet. On March 13, 2003, I received this e-mail:

Hi Bev;

I read your recent article about Diebold Elections systems. Just wanted to let you know that I am the Rob in Georgia that they claimed they didn?t [sic] know about.

Thanks,

Rob Behler

11
Noun *and* Verb?

 rob-georgia.zip

So, what or who is rob-georgia?

When you interview voting system officials, you spend twice as much time following up on their dodgy answers as you do asking the questions in the first place. Flip back to page 129, Chapter 10 and take a look at Joe Richardson, who I believe you might also find in *Webster's Dictionary* defining the word "stonewall." Compare him with Rob's straight-talking interview.

Harris: "What was your position with Diebold in Georgia?"

Rob: "I was a server technician and then Product Deployment Manager for the Georgia project."

Harris: "What was the FTP site for?"

Rob: "One of the problems we had was an issue with the GEMS database. They had to do an update to it, so they just post the update to the Web site."

Harris: "What was rob-georgia?"

Rob: "I believe what that file was for, I did a — well, there were a ton of holes with the programs on those machines. When they all came into the warehouse, I did a quality check; this was something I did on a Saturday. I found that 25 percent of the machines on the floor would fail KSU testing —"

Harris: "What is KSU testing?"

Rob: "Kennesaw State University. We knew basically what they would be testing and the trick was to make sure the machines would pass the testing. So I went and checked a pallet and found it was bad. And I checked another, and another, and I knew we had a problem. ...

"I'd come in on a Saturday, I had two of my sons with me, and I thought, 'I'm going to just look,' and it was bad. Then first thing Monday morning I raised the question, I said, 'Hey, guys, we've got a problem — there's 20-25 percent of the machines that are palletized that are failing ...' "

Harris: "What kind of problems were you seeing?"

Rob: "...One of the things we had wrong was the date wasn't sticking in the Windows CE. The real time clock would go to check the time on the motherboard, and it would have an invalid year in it, like 1974 or something. ...

"They had to do an update in [Windows] CE to fix all those dates. So the way we did that in the warehouse was, they would post whatever the update was on the FTP site. James [Rellinger] would go get the file and put it on the [memory] cards. Because you load everything through the PCMCIA cards. You boot it up using the card and it loads the new software. ...

"I went over to DeKalb [County]. We updated 1,800 machines in basically a day and a half. I still remember ol' Rusty, down at the warehouse, we ended up touching every single machine off the pallet, booting 'em up, update it, we had a couple hundred machines done when in comes a new update over the phone."

Harris: "You mean you used a modem or they called you on the phone?"

Rob: "No. A phone call. They'd say, 'Oh, no, no, the way we had you do, that's not going to work, here's another thing to do.' Okay, we just did a few hundred machines, now we gotta do it this way. ...'"

For some reason, the techs were told to use their own laptops to download files from the Diebold FTP site. According to Rob, he was instructed by Diebold not to discuss anything with Georgia's voting-machine examiner (Dr. Brit Williams) or other state officials. This was awkward because Dr. Williams was working alongside Rob at times, and when Dr. Williams asked questions, Rob made the mistake of answering. This infuriated Diebold managers.

Rob: "They used my laptop. It was not secure, either. They just used the laptop to repro the cards. Diebold never gave us anything [any laptops] with a PCMCIA slot. Then they'd tell us, 'Go download this,' so we'd have to get out our own laptop to do it."

Harris: "Who instructed you about the FTP site? Was it a Diebold employee?"

Rob: "It was Diebold."

Harris: "Was it the people in Ohio or the people in Texas?"

Rob: "The people in McKinney [Texas]."

Harris: "Who were some of the Diebold people? Do you remember any names?"

Rob: "One of the main guys we dealt with was a guy named Ian. He was actually involved in the design of the motherboard. He was very much involved in trying to figure out how to fix the problems ..."

Ian Piper was a stockholder in the company acquired by Diebold, Global Election Systems. The staff directory lists him as Manufacturing Manager, Research & Development division.

Harris: "As I understand it, they send the system to Wyle labs for certification and also to Ciber to test the software. But from what you are describing, I can't understand how the machines got through what they are telling us is 'rigorous testing.' "

Rob: "From what I understand, they ended up figuring out that the cards that we were loading, that fix that Diebold provided for us, well, they were never tested. They just said, 'Oh, here's the problem, go ahead and fix it.' "

Harris: "So what is your opinion about the certification testing?"

Rob: "No, it's not just that. *Nobody* even tested it. When I found that out — I mean, you can't not test a fix — I worked for a billing company, and if I'd put a fix on that wasn't tested I'd have gotten fired. You have to make sure whatever fix you did didn't break something else. But they didn't even *test* the fixes before they told us to install them."

(Time out.) Dr. Brit Williams told us this is not possible. "*After state certification any change to either the Microsoft operating system or the Diebold election system voids the state certification*," Williams wrote. *"The revised system must then go back through the entire ITA Qualification and State Certification."* [1]

Rob: "Look, we're doing this and 50 to 60 percent of the machines are still freezing up. Turn it on, get one result. Turn it off and next time you turn it on you get a different result. Six times, you'd get six different results."

Harris: "Can you give me an example of different results?"

Rob: "Meaning the machine does something wrong different each time you boot it up. One time and it would freeze on you, next time it would load the GEMS program but have a completely different type of error, like there'd be a gray box sitting in the middle of it, or you couldn't use a field."

Harris: "Was this all due to the clock?"

Rob: "I don't know for sure. They [the machines] were not originally doing it. Then they fixed the real time clock, and it was supposed to make it work normal. It fixed the clock problem — the clock problem had caused it to come up and not show the battery at one point. ... I mean, you don't have the machine plugged in, you boot it up, and it starts and says it 'has no battery.' That's like saying, 'This morning I got out of bed and I stood up and I had no brain.' "

A memo from Talbot Iredale dated July 2, 2002, confirms the clock problem. *"The new WinCE 3.00 release is now on the FTP site,"* it says. The memo directs the user to get a file called WCE300-020702.zip and says that the purpose of installing this modification is to *"fix problem with getting and setting persistent Real Time Clock values,"* among other things.

Not only was this modification to Diebold's customized version of Windows CE not certified, but Iredale also indicates at one point that he wants to avoid letting Wyle (the certifier for the touch-screen firmware) look at Diebold's special Windows source code at all. In a memo dated April 15, 2002, Iredale writes:

"We do not want to get Wyle reviewing and certifying the operating systems. Therefore can we keep to a minimum the references to the WnCE 3.0 operating system."

Whatever was on the special Windows system cooked up by Iredale and others at Diebold, it didn't seem to work very well.

Rob: "And then when we loaded the software to fix that, the machines were still acting ridiculous. I was saying, 'This is not good! We need some people that know what this stuff is supposed to do, from McKinney, *now*. These machines, nobody knows what they're doing, but Diebold, you need some people to fix them that know what's going on.' They finally brought in guys, they ended up bringing in about four people. ...'"

You'd think that with such troubles, someone might follow standard company procedure and write up a "bug report."

"*All bugs ever reported have bug numbers,*" wrote Ken Clark in a memo dated Jan. 10, 2003, pointing out that the whole collection can be found in "Bugzilla." So I went looking for Bugzilla reports from Georgia. My goodness. They weren't there.

Bugzilla report numbers 1150–2150 correspond with June–October 2002, but although hundreds of these bug numbers are mentioned in memos and release notes, I only found 75 Bugzilla reports for this time period, none from Georgia. Strange. I was looking forward to reading the explanations about how computers can get up in the morning and announce that they have no brain.

Aha! Here's a memo about missing Bugzilla files. It's dated 8 July 2002, from principal engineer Ken Clark:

Subject: bugzilla down, we are working on it.

"We suffered a rather catastrophic failure of the Bugzilla database," he writes. He warns that recovery of the bugzilla reports "will be ugly" and adds that "there will be a large number of missing bugs."

In a follow-up note on July 16, Clark says, "Some bugs were irrecoverably lost and they will have to be re-found and re-submitted, but overall the loss was relatively minor."

To understand the significance of these two e-mails, you must realize that among programmers, people are fired for not performing a daily system backup. One wonders what happened to their backup. By my estimation, almost a thousand bug reports are missing, including all the Georgia bugs.

Rob: "We assembled the machine, and we ran it though a series of tests. We'd check the power cord, boot up the machine, check the printer, bar-code it, update Windows CE, then send it on to Brit. He did the

KSU testing. The L&A [Logic & Accuracy] was done at the county level, right before the election."

Harris: "So ... the L&A was not done at acceptance testing?"

Rob: "It got so there wasn't time. They did it before the election."

Now, supposedly, this L&A testing procedure is kind of a "mock election," which you do by entering practice votes. I pictured people pushing the touch screen and wondered how many test votes you push before your finger gets really tired. Not that many, apparently.

Rob: "The L&A testing — you would just enter, like, one vote and — you just choose one — you don't need to be specific on which one."

I see. One vote. But then I found out that some of their L&A test involves no touching at all:

> Ballot Station Users Guide: "The automatic L&A test, on the other hand, allows a pre-determined combination of ballots to be <u>automatically selected and marked</u>, according to the voting options selected."

6.1. Test Count

- performing a manual Logic and Accuracy Test
- performing an automated Logic and Accuracy Test

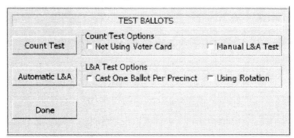

Figure 6-2: Test Ballots Screen

Rob: "I worked there from mid-June to mid-July. The whole time they were upgrading the software and doing some sort of fix to it. ...

" 'You've gotta go take care of this JS [junk shit] equipment,' I told them. Finally, I raised it as high as you go. I raised it to Bob Urosevich. He's the head of it. [Urosevich was president of Diebold Election Systems]. I told him personally, 'This is bad. I don't see us putting an election on with these machines.'

"That's where they finally assembled the teams. They got some big ol' vans; we loaded up as many people as could fit in."

Who paid for the vans? Diebold? Who paid for the people piling into the vans?

Because now I'm having a hard time understanding why Diebold says it had no indication that these patches were done at all.

Rob: "... And then you know, ironically, later on, right before I exited, they were scrambling for a date. They were trying to get us, the teams, into Fulton County to do Fulton County's 1,900 machines.

"They were in the most horrific spot. The place they warehoused them was like 1,900 machines in a little office space. ... I'm talking to this guy ... him and I were scheduling this, figuring it out how to get to these machines and do the update before KSU has to test them. We cannot be doing this at the same time as KSU. ...

"I go back to the office. Brit [Dr. Britain Williams] was there, and he says, 'What's it look like for Fulton?'

"I said, 'There's no way we're going to be able to get to Fulton County by Thursday.' I said we could probably be out there by Friday or Saturday. He said, 'There's no way we can do it at the same time. You know that. ...' "

But Dr. Williams, when interviewed by Kim Zetter of *WiredNews,* "denied that Rob ever mentioned patches to him and said, to his knowledge, no uncertified patches were applied to the machines. He said he would be very concerned if this happened."[2]

The scenario that Dr. Williams describes just does not correspond with what we are learning from Rob. Williams writes:

"... there must be in place well defined and strictly enforced policies and procedures that control who has access to the system, the circumstances under which they can access the system, and the functions that they are allowed to perform on the system."

I must have missed the section of the operating manual that describes people piling into vans and driving around updating voting programs with uncertified patches, using cards they made on their laptops.

"Finally, there must be in place physical security; fences, doors, locks, etc.; that control and limit access to the system."

Well, at least they have our voting machines under lock and key.

Rob: "They were actually swapping parts out of these machines that were on site. They'd cannibalize a machine with a bad printer or whatever, they'd grab the screen off of that to put on another machine with a failing screen, they'd retest it. They were not just breaking them down, they were taking pieces off and putting it back together.

"Even the machines that are updated, that had the right release of the software, exactly like the company wanted it, you'd boot it up and all kinds of crazy things would happen. That led to my belief that when voting took place, there would be problems."

Harris: "Do you remember what release number it was?"

Rob: "Release — I don't remember the number because what they did was it was always the date. ...

"The date was ... let me see ... June 28. No, the last one, the date that was supposed to be on there was July 5. There was about three updates, the CE software, the date that would come up would be the last. After that they came up with another fix; that's the August one at that point."

The more you examine this "electronic patch" thing, the more out of control it looks. From the memos, it appears there were so many patches that the garment might have changed color altogether:

From Talbot Iredale, 13 Jun 2002: "The new WinCE 3.00 and bootloader are on the ftp site. The file is WCE300-020607.zip..."

From Talbot Iredale, 2 Jul 2002: "The new WinCE 3.00 release is now on the ftp site. The file is WCE300-020702.zip..."

From Talbot Iredale, 4 Jul 2002: "The new WinCE 3.00 release is now on the ftp site. The file is WCE300-020704.zip ..."

From Talbot Iredale, 5 Jul 2002: " ... This is fixed in the July 05, 2000 (*sic*) release which is now on the ftp site ..."

From Talbot Iredale, 8 Aug 2002: "The WCE300-020802 release is on the ftp site ..."

From Ian S. Piper, 9 Oct 2002; Subject: AV-TS R6 Bootloader and WinCE version numbers: "... another method for determining the version number of the install files, prior to installation, is to view the creation date of the file on the flash memory card and compare it to the list below. (Unless you trust that someone has labeled the flash card correctly.) ... I've created a list of the file creation dates, and their versions...
Bootloader (filename "fboot.nb0")
Mar. 14th, 2001 Rev 1.00
Jan. 28th, 2002 Rev 1.01
Jun. 7th, 2002 Rev 1.02
Windows CE Image (filename "nk.bin")
May 25th, 2001 WinCE 2.12
Jan. 28th, 2002 WinCE 3.0
Jun 7th, 2002 WinCE 3.0
Jul. 2nd, 2002 WinCE 3.0
Jul. 5th, 2002 WinCE 3.0
Aug. 8th, 2002 WinCE 3.0

" ... Someone wIth the BallotStation install file archives can create a list of BS [Ballot Station software] versions if they want to bother."

There were more patches — the "clockfix.zip" patch is a little addition dated July 7, 2002. According a memo dated Aug. 6, 2002, Kansas may have caught a few bugs from Georgia:

"Steve, it was believed that only units built for Georgia would be affected. However, Lesley had 38 units shipped to Johnson County around the same time, so she was affected as well. There should be no others (famous last words) ..."

The techs were stitching new updates into the voting machines right up to Nov. 5, 2002 — Election Day.

Rob: "This guy came in from McKinney; he was about the second in command. He's a good friend of Bob Urosevich. About second to Bob, at least now, he got a promotion. Greg? Something like that. He flew in and I went to DeKalb County and I tested and together we went through, and we wrote down every single error, and he booted them himself and was looking at the results and seeing how sporadic they were. ...

"Greg Loe is his name. [Greg Loe, controller] I drove him out there. Brit [Dr. Britain Williams] was there; KSU was doing their testing.

They were bombing these machines out left and right.

"I'm telling him, 'They're all like this.' ... We couldn't get enough from the factory because so many were bad. You'd get a shipment of 300, but 75 were bad; they couldn't put them out fast enough to replace all the defects. ... "

Harris: "I understand they did a big demonstration during the summer with the machines."

Rob: "I was there when they told me I needed 1,100 machines for a demo. I thought, 'The trick is coming up with 1,100 machines that actually work.' "

Harris: "Do you know who was writing the fixes?"

Rob: "He had a weird name. He came out of Canada. ... That's it, Talbot Iredale, [he] would actually fix it and say, 'Oh, here's the problem,' and stick it on the FTP site. We'd grab it, stick it on the card and make a bunch of copies and use it.

"They produced it and got it to us in 24 to 48 hours. If I'd known they hadn't tested it, I simply wouldn't have installed it. My background tells me that's a no-no."

On the concept of locks, keys, fences and warehouse security:

Harris: "How secure were the machines, from what you saw?"

Rob: "I'll tell you something else — we didn't have badges. People could just walk right in and get to the machines."

Harris: "Do you think anybody could have tampered with a machine, if they wanted to?"

Rob: "Well, when we did the quality-control check, we'd open it up. They have a little box for the printer. We would find the key still in the printer. Someone could literally take that. We found cards left in the machine. [Voter cards activate the vote; memory cards store the votes.] I wondered what would happen if the wrong person got it. ..."

Harris: "Were there any protections to keep you from duplicating memory cards, or to have them serial numbered or whatever?"

Rob: "The memory cards, you can just duplicate them. You have to have the proper info on the card for the machine to boot up, but you can just make copies of the cards."

If what Rob is describing sounds pretty slipshod to you, you're not alone. In a September 2003 letter from a member of the Georgia Elections Board to Secretary of State Cathy Cox, we learn that voting-machine security is rather lacking.

"*A missing DRE* [touch-screen voting machine] *for the State Board of Elections is tantamount to a missing ATM for a bank,*" J. Randolph Evans states in his letter. He then goes on to report that voting machines have been found in hallways, stairwells and trunks of cars.[3]

* * * * *

Now every good fiasco has a little shoutin' and lyin'. This one has it all — office politics, regular politics and people scrambling to protect the company checkbook.

Harris: "When I asked Diebold if there was anyone named Rob in Georgia, they said no. Did they know about you?"

Rob: "They knew me and they knew me well. I met Bob Urosevich [president of Diebold Election Systems] a couple different times, and Ian, and then Greg Loe, he got promoted, he was basically Bob's right-hand man.

"You know, one of the main things that really just made me so upset, they were just, like, 'This Brit guy, don't even speak to him. It's a political game; you've gotta play the politics.' Well, he walks in and says, 'What are you guys doing?'

"I said, 'We're putting in an update.' He said, 'Will it change what it does?' We said, 'Just do your normal test; we're supposed to get the machines ready for you.'

"He tells someone at the office and they freaked out. They were, like, 'What the heck are you doing?'

"I wasn't supposed to talk to him at all, I guess. The guy had a flannel shirt on; he was kicking it and he was very genuine and open and there we are in the same room together, but because I actually spoke to him I got reprimanded. They said, 'If they ask you any question, you gotta say, "Talk to Norma, to one of us. ..." ' "

Harris: "What did you say to him, anyway?"

Rob: "He [Williams] said he wanted to talk to me, so I met him in this little side office and [he] asked me what was going on. I basically said I was updating the machines, doing a quality check, making sure the machines are the same, making sure they had the right release of Windows.

"Essentially, when I got back there was a meeting called. Urosevich was in it with a conference call. I went in, la-dee-dah, thinking I'd been doing a great job, and it caught me by surprise. It just totally blew me away that they would be so incensed and just absolutely angry about something so frivolous as the basic information I gave Dr. Williams. I've never been told to shut up so many times by so many people."

Harris: "You mean, 'Shut up in this meeting,' or shut up by not talking to other people?"

Rob: "I'll tell you exactly, I'll give you a quote — this came from Urosevich: He said, 'We don't need you airing our dirty laundry.'

"It was during that meeting the details came to light for me about patches and certifying them. I wasn't aware of that before. There was this big discussion about what needed to be certified. In the course of trying to determine whether they needed to be certified, they were saying, 'What do we tell Kennesaw State?' Everybody went around and gave opinions except for James Rellinger, who didn't know. Wes [Krivanek], Norma [Lyons], Darrell [Graves], Bob [Urosevich] on the phone, each gave opinions on how it should be spun as to what we were trying to do. During the course of the conversation I said, 'Can't we just tell them? What's wrong with that?'

"[They said] 'No you can't do that, it may be a certification issue.' We were sitting around tables with Urosevich on speaker phone, trying to decide whether to tell the truth, half the truth, or a complete lie."

Georgia had just ordered $53.9 million in voting machines, and the ink on the check wasn't quite dry.

"If they started erring in mass quantities, Kennesaw State's going to raise a red flag, the secretary of state's going to raise a red flag and Diebold wouldn't get paid," Behler told Kim Zetter of *WiredNews*. "I understand if a company has information they need to keep under tight lip. But when you sit around discussing lying to a client in order to make sure you're getting paid ... it's an ethics issue."

Certification Requirements Summary

Governing Entity	Certification Required	Need NASED #	Need Wyle Cert	Need CIBER Cert	Modification Requires Recertification	Submission Form Required	Technology Escrow Required
Alabama	☑	☑	☐	☐	☑	☐	☐
Alaska	☐	☐	☐	☐	☐	☐	☐
Arizona	☑	☐	☐	☐	☐	☐	☐
Arkansas	☑	☐	☐	☐	☐	☐	☐
California	☑	☑	☑	☑	☑	☑	☑
Colorado	☑	☐	☐	☐	☑	☐	☐
Connecticut	☑	☑	☐	☐	☐	☐	☑
District of Columbia	☑	☐	☐	☐	☐	☐	☐
Florida	☑	☑	☐	☐	☑	☐	☐
Georgia	☑	☑	☐	☐	☑	☐	☐

Diebold officials knew they weren't supposed to modify programs without certifying the changes. This was found in a file in the Diebold memos.

Rob: "The rumor around the office was that Diebold lost maybe $10 million on the Georgia thing. I mean, they only sold the machines for, what, $2,000 or $2,500, and then you have to build them and then you're paying people $30 an hour and you are out touching 22,000 machines *four times* — there's no way they didn't lose money on this deal. ...

"The gist of the conversation was, you screw around with this and they might decide not to pay us."

* * * * *

How credible is Rob Behler?

Dr. Brit Williams told *WiredNews* that Behler was a disgruntled employee who was fired from the project by Diebold and Automated Business Systems and Services. Rob's personnel records discredit this assertion.

" 'He was released because his part of the project was completed,' " [ABSS's vice president for the southwest region, Terrence] Thomas told *WiredNews*, explaining that there was no performance issue with Behler's work.''

James Rellinger, a Diebold contractor who worked with Rob, also rejects Williams' interpretation of events. Rellinger told *WiredNews* that both Diebold and ABSS seemed happy with Rob's work.

But there are additional reasons to believe Rob.

I spoke with Rob in March 2003. He had no way of knowing which files were sitting on the Diebold FTP site in January 2003 since he had not worked for the company in months — yet in his interview, he mentions specific electronic patch files, and I was able to find the files he mentioned among those on the Diebold FTP site. The file dates matched exactly, and the information in the accompanying release notes supports Rob's story.

Rob could not know that internal memos from Diebold would surface. He recalled that people with the names "Talbot Iredale" and "Ian" were involved with the fixes. Now we know that memos written by Talbot Iredale and Ian Piper reveal patches exactly like those reported by Rob. These 2002 memos, which were leaked on July 29, 2003, contain 13-character passwords that open files found on the Diebold FTP site in January — files which had never been opened because they were locked with complex passwords.

I interviewed Rob in March 2003. Kim Zetter from *WiredNews* interviewed him in September 2003. I interviewed him again in October. He never evaded questions, and his answers stayed consistent over this six-month period.

Rob was told to download information to his laptop. He has saved several files. He has the notes taken while demonstrating problems to Greg Loe and has provided a copy of his notes (and a videotaped deposition) to James Penland, a lawyer who is working on a case with Georgia activists.

Rob: " ... I went into this Diebold thing with no real knowledge of the voting industry. When I left, I not only had a complete grasp, but I had a complete disrespect for these machines.

"And with the folks in the office who were so — you know, 'I'm the political person; you have to know how the system works' — they were so much more concerned about their own self-importance, they were losing track of do the machines count the vote properly.

"Because that's what the people in Georgia need.

"And I'm one of them."

* * * * *

Rob jeopardized his employment future by stepping forward to tell us what really happened in Georgia. He has never asked for anything. This is especially impressive when you learn about a method that citizens like Rob can use to enrich themselves (albeit at the expense of the public interest).

In cases in which a government agency has spent taxpayer money based on fraudulent claims, the first citizens to file a *Qui Tam* lawsuit can collect as much as 30 percent of the money misspent by the agency in question — in this case, for Georgia, nearly $54 million. The catch? The case must be filed under seal. No congressional investigation, no public disclosure, just a secret filing that may or may not get unsealed.

But citizens need to know the details about these voting machines. There are bills pending in Congress and states considering purchase as of this writing. Time is of the essence. Secreting the evidence away just seems wrong.

I told Rob about *Qui Tam* and suggested that he consult someone for guidance to decide whether to pursue this path. He did.

He consulted the Bible. He looked up what the Proverbs have to say and shared their wisdom with me.

"I'm not interested in it," he decided. Now, Rob Behler is a man who is raising seven children with little material wealth. He could probably use 30 percent of $54 million. Instead, he has chosen to protect the security of your vote by telling the truth publicly.

In Rob Behler we meet the kind of quiet, patriotic citizen that makes us proud to be Americans.

* * * * *

 rob-georgia.zip

rob-georgia: Epilogue

Harris: "Do you remember when you got this job back in June?"

Rob: "Yes. Late June."

Hmmm.

Harris: "Are you sure?"

Rob: "Yes. June 24, at the earliest, June 16."

Date on the rob-georgia files: June 4. At least two weeks *before* Rob was hired.

So who — or what — is "rob-georgia?"

12
Open Source Exam

This chapter delves into unavoidably technical areas. This presents a challenge to the reader if, like me, you don't have a computer background. Even if you don't understand the specifics of the flaws uncovered, the gist of the problem is apparent. You will see our evolution from curiosity, to concern, to alarm as we unravel computer programming that runs the Diebold voting system.

Aside from looking at file names, I wasn't much help in analyzing what was in the FTP files. But in June 2003, Diebold voting files began to be examined at a forum called DemocraticUnderground.com, and we learned that people are deeply interested in how their votes are counted.

"This is dangerous," someone explained, to everyone's surprise. "Bad things could happen. Very bad things."

Can someone please explain to me how our "democracy" turned into something where ordinary citizens can get arrested just for looking at how their votes are counted? No, I'm not asking you to explain the "Digital Millennium Copyright Act" (DMCA),[1] which in Internet circles is almost as controversial as the Patriot Act. The DMCA was designed to clamp down on music swapping, but somehow it turned into a tool that can eliminate free speech without due process. It may punish copyright violations with jail time. Some people say the DMCA might be used against anyone who studies the software that counts his votes.

What I want to know is this: How can we call ourselves a democracy if we are so afraid of the consequences that we don't dare to inspect our own vote-counting system? What I'm looking for is an explanation of how *scaring* people who simply want to make sure their votes are counted properly can possibly be the right approach to a robust democracy.

Apparently, this looking at how we count votes is dangerous and (possibly) forbidden — but no one seems to know for sure. Lawyers confess to uncertainty as to whether looking at vote-counting files found on an open Web site can be permitted.

For several months, I considered this issue. As of the writing of this book, I've not yet been able to get a straight answer out of anyone. Here is what *I* came to believe, after much thought: I think that examining our voting machine software is not only a legitimate activity, but it is also our civic duty. For queasier souls, I offer these statements in defense of this endeavor:

1) These files were publicly available.

2) Examining them is in the public interest.

3) Our objective is study and review, not copying and selling voting systems.

4) In a democracy, vote-counting should not be secret in the first place.

The Internet is alive with message boards, chat rooms and forums. People go to these Web sites to meet and converse with each other, using "screen names" so that they can feel free to express any opinion they like. DemocraticUnderground.com (DU) is a rapid-fire political discussion board with more than 35,000 participants. Because this kind of venue provides a feeling of safety and anonymity, citizens used it to examine our voting system.

I perused more than 5,000 comments about voting systems from DU, and I think you'll agree that the excerpts from this body of work (screen names changed) show a remarkable picture of democracy in action.

"I haven't seen the Diebold machines or how they operate," commented "Cleaver" on DU, "but in my precinct, we have a numbered ballot we fill out that is scanned into a machine. In case of a questionable result, the numbered paper ballots can be used to verify results by a hand count. The Diebold machines should have something similar."

Three months later, Cleaver got a rude awakening. He learned that he has indeed been voting on Diebold machines and that a security breach was discovered right in his home county.

After sitting on the files for four and a half months, I was dying to know what was in them.

"What could this thing possibly be doing to need so much source code?" asked "Romeo," a computer programmer. "I have built systems ten times more complex than any imaginable voting machine in one-hundredth the source code space. Sometimes when programmers don't know what they are doing this is the result – lots of cut and pasted functions that are almost the same, tons of obsolete but not removed code. ... Ugh."

Another programmer did not find the quantity of code unusual.

"Given that professional programming is complex by its nature and professional programmers are often messy tasteless people by 'normal' social standards," said "mortal," "I'd be surprised if it didn't look like this. In fact, while the sample in question is small, it looks like at least half of the source is visual C++ generated from templates by click&drag, by virtue of its unpleasant-to-type words.

"Once the compiler gets hold of it, chops logicals and optimizes loops, you'll never know how crappy the source looked anyway ... there are actually contests (such as the infamous 'obfuscated C contest') to write the most convoluted and inscrutable programs possible."

A participant called "BettaWatchYerVote" didn't think we'd find evidence of tampering in the computer code.

"I don't think it's likely that you can prove anything with the source code. You won't find a function called 'double_GOP_Votes' that does fake counting ... nevertheless, we could very well find back doors, which aren't that uncommon, that would allow tampering."

Some participants argued about the discussion process itself.

"The thought struck me after reading the third or fourth message that this dialogue should not be on a public forum," said "ErgoWeAre."

"Why not? This is the very underpinning of democracy we're discussing here. If there was ever a need-to-know issue for the general public, this is it," replied mortal.

Others suggested the most efficient ways to hunt for vote fraud.

"Have any empirical tests been done?" A citizen we'll call "Ovaltina" often defended Diebold and provided an alternate point of view. Here, Ovaltina suggested ways to test the code.

"Meaning, generate a large amount of output with the code, and analyze that output, looking for anything the least bit funny, then going back and then focusing on those funny results to look for foul play."

A forum participant called "Bibbidi-Bobbidi-Boo" had a different approach.

"OK, so you've got your haystack and you're looking for the needle ... Here's how I'd approach this problem. ... I'd begin by doing a bit of analysis on how the system is structured. Isolate the important data types (that voter info one is a good example) that someone might be interested in modifying. ...

"After that, I'd go a few levels deeper with the functions that are doing the data modifications (look at the functions that are called by those functions). I'd begin to chart out the 'life of a vote' in the system. ...

" ... [I'd look for] code that does not appear to do what its comments say it's supposed to do; code that is completely undocumented; any code that seems to be manipulating memory in 'weird' or unnecessary ways. God help you because this is in C++."

One participant pondered new DMCA legal issues.

"Discussion cannot be considered illegal under the DMCA," said "Clark Kent," a programmer who had noticed that Diebold passed around other people's proprietary code on its site. "... By making this third party code available freely, Diebold was violating the DMCA. ... It's unfortunate that Diebold allowed Microsoft source code to be publicly available on one of their FTP servers."

Participants debated whether the curious phrasing in some of the user manuals indicated security weaknesses, or simply imprecise writing.

"Look at this sentence," said "Jolio," — "*When you have finished entering the totals for a precinct, all Check values must be zero in order for you to proceed to the next precinct. If necessary, you can make up the difference by putting the number in the Check tally in the Times Blank field if the race is a Vote For One race. If not, you may have to perform some additional calculations to make the Check value equal zero.*"

Several technical writers participated in the analysis. One, who called himself "Crapper Dan!" couldn't decide whether the previous passage was badly written or contained instructions on how to fudge the numbers.

"I'm a technical writer, and even *I* can't figure out if that says what we think it says or not. Enter that one in the STC's 'Worst Manual of the Year' contest," he said.

Citizens examined the built-in "manual entry" feature, wondering what it was used for and what controls were in place to prevent its abuse.

"Why are they entering manual votes?" asked Jolio. "If we have optical scanners reading absentee and touch screens reading polling votes (and the touch screens also read the challenge votes) — what is the purpose of manual entry?"

"My guess," replied "K3Park," "[is that] the optical scan machines may not be integrated into the same computer system as they are using to run the GEMS software. So (I am guessing) the data has to be entered manually. Even [if] the optical scan machines WERE on the same computer, it might be necessary to enter the data manually if there is no standard protocol for transferring the data from the 'optical scan' app to the GEMS software. Another possibility is write-in votes or provisional ballots."

This seemed like a good explanation, though an examination of internal memos, which surfaced later, indicated that both touch-screens and optical scans are integrated into the same GEMS program.

Jolio was still concerned. "That could be the reason for it, but if so ... what security measures should it have, at a minimum? Because, manual entry might have a legitimate purpose for entering absentee votes, yet provide a back-door for tampering also."

Clark Kent went looking for the source code which controls the manual entry function.

"Unfortunately, a key piece is missing, manualentry.cpp," he said. "It's documented, but is not there."

The discussions began to attract more programmers. One, who we'll call "Rummage," was particularly interested in the central count "GEMS" system, recognizing that it could provide a key attack point.

"That's right," he said. "The code for the GEMS Server is the key and it ain't here."

Concern soon turned into criticism, as citizens noticed omissions and weak auditing procedures.

"It took 'em three years to log manual entries, said "Lucille Goldman," a programmer whose criticism stung all the more because she often defended Diebold. "Sheesh!"

"I see the section on manual entry," said Jolio, after reviewing the user manuals. "Not a word in it on who is allowed to do it — presumably, must be someone with admin privileges, but I note this manual also has a section for remote access to the database (why does any election supervisor need remote access to their computer for voting program tasks?) And uh — wouldn't you say that a key event to log [in the audit] after launching the election would be to log the closing of the election? Not a peep, they just go on and open another election."

"You call that an audit log?" asked Lucille Goldman. "Everybody's [logged in as] 'admin.' "

"Topper," who works with government procurement and computer programming, was concerned about holes in the documentation. "More damning ... is that there doesn't seem to be a document detailing policies and procedures for security both at the user/institutional level and the hardware/software level. There needs to be a document detailing who is entitled to do what with the system."

A programmer who I'll call "BlueMac" pointed out a series of agonized comments by Diebold programmers, found in the source code for card readers and touch-screens.

"They have had one hell of a time with standard magnetic card readers. Programmer frustration comments are rampant in this series of modules."

"The thing that disturbs me," said a participant we'll call "OutofTouch," "is the comment saying 'add this after it get backs from certification' (or however it's worded). While it's not necessarily nefarious doings — it could be they modified a function, and the mod was crashing, so they didn't want to insert the update until it was 'stable' — the note does imply that there may be a non-certified build in use."

Of course, anonymous participants on an Internet message board are of no help at all if you want to document problems in a formal way. With the Internet, you never really know whom you are dealing with; a fellow who joins a singles forum may think he's chatting up a buxom blonde named Inga from Denmark while he's actually charming a 400-pound farmer from Iowa named Ralph.

Among the advantages of this informal review format was the perception of protected freedom of speech, facilitated by anonymity. A disadvantage of doing an open-source investigation using a public forum was that we knew very little about these people's credentials, except what they volunteered.

This public "open-source investigation" had many drawbacks, but it did attract intellectual talent and ultimately led to the first public evaluations of the software outside the voting industry itself. One of the contributors, whom I'll call "Goody Two-Shoes," explains how he came to be concerned about the Diebold software:

"I'm the poor schmuck who configures brand new, untested, computer systems designed by teams of highly educated hardware engineers and loads brand new untested software designed by highly educated teams of software engineers and then performs the 'debug' to make them work together. The systems rarely, if ever, work the first time. It's been my job to be the final arbiter of the finger pointing battles between the two engineering groups who each claim the others product is at fault."

He goes on to describe how he can quickly locate problem areas in the source code.

"...Programmers tend to be extremely logical thinkers. They exhibit that logical thinking in the way they write their comments into the source code. Each section of code produced by a 'good' programmer has a 'plain english' explanation of what that section does. You might call it a 'professional courtesy' to other programmers who have to work with their code downstream. It's [looking at the comments] a shortcut that quickly lets you know where to focus your attention rather than study every line of code to find what you're looking for."

"When you find comments [in the source code] that say things like: *'this is baloney, you don't have to do this, this function is already built in to XXXXXX, just use the XXXXX command'* or *'the (insert critical flag here) flag is broken so I did this and that to get around it'* and even things like *'I don't know why you want me to do this, it will let this and that happen....unless that's what you want to happen then I guess it's OK'*!

"Comments of this type naturally lead a good programmer looking for problems to investigate what is going on in those routines."

The contributor known here under the screen name "Rummage" studied computer science under a Nobel laureate at Carnegie-Mellon University. In real life and under his normal name, he designs databases for critical applications in the medical field.

"So far, that's the story of the last few days," he wrote. "From databases with no foreign keys (read no referential integrity), unprotected transmission code, ample opportunity for buffer overruns right to PCMCIA slots for wireless modems. Not so much nefarious code as a system with so much opportunity for hacking/fraud as to invite cheating. "

"...as for structure and understanding the DB [database], there are no relationships and the Primary keys are not defined as Access Primary keys. This will make reconstructing the schema a little harder. I don't think a DBA [database analyst] designed this.

"No referential integrity — no autonumber primary keys. Bad for maintaining a reliable database — good for adding and deleting data at will."

I've spoken to many of the participants of the voting machine examination who seemed especially insightful, and they often have impressive credentials, but to most of the world they are anonymous so you can't really know. These informal forum discussions are more akin to casual conversation in the cafeteria than to academic research.

Here are comments from "t_device," a European participant who concurs with "Rummage" about weaknesses in the database design.

"The fact that they're using Access disallows relationality. ... When using a decent database, SQL Server Sybase etc, for example, constraints, triggers, stored procedures, packages, relationships, views, etc are all maintained inside the database — that's where all the business logic resides in a well crafted modern application.

"With Access, however, you're dealing with basically a toy database, and since all of the above are missing, it is common to join tables on the fly using the data connection and SQL code embedded into the program itself. ...

"... I could be wrong, but in Access, if you have write capability, you have delete capability ... the security features are very limited.

"Security is not something I would consider claiming to have for *any* Access-based application since about any user can gain access fairly easily ... and if you'd ever tried to upsize from Access you wouldn't be touting it as a good thing. Data types get changed, boolean fields don't translate ... it certainly shouldn't be used in a mission critical voting application."

On forums, people are free to make opinionated, dogmatic and sometimes mistaken statements, just as we do in casual conversation on the subway or in a bar. The Internet culture uses forums and message boards to consider perspectives and ideas, but never for a definitive answer. One reason: It all depends who's chatting that day.

Lucille Goldman took issue with criticisms posted by t_device.

"Let's not get into a pissing match," she wrote. "My upsized applications run very nicely to this day. Yes, it's not perfect, but I've used ERwin for documentation and Access is much easier for smaller projects. You get the application running, produce the relational schema and put it on the server. You may choose to develop on the target system. I prefer my method. I hope we can treat each other respectfully."

"I believe we have been civil," said t_device. "If that's not the case, let me know. Apparently we have a difference of opinion. That's healthy. I have upsized a few Access apps and I've developed in it, so I'm not speaking off the top of my head. ... Anyway, let's drop the Access better/worse convo and stick to the voting application."

Most programmers concurred that Diebold's use of the Microsoft Access program indicated weaker security than desired.

"Go over to slashdot," said "abcxyz." Slashdot.org is a forum for computer people. "Try talking about 'security' and 'Access' in the same breath and see how seriously they take you over there — they won't even dignify you with a response, they'll just laugh at you and spray you with onomatopoeic responses like this:
choke
wheeze
bwahahahahahahahahahahahah
gasp
Wait, these things are already in use?!?
thud
... because all programmers know there is no security in Access."

"If you want to know why Access is a bad idea," said Goody Two-Shoes, "just do a Google search for 'Access, vulnerability' and browse through the 951,000 hits!"

"Now THAT is a legitimate beef re: Access," agreed Rummage. "And the lack of referential integrity (which could have been done, but wasn't) only fuels my suspicions."

By now, many people have read criticisms about the Diebold voting system, but back in June 2003 no such reports had surfaced. I found myself staying up late into the night, just to see what else the programmers would find. They were especially critical of the audit log, cited by Dr. Brit Williams as a key component to the security of Georgia's voting system.

"Good point about database audit log tables," said a programmer we'll call "gandalf." He pointed out that the Diebold audit log was not constructed properly. "Very easy to delete any entries. Though there should be some sort of audit ID (in any good database design) that records the sequence of audit log entries which would indicate that a log entry had been deleted."

The audit log. The more people looked at it, the greater the dismay. What citizens were finding simply did not match claims made by Diebold and its regulators. From Dr. Brit Williams:

> "Overall security of any computer-based system is obtained by a combination of three factors working in concert with each other: First, the computer system must provide audit data that is sufficient to track the sequence of events that occur on the system and, to the extent possible, identify the person(s) that initiated the events." [2]

The following statement, taken from the Diebold document used to sell its system to the state of Georgia, refers to a touch-screen audit trail:

> "Generated entries on the audit log cannot be terminated or interfered with by program control or by human intervention." [3]

Not quite. The server at the county that accumulates all the incoming votes (GEMS) is an attractive tampering target, and altering the critically important GEMS audit log is quite easy.

"Bev, in what way is it significant that the audit log can be rewritten?" asked a programmer we'll call "Mae West." "I'm puzzled by that," she said, "because as several people said (I among them) early on, physical control of a machine always means you can overwrite whatever you like. The trick is to keep the bad guys from gaining physical control."

"The significance is that in letters from certifiers and in documentation provided to certifiers and to the public, they took the curious position that the 'audit log' was a primary means of security protection," I replied, referencing Dr. Williams' report.

"Hmmm ... did they say in what way?" she asked. "Because if they said it as you implied here (i.e., the existence of an audit file is enough), that would actually be hilariously funny if it weren't so serious. Nerds the world 'round would be cleaning their keyboards and monitors after failing to laugh and swallow at the same time."

Looking at the Microsoft Access database used in the county vote tabulation system led to concerns about the integrity of the GEMS program as a whole. Interest in the GEMS program began to take on a life of its own on the forums.

"Here's the best part," said BlueMac, "With GEMS (server) installed on my computer, I was able to create a user name ("me") with a password of my choosing ("mac") and assign myself ADMIN capabilities. This was without ever signing into GEMS. ... all I had to do was create a new database and I was in like Flynn."

Diebold was not without its supporters. "Ovaltina" pointed out that a database maintenance application might provide the security that GEMS was found to lack.

"The votes end up in a database. Whenever there's a database, it makes sense that there would be a database maintenance application. Always preferable to have such an application controlling data entry, to control access and make sure everything agrees, catch entry errors, log activity, etc.

"Without this data entry procedure, what would stop someone from going directly into the database and committing fraud that way? I think you said before that it's an Access database? So open up the database with Access and put your phony votes in. So what I'm saying is the mere ability to edit votes isn't all that menacing to me, because it doesn't say that there are no procedures to prevent it from being abused. Maybe elsewhere in the system, or maybe completely outside the system."

The GEMS program at the county, which pulls in all the polling-place votes, would not be as vulnerable if a report was run directly from the voting machines themselves before any data was sent to the county tabulator. That way, if someone tampered with GEMS (even if they also tampered with the incoming data from the polling place), the numbers wouldn't match. A forum member called "DanglingChad" who had election experience weighed in:

"Full precinct reports are required by California state law as well as others. The Diebold system better be complying with the requirement ... California Code 19370 states ... 'At the close of polls... at the precinct ... one copy of the statement of return of votes cast for each machine shall be posted upon the outside wall of the precinct for all to see. The return of votes includes each candidate's name and their vote totals at the precinct. During certification of voting machines, the Voting Systems Panel requires evidence that the procedures of each vendor include this process. ...' "

If someone tries to hack the GEMS program, posted reports at each precinct (as long as they were printed before any upload of data) would make fraud at the central tabulation stage significantly more difficult, though a clever insider could get around this safeguard. Unfortunately, as you'll learn in the next chapter, this procedure was not followed in the 2003 California gubernatorial recall.

* * * * *

Most of us are given some amount of common sense (as long as sex or money isn't involved), and when we meet up in a group and bring our experiences into the picture, we can make some good, solid decisions. People familiar with accounting and bookkeeping began to weigh in on the online voting system examinations, and they sometimes took software engineers to task for their failure to understand basic accounting principles.

At issue in this conversation were statements by computer scientists that it was sometimes permissible to design tabulation systems in which totals could be manually overwritten.

No way, said a citizen who went by the moniker "ItAllAddsUp." "Each and every vote should exist as a distinct and unadulterated record of one citizen's transaction, probably one or more copies should be generated simultaneously, and everything should be 'journalled' ...

"Since voters are not allowed to recast votes, no possible set of circumstances can possibly exist to justify changing those records. ... Every change, every addition or subtraction to votes, has got to be a separate transaction. As a matter of fact, what reason should ever exist to make a change that has an intrinsic value of more than one?

"If a fifty vote change has to be made, then you had better show fifty transactions. ... If you need to cancel fifty votes, then you had better show which fifty votes that you are cancelling. Damn and double damn. There is absolutely no technical reason in the world why this cannot be done.

"One vote today is the same as one vote in 1776, which is the same as one vote in 1876, which is the same as one vote in 1976, which should be the same as one vote in 2076.

"What is so hard to understand about that for these computer geeks?"

"Cleaver" pointed out that counting votes was a form of bookkeeping and explained why the same kinds of safeguards should be used.

"Accounting practices are double entry, not only because of mistakes, but also fraud. Two sources are better than one. So there should be an accounting trail to verify results, especially when there is a question of accuracy. ... It doesn't have to be paper but it should be a traceable source document."

Most of all, citizens weighed in with demands for transparency. They chafed at corporate claims to privacy for votes that belong to all of us:

"Government has no business hiding behind proprietary computer code in proprietary voting machines," said ItAllAddsUp. "If the government wants us to use a number 2 lead pencil to mark the ballot, then we damn well better be able to examine that number 2 lead pencil ourselves. We should be able to buy a box of those very same, identical, number 2 lead pencils if we so desire. The paper used for the ballots has got to be paper that can be examined by any who wish. The boxes where the ballots are stuffed need to be able to be examined ... "

As citizens became more concerned about the security of the Diebold voting system, they began to look for remedies and found that state law often lacks adequate protections.

"States like Georgia have written provisions into their laws that make it impossible to get a machine in dispute adequately inspected," said Goody Two-Shoes. "The Georgia law stipulates that three people, a patent attorney and two *mechanics*, be appointed by law to look at the computerized machines! This is tantamount to appointing two blind men and an attack dog to inspect the machine. If either of the 'mechanics' asks about how the machine works the attorney is there to tell them, 'It's proprietary information, you're not allowed to know!' "

Every now and then someone still pops up to tell us that the voting system topic has no legs or that people just don't care about it. Then explain this: Voting system analysis at DemocraticUnderground.com became kind of an attraction. More and more people tuned in, but at the same time, the subject matter became increasingly technical, while the tone of discussions reflected more urgent concerns. Occasionally someone would sigh and raise a hand:

"Can anyone explain what is happening here in simple language for those of us who are non-techies?" asked a citizen called "SkiBob." "I can't make heads or tails about what you may have found here."

Well, we're talking about the systems used to count our votes.

"But have you guys found anything? Everybody seems to be talking in very excited tones using terms I can't understand."

(Sorry.) Yes, people were finding things. Many of the things they found were eventually found also by researchers at Johns Hopkins and Rice universities,[4] in a report that ended up in *The New York Times.* It was the "increasingly excited tones" that directly led to the events that produced that report.

"Attn: Bev Harris ... look at the cryptographic routines of the voting system. I've just started to go through this system and have a few little snide remarks to make," said the computer professional who went by the name "Topper." She was concerned about the possible use of a free, open-source cryptography program which is no longer supported.

"The problem with using open source with no support is getting a timely answer to your question," she said. "Ergo, if there is a security problem during an election, you are stuck with fixing it — which you may not be able to do yourself in a timely fashion."

"Actually it's not so bad," countered a programmer called "MidniteMunchies." "I'm a programmer and have used that code before. It isn't very well documented and the code is very confusing due to some funky overuse of C++ templates.

"... However, I would have to agree that any kind of election software encryption should be based on a standard commercial or government supported encryption solution rather than someone's hobby encryption project."

Encryption is important because we don't want people intercepting and changing the votes as we record, transfer and tally them up.

Used correctly, encryption can prevent some kinds of unauthorized access. Discussions about encryption were about as opaque as it gets on a political discussion board, but even those of us who are not techies could tell that Diebold's encryption was causing significant concern.

"I'm not sure any of the encryption is actually used anywhere," said "PoodieToot." This was not reassuring.

"Since you brought it up, I thought I'd see what algorithm they ended up using. The problem is, I've grepped all over the files, and I don't find any header file inclusions from the crypto library *anywhere,* other than the crypto library. I can't see where the other CVS modules call any of this stuff at all.

"You know," PoodieToot continued, "they *could* have gone with OpenSSL — it's free, and supported by far, far more users (and corporate users, such as Apple and IBM for example). But, then again, it doesn't look like they are using any of it anyway. ..."

Uh-oh. When answers about Diebold's cryptographic methods were found, they weren't the right ones.

"Mystery solved," said PoodieToot, "but ... oh, no ... I found what they are actually doing for encryption. They have their own implementation of DES in Des.h. Here's the bad news ... it looks like the DES encryption key is *hard coded as a macro*!!!!!

"AAAAIIIIIIIEEEEEEEEIIIHHHHHHH!!!!!!!!!!!!

"I'll leave discovery of aforementioned key as an exercise for the reader. ... Good God. ..."

PoodieToot's discovery brought the Internet board alive with the forum equivalent of shrieks and moans.

"Ooorah!!!!!!! Yeah," said Topper. "I've found the DES.h file ... and will start trolling through this. ... If you've hard coded your key and left it just like the public implementation, then it would not be that hard for a hacker to figure out how to get into your system."

Programmers were beside themselves upon viewing the blatant security flaws, and soon they were finishing each others' sentences.

"—It would end up as a static string in the executable file," said PoodieToot. "And you can tear the static strings out of an executable to view them faster than you can blink your eyes."

"In your best '50s announcer voice," said Romeo sarcastically, "now *that's* real data security! (cough, cough.)"

The more people learned, the more alarmed they became.

"These things actually use PCMCIA cards?" asked Clark Kent in dismay. "Huge potential security breaches! Think of the new stuff out there. This is Windows CE-based code. Couldn't the existence of these drivers open up any one of these machines having a PCMCIA based wireless network card installed surreptitiously, allowing remote access via airwaves?

"They're using simple PCMCIA ATA disks These things are basically notepad PC's and the security is almost non-existent. How many local governments will be up on the sophistication required to implement WEP with encryption and hiding SSID's for wireless networks? Heck, you wouldn't even have to hack the wireless network to get around these things, all that is necessary is to pop out one hard drive of results and pop in another with new results preconfigured."

A tech who went by the name "Razmataz" was shocked at finding evidence of wireless communications in the voting system.

"Wireless programming required? Are they nuts? I thought I'd been following all the 'electronic voting machine' strategies but that's one I missed. I'm a techie, 36 years in the business, some of it with reading punch card votes and optical votes. Wireless programming capability is just plain nuts. That's a security hole the size of a 747.

"That would mean somebody could walk near the voting area (even outside the building), connect to the voting machines via wireless network, and make changes to the voting programs and/or the vote counts."

"I think we've found a potential hole where somebody could alter results remotely with nothing going over any wire," said Clark Kent. "Somebody needs to seriously wardrive elections sites using these things."

"Ah. ... That is serious bad news if they are running these terminals wirelessly and only relying on WEP for security," said "RescueRanger." "That is enough to fail a security audit at any Fortune 1000 company."

Yet, RescueRanger held onto hope for a bit of good news.

"On the other hand, wireless can be extremely secure, more secure in fact than most wired communication if done properly and with the right equipment and design. To do it securely, would require fairly recent (and proprietary) technology ... certainly not anything that is anywhere near five years old."

Perhaps we should all calm down, intoned a forum participant who went by the name "spock."

"You are assuming no encryption. Because this is wireless does not mean no encryption is being used. WEP anyone? Proprietary encryption perhaps? But then again it could be none is."

"The onus is on the local election administrators," said Clark Kent, "though I have my home wireless network locked down so tight most wardrivers will take one look at all of my security measures and drive on down the street to the guy who is advertising an SSID that is the default on the access point he installed and has never changed the admin password."

To most of us, this conversation might as well have been conducted in Greek, but we couldn't stop tuning in. Clark Kent explained the security flaws in language only a cryptologist could love.

"Even I know that with 128 bit encryption using WEP, no advertised SSID, and a MAC Address list can still be cracked. MAC addresses can be spoofed relatively easily and brute force can break the 128 bit encryption if you've got the processor power. Even with encryption, it can be cracked. Now tell me how many of the local election boards you've had experience with are sophisticated enough to implement WEP, let alone MAC Address access lists? Add to that the fact that there is a ton of code that could hold back door access and this thing is rife with potential abuse.

"Nope, this doesn't even compare to the potential for pushing out chads on hundreds of cards with a pin so they register as double votes and thus are spoiled ballots. The potential for abuse is magnitudes above this. If the government does not require an independent code review by at least three different companies, it's not doing its job."

Remain calm, spock suggested: "I trust you are aware... The chances of breaking 128 bit encryption with a brute force approach could very well take centuries with just about any computer on the planet?"

No, no, no. "A 128 bit encrypted file and the encryption level on WEP are two different things," said Clark Kent. "I assure you, WEP is crackable. A PGP file with 128 bit encryption is, as you stated, not easily crackable. And when database files have passwords that are the name of the county where votes are counted, how secure is this system?"

It got worse.

"Perhaps this programmer's comment in the Results Transfer Dialog file [TransferResultDlg.cpp] will answer that question for you," said BlueMac. " 'Changed the election.dbd file to only store ASCII code not unicode to make it compatible between windowsNT/95/98 and WinCE. The conversion from ASCII to unicode, if required, is done when the data is retrieved from the database. Note: This does not affect RTF data since it is always stored in ASCII.' "

Though many of us didn't exactly understand it, this last news, apparently, was pretty bad.

"Straight ASCII????????" wrote Clark Kent. "For compatibility with Windows 95/98/NT???? On February 15, 2001?????"

A typographical wink was spock's response: "Why not? ;o"

"That's some encryption there! Straight ASCII for backwards compatibility on operating systems that are obsolete," said Clark Kent. "This makes a lot of sense for a system we are supposed to trust the future of the world to."

He wasn't sure it was a disaster, but spock ceased to be at all reassuring.

"I believe it is talking about the unencrypted values for backwards compatibility when being viewed. But then again that's another problem with leaked source that may or may not be final, you can't be sure."

"And that's the problem with computer voting systems, isn't it," said PoodieToot. "You can't be sure."

But why not use widely accepted encryption techniques?

"If I were the guys doing openssl, I'd be real pissed off right now," said mortal. "That blows chunks. I guess assigning a public/private key pair to each networked voting machine is too difficult for the people entrusted with the lifeblood of democracy?"

"Seems a Congressional investigation should be next," said "SPacific."

If anything should have a congressional investigation in full view of TV cameras, the voting industry should, but as of the writing of this book, it hasn't happened.

* * * * *

What came next was a quiet phone call on a Sunday morning.

Over the course of a year, I had consulted with about two dozen computer techs. Several are not on DemocraticUnderground.com because they are Republicans. I met one on Free Republic, a conservative forum. Voting-system integrity is a truly nonpartisan subject. Democrats, Republicans, Libertarians and Greens — everyone but the Charlatan Party, I guess — all respond the same way when someone says, *By the way, we won't be auditing the vote, thank you.*

Among my sources is a computer programmer I'll call "Cape Cod." He rarely calls me and has always been irritatingly discreet about his examinations of the Diebold files. When he calls, his clipped, East Coast voice provides no unnecessary words and gives very tidy explanations.

The best programmers explain things in a very concise way. I'll keep asking questions until I understand the answer or the other person starts shouting at me, whichever comes first. But highly skilled programmers are extremely organized thinkers, and it is easy to follow their explanations. Cape Cod is such a person. His explanations of complex computer concepts follow this simple, linear fashion: *Here is A, and I'm going to take you to B. Take hold of A, and walk just this way, and I'll describe the scenery as we go. Now, here we have arrived at B; did you enjoy it?*

He never calls unless he has something to say. He made one efficient, four-minute call to explain how a voting system might be able to cheat with "zero reports," for example:

"It's quite simple, really; your goal is to stuff the electronic ballot box while at the same time generating a report at the beginning of the election which tells you that zero votes have been cast, proving the ballot box has *not* been stuffed.

"Here's what you do: You stuff the ballot box by entering two vote totals that cancel each other out: 'plus 50 for Truman, minus 50 for Dewey.' You have thus created a spread of 100 votes between the candidates before the election begins — yet because +50 and -50 sum to zero, you have added no extra voters.

"To make the report read zero when you start the election, simply instruct the code to put a string of zeroes into the 'zero report' if there are any negative numbers in the ballot-stuffing area, but it must only do this if there are no other votes in the system. And by designing a database without referential integrity, you can arrange for the evidence of this ballot-stuffing area to fall off the radar."

One Sunday morning while I was still in my bathrobe, I received one of Cape Cod's rare phone calls.

"Go to your computer. I want to show you something."

He proceeded to walk me through the process of rigging an election using a real Diebold "GEMS" program, with a version used in a real election, with a vote database for Cobb County, Georgia.

Bypassing the supervisor password

If you install GEMS and make a new "test election," the manual tells you to use the password "GEMSUSER." Close your test election and open the same file in Microsoft Access, and you will find an encrypted version of the "GEMSUSER" password. Copy the encrypted password and paste it into any election database. You don't really need Microsoft Access; a simple text editor can also be used. By doing this, you can bypass the password in any GEMS vote database.

You can grant yourself supervisor privileges by making yourself an "admin."

You can add as many friends as you want. (I added 50 of mine and gave them all the same password, which was "password.")

It gets worse: If you go in the back door, you don't even need a password.

A triple set of books

The GEMS program looks and feels very secure when you work with it. However, running behind the GEMS program is a database using Microsoft Access. When you open an election in GEMS, it places an election database in a folder on your computer. Anyone who can get at the computer, either with physical access or by hacking in, can open this election file; right-click it, open it with a text editor or with Microsoft Access, then just go right in the back door. This technique is not certified or authorized, but it can be done anyway. You don't need any special computer skills. At the time we examined the files, if you could right-click a file and type, you could alter the votes in GEMS.

Back to Cape Cod.

"Here's what we're going to do," he said. "We'll go in and run a totals report, so you can see what the election supervisor sees. Then I'll show you something unusual."

I opened the GEMS program and ran a totals report, showing the overall election results. Then I ran a detail report showing the results in each precinct.

"Now, open the file in Microsoft Access."

"Close out of GEMS?"

"No, Access is configured for multiple users."

OK, I didn't know that. Two people can wander around in the vote database at the same time without bumping into each other.

Remember that there are two programs: the GEMS program, which the election supervisor sees, and the Microsoft Access database (the back door) that stores the votes, which she does not see.

You can click a table called CandidateCounter, which will show you how many votes the candidate has accumulated for each polling place.

Cape Cod showed me another table in the vote database, called SumCandidateCounter. This table had the same information as CandidateCounter, but we observed that it had two complete sets of the same information. One set was marked by a flag, the number "-1." Notice that this gives us three sets of votes.

"Change some of the vote totals in SumCandidateCounter."

"Now go into GEMS and run the totals report."

The totals report showed my new numbers, proving I could alter the report by going in the back door and replacing vote totals with my own.

"Now go back and look at that detail report."

The detail report had the original votes, not the ones I changed. In accounting, this is called having two sets of books. (Or in this case, three. I never heard what the third set of books does. Cape Cod called it the "Lord only knows" table.)

"Why would it be good to have the detail report show the real votes while the summary shows the ones I changed?"

"Because it would allow a manipulated system to pass a spot check."

Altering the audit log

Any time you open the GEMS program, it will show up in the GEMS audit log. (If you go in the back door using Microsoft Access, however, your work will not show up in the audit log.) But suppose you need to erase your activities in GEMS?

In the Diebold system, it seems that everyone uses the same name when they go into GEMS (they all call themselves "admin"), but I wanted to see whether I could become someone new, play around in GEMS and then erase myself from the audit log.

I created a new user by the name of "Evildoer." Evildoer performed various functions, including running reports to check his vote-rigging work, but only some of his activities showed up on the audit log. For some reason, a few of his activities omitted themselves from the audit log even before I tampered with it. But I wanted to erase *all* evidence that Evildoer had existed.

I went in the back door. I expected the audit-log entries to be numbered automatically with something I could not edit. That way, if I erased some Evildoer activities, the numbers would still be there, marking an activity that had disappeared. I was surprised to find that I could just type new numbers over any of the GEMS audit-log numbers, and I could also erase events altogether.

In every version of GEMS that I examined, the autonumbering feature was disabled, allowing anyone to add, change and delete items from the audit without leaving a trace. I simply erased Evildoer.

Going back into GEMS, I ran an audit report to see if Evildoer had indeed disappeared. *Poof!* Gone. As Verbal Kint said in the movie *The Usual Suspects* (1995), "The greatest trick the devil ever pulled was convincing the world he didn't exist."

Another thing that seemed improper in the GEMS program is this: You can enter *negative* votes. It is a simple matter to program the software so that it will never accept a negative number. Why should it? A vote total that is less than zero can only be illicit.

The entire process — bypassing the password, changing the vote totals, cleaning up the audit log — took less than 10 minutes.

* * * * *

Scoop Media's publisher knew from my communications on the forums that we had something big.

"Hi, Bev. (New Zealand pronunciation: 'Bivv'). Alastair here. (New Zealand pronunciation 'Alasteh'). What's up?"

"Well, we have a story. With the GEMS program, using one of the databases found on the FTP site, we were able to rig it," I said.

"Hmm!"

"I'm writing it up. I'm not sure which outlet I'm taking it to, though."

"You know, I rather thought this might be a good time to publish the link," said Thompson.

"What link?"

"Oh you know. To the files."

"The files from the FTP site?"

"It seems like a good time, don't you think? I think we should come out with your story at the same time. Get people to it, right?"

"Alastair, that set of files is huge. Do you have the bandwidth?"

"Oh, I think we'll be all right. They have bandwidth to burn."

The story went out on *Scoop Media* on July 8;[5] Thompson ran my story about the hackability of GEMS, along with his own editorial which he titled "Bigger than Watergate!" He has since been roundly criticized for that choice of title, but remember: Watergate took two years to get as "big as Watergate."

Just 16 days later, *The New York Times* ran a scathing report on the Diebold voting-system software by computer security experts from Johns Hopkins and Rice universities. They had downloaded the files, originally from the Diebold FTP site, from *Scoop Media*. At least one new story came out in a major media outlet every day for the next two months. In September, a report written by Pentagon contractor Scientific Applications International Corp. (SAIC) was published that detailed 328 security flaws in the Diebold voting system, 26 of which it deemed "critical."

The Johns Hopkins/Rice universities report

On July 24, 2003, *The New York Times*[6] ran an exclusive story about "stunning, stunning security flaws" uncovered by four researchers at Johns Hopkins and Rice universities. The report, titled "Analysis of an Electronic Voting System," described many of the findings pointed out by the irreverent bunch at Democratic Underground, but these computer scientists — Avi Rubin, Dan Wallach, Adam Stubblefleld and Yoshi Kohno — did a gutsy formal study and put their names on it.

The Johns Hopkins/Rice report was blistering. It quoted source code and delved into Diebold's smart-card security and its cryptographic weaknesses. The report also revealed that one flaw had been pointed out by voting examiners five years ago and still had not been corrected.

Diebold Election Systems came out swinging: The software was never used in any election! Well, it was used in some elections, another Diebold spokesman was reported by *WiredNews* reporter Louise Witt to have said.[7] I called her to ask how solid this quote was. Rock solid, she said, but the quote was pulled a day later in favor of this: "*A small part of the software may have been used in some elections.*"

We were told by Diebold that the problems had been fixed and also that they were never a problem in the first place, because the Diebold software is surrounded by election procedures and physical security, which have neutralized the problems all along. Diebold tells us this, but will not prove it to us.

There are weaknesses in the Hopkins/Rice report. Several sections seem to assume that touch-screen machines are connected to the Internet, but nothing I've seen indicates that to be the case. GEMS servers can connect to the Internet, and GEMS also connects to modems which, in turn, connect back to touch-screens.

The criticism that the Hopkins/Rice report doesn't take into account all the election procedures is, in many ways, correct. It doesn't appear that the authors read the user manuals that go with the software; they apparently did not interview any election officials.

Other areas of the report describe hacks that would be impractical or could not affect many votes at a time. The most publicized security flaw in the report has to do with making extra voter cards (or reprogramming one so that it can vote as many times as you want). These are valid concerns, but checking the number of voters signed in against the number of votes cast is a required safeguard in most states and would reveal such a ploy. This type of hack would also be difficult to achieve on a grand scale; you would have to make rigged smart cards and send people in to cast extra votes at hundreds of polling places at once, which gets into the crazy conspiracy realm.

The biggest taint applied to the Hopkins/Rice report is a conflict of interest on the part of one of its primary authors, Aviel Rubin. Lynn Landes, a freelance reporter, revealed that Rubin had been an advisory-board member for VoteHere, a company that claims its software solves many of the problems in the Hopkins/Rice report.[9] Rubin also held stock options in VoteHere; he resigned and gave back his stock options after Landes had published her article. Rubin told Landes that he had forgotten about this conflict of interest when he wrote the report.

Three more researchers — Dan Wallach, who is a full professor at Rice University, and Adam Stubblefield and Yoshi Kohno, of Johns Hopkins — also wrote the report, and none of them appears to have any conflicts of interest. It seems unlikely that all three would help Rubin slant a report just to help him sell VoteHere software.

The importance of the Hopkins/Rice report:

1) It correctly identifies weaknesses in Diebold's software-development process. The code seems cobbled together to fix and patch.

2) It identifies very real security flaws that can jeopardize vote data, especially during transmission to the county tabulator.

3) The Hopkins/Rice report pushed media coverage into the mainstream. When you are researching this story, you can't even sneeze without finding something new, so coverage of the integrity of our voting system will continue to gather momentum. The longest leap forward in a single day was attributable to the Hopkins/Rice report.

4) The report triggered another evaluation, this time by Science Applications International Corporation.

SAIC report

In August 2003, the governor of Maryland, which had placed a $55 million order for Diebold touch-screen machines, ordered an evaluation by Scientific Applications International Corp.[10]

If Rubin is said to have a conflict of interest, then SAIC had a whopper: The vice chairman of SAIC, Admiral Bill Owens, was the chairman of VoteHere. Like the Johns Hopkins/Rice report, the SAIC report identifies areas for which VoteHere claims to have a solution.

The SAIC report did a bizarre thing: It redacted the version numbers for the software it studied. Now, the version numbers are what is certified by the ITAs, and it is the version number that gets approved by the states. Refusing to say what version number was studied pretty much eliminates the usefulness of this report.

The report also redacted the entire section on GEMS, stating simply that the program was unsatisfactory. All in all, 131 pages out of 200 were redacted, and if we are to believe Washington State Elections Director David Elliott, even state election officials are not privy to this information. Here is what Elliott wrote when I inquired about how he can oversee elections that use GEMS if he can't read the SAIC report:

"As to your questions about the SAIC report. I share your frustration about the redactions contained in that report. I have read what was published in its redacted form. I have not been able to secure an un-edited copy."

If there was ever an indictment of the concept of privatizing a public trust, this is it. Here we have a for-profit corporation asserting privacy over a report commissioned by the state of Maryland, and the state of Washington, which uses the voting program developed by this company, cannot even find out what this government-commissioned report says.

The SAIC report does validate important findings in the Hopkins/Rice report and identifies many new areas of concern. Because it is heavily redacted, we don't know the details on all of the flaws it found, and many are specific to Maryland. Still, these words, taken from the SAIC report, reverberate:

"The system, as implemented in policy, procedure, and technology, is at high risk of compromise."

Or, to put it succinctly: "328 security flaws, 26 deemed critical."

As this book went to print, another independent study was released, this time commissioned by the state of Ohio,[11] and this time, the study examined systems from Diebold, ES&S, Sequoia and Hart Intercivic.

The study found multiple, critical security flaws in all four systems.

13
Security Breaches

San Diego County and the states of Maryland, Arizona and Ohio planned to buy new voting machines, and Diebold planned to sell them. All told, these contracts were worth more than a quarter of a billion dollars. Despite all the information that had come out, officials were barreling right ahead with their purchase orders.

Such confidence must be supported by a powerful factual underpinning, but so far I haven't been able to find it. Could someone please share the secret decoder ring with us, so we, too, can see why these machines should be trusted?

Election officials explained that all this criticism was just so much hooey; they trusted the machines and those computer scientists didn't know what they were talking about. Diebold announced, after the SAIC report gave it a failing grade, that the report (yes, the same one) said its voting system gave voters "an unprecedented level of security." Er — I guess you could call it "unprecedented."

Many election officials are still giving Diebold's encryption scheme a clean bill of health, but I'm not sure many of them can spell the word "algorithm," much less explain it. Why are we allowing election officials to pronounce an opinion on computer programming anyway?

I have yet to see any of Diebold's programmers answer a single question about these software flaws. Public-relations team, yes. Diebold software engineers? Total silence. I, for one, would like to hear from principal engineer Ken Clark, who replied to the following e-mail two years before my article about altering the audit log in Access:

From: Nel Finberg, 16 Oct 2001: "Jennifer Price at Metamor (about to be Ciber) [Independent Testing Authority – ITA – certifier] has indicated that she can access the GEMS Access database and alter the Audit log without entering a password. What is the position of our development staff on this issue? Can we justify this? Or should this be anathema?"

From: Ken Clark, 18 Oct 2001 RE: alteration of Audit Log in Access; "Its a tough question, and it has a lot to do with perception. Of course everyone knows perception is reality. Right now you can open GEMS' .mdb file with MS-Access, and alter its contents. That includes the audit log. This isn't anything new ... I've threatened to put a password on the .mdb before when dealers/customers/support have done stupid things with the GEMS database structure using Access. Being able to end-run the database has admittedly got people out of a bind though. Jane (I think it was Jane) did some fancy footwork on the .mdb file in Gaston recently. I know our dealers do it. King County is famous for it. That's why we've never put a password on the file before ... Back to perception though, if you don't bring this up you might skate through Metamor.

"There might be some clever crypto techniques to make it even harder to change the log ... We're talking big changes here though, and at the moment largely theoretical ones ...

"Bottom line on Metamor is to find out what it is going to take to make them happy. You can try the old standard of the NT password gains access to the operating system, and that after that point all bets are off ... This is all about Florida, and we have had VTS certified in Florida under the status quo for nearly ten years.

"I sense a loosing *[sic]* battle here though. The changes to put a password on the .mdb file are not trivial and probably not even backward compatible, but we'll do it if that is what it is going to take. " — Ken

Nel's reply: "For now Metamor accepts the requirement to restrict the server password to authorized staff in the jurisdiction, and that it should be the responsibility of the jurisdiction to restrict knowledge of this password. So no action is necessary in this matter, at this time."

We are leaning heavily on local election officials to set up security. Setting aside the references to doing "end runs" around the voting system, four examples show that local officials have been unable to restrict access to authorized staff and approved software:

1. A San Luis Obispo County, California, vote database popped up on the Diebold Web site during the March 2002 primary, tallied hours before the polls closed. Election officials can't explain how it got there.

2. A cell phone was used to transfer a vote database in Marin County, California. This is insecure and was never approved by anyone.

3. In November 2000, an unexplained replacement vote database in Volusia County, Florida, overwrote the original votes, causing TV networks to erroneously call the election for George W. Bush.

4. Voting software in 10 states, certified by the ITA and NASED and escrowed by the secretary of state, was replaced by unauthorized versions which came from five men in Canada.

SLO County Mystery Tally

A vote tabulation saved at 3:31 p.m., five hours before poll closing for the March 5, 2002, San Luis Obispo County primary ("SLO County" to the locals) was found on the Diebold FTP site. SLO County Clerk-Recorder Julie Rodewald says that she doesn't know who put that file on the FTP site, and only two people have access to the GEMS computer — the Deputy Registrar of Voters and Rodewald herself. [1]

The SLO file contains votes from a real election. It also contains a problem for Diebold, because in California it is illegal to tabulate votes before the polls close. According to California law, counties are allowed to begin counting mail-in and absentee ballots prior to election day, but results may not be posted before the polls close at 8 p.m.

"We don't release those results. In fact, we don't even print results. We don't know what the results are until 8 p.m.," Rodewald said.

This file contains an audit log which documents GEMS activities step by step for months leading up to the election, stopping precisely at 3:31 p.m. on March 5, 2002.

The votes in the file correspond with the final vote tally, which can be found on the San Luis Obispo County Web site for that election — but only about 40 percent of the votes had come in by 3:31 p.m. Computer programmer Jim March discovered that this file contained real votes.

Maybe the clock was off? It was for a different time zone? When it said 3:31 it was 8:31? Checking the date and clock is part of the election procedures, marked "important." But more than that, after the polls closed there were more votes.

Was this file used for training? No one trains poll workers during an election.

How do the votes correspond to the final vote tally? The vote distribution parallels that of the final tally.

The SLO vote file was assigned a password and placed on a Diebold-owned FTP site. The password was: "Sophia." Sophia Lee was a Diebold project manager. Was she there that day? Yes. Did Sophia put that file on the Diebold site?

"She's saying she did not post (the data) on election day," Rodewald said. "She said it's something she never would have done."

Did Rodewald give Sophia access to the GEMS computer and the vote database? Rodewald says that neither she nor any of her staff put that file on the Diebold site, nor does she know how it got there.

"Only the deputy (registrar of voters) and myself have access to the computer on election day or any day," Rodewald said.

The large file, which was on the GEMS computer, takes time to upload to an FTP site — even with a fast Internet connection. Rodewald said that the GEMS computer does not connect to the Internet.

Somehow this file made its way from the secure, inaccessible, locked-in-a-room, not-connected computer onto the Diebold company FTP site. Diebold denied that the information was posted on Election Day.

"Diebold is trying to track down when the information was posted," said Deborah Seiler, western regional representative for Diebold. (If Diebold was trying to find out when it was posted, why did Diebold state that it was not posted on a particular day?)

Rodewald says that the votes in the SLO file were absentee votes, which were counted before March 5. She says they are not votes cast at the polling place, which is reassuring, because the only way polling place votes could be on a Diebold company site at 3:31 in the afternoon is if the machines had an E.T. moment and decided to phone home while the election was in progress.

However, the absentee explanation doesn't exactly correspond with the tags in the file. And it doesn't explain why a partially-voted backup file would be parked on a Diebold FTP site. [2] Why should Diebold take any election vote file and keep it on a company site?

Perhaps because just 21 hours before the election, the software wasn't working correctly.

From: Sophia Lee, 4 Mar 2002: SLO County — "Cards cast for precincts in multiple vote centers are incorrect."

Sophia's memo is a bug report showing that the software is miscounting the day before the election. It references "GEMSReport 1-17-21," a version that does not have a NASED certification number.

Whether or not anything unscrupulous is involved with this file, it seems that unauthorized access was allowed into the system on Election Day, and also that machines were using uncertified software which wasn't working properly.

Transferring votes by cell phone

On October 8, 2003, I spoke with Marc Carrel, assistant secretary of state for policy and planning for the state of California. I asked Carrel about a set of memos indicating that Diebold has used cell phones to transfer vote results.

"That's not certified," he said. True. "Not in California, they haven't," he said, after a stunned pause. Yes, they have. In Marin and Tulare counties, according to the Diebold memos.

I passed the memos to an investigative writer named Tom Flocco (www.tomflocco.com). In his blog he wrote:

"Diebold sales representative Steve Knecht wrote on April 12, 2000 that 'We are using cell phones in Tulare and Marin,' while also introducing a rather curious, unfamiliar electronic election official called a 'rover:' 'Rovers are the ones who are given the cell phone with the modem for end of night totals upload, not the precinct worker, at least in these two locations.'

"Guy Lancaster, Diebold software programmer, wrote on April 12, 2000, regarding cell phones: 'I know of no written instructions,' leading us to wonder if there were rules and traceable documentation, or why cell phones were being used in the first place. ...

"[Diebold sales representative Juan Rivera wrote] 'Also, we did not have to dial the phone manually; the AccuVote did that just as if it was connected to the wall jack.' ... So now we have private cell-phones, lap-top computers — and rovers, ostensibly uncertified by any government authority. ...

"On April 17, 2000, Guy Lancaster wrote more about the Diebold AccuVote internal modem: 'We use what's called 'blind dialing' (ATX0) which means that it'll dial with nothing plugged into it. Thus if the AV won't work without this Dial Tone Emulator, then it's doing something in addition to providing a dial tone.'

Dr. David Dill's webmaster, Greg Dinger, arranged for a friend to assist as an official pollworker.

"OK, I have some news," Dinger wrote shortly after the October 2003 gubernatorial recall election. "At the end of the day, the 'head' of the scanner was removed from the base. It was connected to some sort of cell phone for transmitting the results. ... It was wireless. ...

"During the transmission process, errors occurred. The phone apparently reported that a ballot was 'stuck' in the reader. The precinct folks confirmed that this was not the case. There was a phone call placed to some 'support number' which turned out to be a bad number. The lead precinct worker happened to have another phone number, reached some unidentified (to my friend) person, and eventually resolved the issue after a lengthy delay. ...

" ... The precinct leader was provided a cordless phone of some sort. At the end of the day, she pulled the scanner out of the base and moved it to a table. Then the phone was attached (as I understand it) with a short cable. I do not believe the unit was built into the scanner, nor was it connected during the day." [3]

Yeesh. A well-financed operation can penetrate the voting system with the right equipment and the correct information. Cell phones connect to the access tower with the strongest signal. It is relatively easy, though not inexpensive, to set up a rogue access tower. If you do, this cell phone will automatically communicate with you. You would then connect the call to your own GEMS server, load the real results, modify them and then call up the real GEMS server to upload your results.

Volusia County, Florida:

John Ellis, hired as an analyst for Fox TV News, knew exactly what margin was needed in order to call the 2000 presidential race for George W. Bush. He was privy to the Voter News Service data, and he spoke several times during the evening to his two cousins: Jeb and George W. Bush. [4]

At 2:09 a.m., the required vote margin appeared from Volusia County, Florida. At 2:10 a.m., this margin was enhanced by a 4,000-vote bump in Brevard County, and at 2:16 a.m., Ellis called the race for George W. Bush. Within four minutes, NBC, CBS and ABC followed suit. [5]

Precisely the right margin appeared on a Volusia County machine (Global Election Systems, now Diebold), amplified by a Diebold/Global Election Systems machine in Brevard County. Unfortunately, these vote totals were incorrect and soon disappeared, along with a "card no. 3" which helped to create them.

If Al Gore had publicly conceded on election night, would we ever have learned that these votes were bogus? Would there have been a recount, and could the "Help America Vote Act" have passed, triggering the rush to touch-screen machines?

We'll never know, but thanks to an internal CBS report and a memo written by Talbot Iredale, vice president of research and development at Diebold Election Systems, we now know that the unexplained replacement of a set of votes on a Diebold optical-scan machine in Volusia County triggered a premature private concession from Al Gore to George W. Bush and resulted in TV networks' erroneously calling the election for Bush instead of deeming it too close to call. The final "offical" tally showed Gore losing by 527 votes, though the hand recount stopped by the Supreme Court later gave the election to Gore.

* * * * *

Fox News Network, 29 November 2000: Brit Hume, host: " ... It seems a broken computer modem and a faulty memory card were culprits in the erroneous election-night call of George W. Bush as the Florida winner ... computers with a bad memory card caused it to appear for a time that Al Gore had lost more than 16,000 votes, which seemed to put George W. Bush up by 50,000 — at that stage in the night, an insurmountable margin. Every network saw that as a basis for calling the state for Mr. Bush. ... " [6]

Was it a "bad memory card" that produced the 16,000-vote spread? Or is there another explanation? And is it true that these 16,000 mystery votes caused the networks to call the election for Bush?

Let's look at the symptoms of a bad memory card. A memory card, as you'll recall, is like a floppy disk. If you have worked with computers for any length of time, you know that a disk can go bad. When it does, which of the following is most likely:

a) In an Excel spreadsheet that you saved on the "bad disk," is it likely to read a column of numbers correctly the first time: "1005, 2109, 3000 ... " but the second time, replace one of the numbers like this: "1005, 2109, –16,022 ... "?

b) Or is it more likely that the "bad disk" will do one of the following things: Fail to read the file at all; crash your computer; give you an error message; or make weird humming and whirring noises while your computer attempts unsuccessfully to read the disk?

For most of us, the answer is b). But according to news reports, the official explanation from Global Election Systems was that a "bad memory card" reported votes correctly in every race except the presidential race, where it changed Gore's total to minus 16,022.

This kind of explanation gets my nose twitching. Really? Is that what a "bad memory card" does? If so, how many "bad memory cards" have been out there changing vote totals, unbeknownst to voters?

If the symptom of a corrupted memory card was arbitrary vote-changing, as explained to the media in Volusia County, we'd be in real trouble — according to Diebold sales representative Steve Knecht in a March 24, 2000, memo: "*Cards were corrupted throughout California at a rate exceeding our normal 1 in 100 that we've been seeing. Marin is now up to 8 cards corrupted out of 114.*"

With these numbers, we'd better hope that the symptoms do *not* include randomly changing the vote totals.

According to an exchange between principal engineer Ken Clark and Donna Daloisio, who was systems administrator for Supervisor of Elections Gertrude Walker in St. Lucie County, Florida, the following symptoms typify a corrupt memory card:

When beginning to upload results the following message appears: "*Please re-insert memory card.*" If you take the memory card out and put it back in, you are likely to see this error: *"Pct data error OK to continue?"* If you say yes, this message appears again: *"Please reinsert memory card."*

When Daloisio described these symptoms, principal engineer Ken Clark shot back this diagnosis: *"Garden variety corrupt memory card."*

The Diebold memos reveal that the story given to the media about Volusia County's sudden vote discrepancy isn't quite the whole story.

On January 17, 2001, Volusia County employee Lana Hires asked the technical staff at Global Election Systems for help. She was being put on the hot seat over Al Gore's strange tally of negative 16,022 votes.

"I need some answers!" she wrote. "Our department is being audited by the County. I have been waiting for someone to give me an explanation as to why Precinct 216 gave Al Gore a minus 16022 when it was uploaded. Will someone please explain this so that I have the information to give the auditor instead of standing here 'looking dumb.' " [7]

Global Election Systems' John McLaurin tossed the hot potato to Sophia Lee and Talbot Iredale. "Sophia and Tab may be able to shed some light here, keeping in mind that the boogie man may me *[sic]* reading our mail.* Do we know how this could occur?" [8]

Talbot Iredale, senior vice president for research and development, explains: "Only the presidential totals were incorrect." Iredale then hits us with this bombshell: [9]

"The problem precinct had two memcory *[sic]* cards uploaded. The second one is the one I believe caused the problem. They were uploaded on the same port approx. 1 hour apart. As far as I know there should only have been one memory card uploaded."

Where did this second card come from? Iredale then gives a cursory nod to the official explanation given to the media:

"Corrupt memory card. This is the most likely explaination *[sic]* for the problem but since I know nothing about the 'second' memory card I have no ability to confirm the probability of this."

Again, where did the second card come from?

---

*That's a damned curious remark!

"Invalid read from good memory card. This is unlikely since the candidates results for the race are not all read at the same time and the corruption was limited to a single race. There is a possibility that a section of the memory card was bad but since I do not know anything more about the 'second' memory card I cannot validate this."

There's that pesky second card again. He then suggests that perhaps the second card might have been — well — another way to say this would be "election tampering," I guess:

"Invalid memory card (i.e. one that should not have been uploaded). There is always the possibility that the 'second memory card' or 'second upload' came from an un-authorised source."

So, who is investigating this unauthorized source?

"If this problem is to be properly answered we need to determine where the 'second' memory card is or whether it even exists.

But it turns out that this second card did exist:

"I do know that there were two uploads from two different memory cards (copy 0 (master) and copy 3)."

There were two uploads from two different cards.

• The votes were uploaded on the same port approximately 1 hour apart.
• Only one memory card was supposed to have been uploaded.
• "Copy 0" uploaded some votes.
• "Copy 3" replaced the votes from "Copy 0" with its own.
• Iredale believes the second one is the one that caused the problem.
• The "problem": 16,022 negative votes for Al Gore

We know that the "problem" was noticed and corrected. An election worker noticed Gore's votes literally falling off the tally, and the number of votes in Precinct 216 was totally out of whack. Eventually, a manual recount was done. No harm, no foul?

That depends on how you look at things. I found a report called "CBS News Coverage of Election Night 2000: Investigation, Analysis, Recommendations prepared for CBS News." [10]

"It would be easy to dismiss the bizarre events of Election Night 2000 as an aberration, as something that will never happen again," the report begins. " ... But, this election exposed flaws in the American voting system, imperfections mirrored in television's coverage of the election results."

Yes. This election exposed flaws, but the imperfections were not really quite "mirrored" in television's coverage of the results. A more apt metaphor would be that the imperfections exposed the tip of an iceberg and then, with the HAVA bill, everyone in America decided to buy a ticket on the *Titanic*.

It is, as one of the computer scientists I've talked with likes to say, like "The Amazing Randi." Don't look there — look here! An illusion. Ridicule the dangling chads. Voter News Service blew it. Don't worry, we caught that crazy error of minus 16,022 votes; it made no difference. We'll give you the Help America Vote Act (HAVA) and promise $3.8 billion (much of which may never materialize) to prevent this fiasco from ever happening again.

Look over here: Chads are bad. Look over there: Let's vote on a black box!

Don't look there. No one paid much attention to the optical-scan machines, which, we now know from Greg Palast's research, used different settings depending on whether you were in a minority district or an affluent suburb. White? Suburban? Set the machine to provide an error message if the ballot was overvoted, so the voter can correct it. Minority? Poor? Accidental overvotes discarded, thank you. Back that up with statistics, of course: "Too dumb to vote." [11]

While we fixated on a butterfly ballot, no one asked about the GEMS program, or demanded to see "card number 3" from Volusia County, or asked who made this card and how it got past all the election procedures and physical security, or whether any other counties had a card number 3.

Here is a chronology of how the election was called for Bush. You decide whether card number 3 made a difference: [12]

7:00 PM: CBS News' estimate, based upon exit-poll interviews, shows Gore leading Bush by 6.6 percentage points.

7:40 PM: Voter News Service (VNS) projects Florida for Gore.

7:48 PM: NBC projects Florida for Gore.

7:50 PM: CBS projects Florida for Gore.

7:52:32 PM: VNS *calls* Florida for Gore.

8:10 PM: CBS News analysts recheck the Florida race and feel even more confident about the call for Gore.

9:00 PM: A member of the CBS News Decision Team notices a change in one of the Florida computations. One of the estimates, the one based solely on tabulated county votes (voting-machine results rather than exit polls) is now showing a Bush lead.

9:07 PM: VNS reports vote data from Duval County that put Gore in the lead. This was then deemed to be an error.

9:38 PM: VNS deletes the Duval County vote from the system. Gore's total in Florida is reduced by 40,000 votes.

10:00 PM: CBS withdraws the Florida call for Gore.

10:16 PM: VNS retracts its Florida call for Gore.

At some point between 10:16 p.m. and 1:12 a.m., Bush took the lead.

1:12 AM: Associated Press, which collects its numbers separately from VNS, shows the Bush lead dropping. VNS differs. Correspondent Ed Bradley begins warning people in the CBS studio of irregularities.

1:43 AM: Bradley points out that more than 30 percent of the vote is still uncounted in Dade and Broward counties, Democratic strongholds.

1:48 AM: Bradley does the math: "Bush is ahead by 38,000 votes. And still out there, about 5 percent of the vote is still out, 270,000 votes. So that's a big chunk of votes." Bradley seeks more information from the AP wire and from CBS News correspondent Byron Pitts.

2:00 AM: According to VNS, Bush leads by 29,000 votes. Heavily Democratic counties have not weighed in yet. Ed Bradley is talking about the AP reports, but CBS is not using that information.

2:09 AM: VNS adds Volusia County's incorrect numbers to its tabulated vote. This change increases Bush's VNS lead to 51,000 votes.

2:09:32 AM: Bradley sounds an alarm, but no one pays attention: "Among the votes that aren't counted are Volusia County. Traditionally they're ... one of the last counties to come in. That's an area that has 260,000 registered voters. Many of them are black and most of them are Democrat."

2:10 AM: Brevard County omits 4,000 votes for Gore.

Bush's lead in the VNS count includes 16,000 negative votes for Gore and unspecified other voting problems such that Bush's lead appeared to increase by 20,000 votes in Volusia (plus the 4,000 missing from Brevard).

According to the CBS News report: "These 24,000 votes would have nearly eliminated the 30,000-vote final Bush margin the CBS News Decision Desk has estimated. There would have been no call if these errors had not been in the system."

2:16 AM: John Ellis calls Florida for Bush.

2:16 AM: NBC calls Florida for Bush.

2:16 AM: The AP lead for Bush drops by 17,000 votes, to 30,000. This 17,000-vote drop, occurring in only four minutes, is a Volusia County correction. But VNS does not use the correction, and no one at CBS is listening to Ed Bradley or watching the AP wire.

2:16:17 AM: Dan Rather talks with Bradley about the large number of votes still out in Volusia County.

2:17:52 AM: CBS calls Florida for Bush.

2:20 AM: ABC calls Florida for Bush.

2:47 AM: The AP reports that Bush's lead has dropped to 13,934.

2:48 AM: VNS still shows the Bush lead at 55,449.

2:51 AM: VNS corrects part of its Volusia error, and Bush's lead drops to 39,606.

2:52 AM: The AP reports the Bush lead down to 11,090.

2:55 AM: Palm Beach County weighs in with a large number of votes, and VNS reports the Bush lead down to 9,163.

3:00 AM: Rather preps viewers for a Gore concession speech: "We haven't heard yet from either Al Gore or from the triumphant Governor Bush. We do expect to hear from them in the forthcoming minutes."

3:10–3:15 AM: * Al Gore telephones Mr. Bush to concede.

3:10 AM: CBS begins investigating the VNS numbers. It also, finally, begins watching numbers from the AP. CBS also looks at the Florida Secretary of State's Web site. The three sets of numbers don't match, but all of them indicate the race is much closer.

3:32 AM: From 3 a.m. until now, there is much talk about the expected Gore concession speech.

---

* At this point I have drawn the timeline from three sources: CBS report, an Agence France-Presse [13] (*) report, and Dow Jones News [14] (**). The events reported after 3 a.m. sometimes differ by a few minutes between these reports.

3:30-3:45 AM:** Gore boards a motorcade for a 10-minute journey to War Memorial Plaza in Nashville, Tennessee, to deliver a concession speech to the nation.

3:40 AM: Bush's VNS lead drops to 6,060 votes.

Around this time, Gore Campaign Chairman William Daley places a call to CBS News President Andrew Heyward. Daley asks whether CBS is thinking about pulling back its call for Bush. Heyward wants to know what Gore is planning to do.

According to the CBS report, "Daley says, 'I'll get right back to you,' hangs up and does not call back."

When the lead is down to 6,000 votes, Daley asks whether CBS is thinking about pulling its call for Bush. The answer is they want to know what Gore is planning to do. Is it just me, or does this response bother you?

3:48 AM: "Rather says, 'Now the situation at the moment is, nobody knows for a fact who has won Florida. Far be it from me to question one of our esteemed leaders [CBS management], but somebody needs to begin explaining why Florida has now not been pulled back to the undecided category. ... A senior Gore aide is quoted by Reuters as confirming that Gore has withdrawn [his] concession in the U.S. President race."

3:45-3:55 AM:* Two blocks away from the plaza, Gore field director Michael Whouley pages traveling chief of staff Michael Feldman to tell him the official Florida tally now shows Bush up by just 6,000 votes, with many ballots left to be counted. By the time the Gore motorcade reaches the plaza, according to Agence France-Presse, he is down by fewer than 1,000 votes. Gore does not, then, give the speech he had planned to give. Instead he consults with his staff.

3:57 AM: According to CBS, the Bush margin has narrowed to fewer than 2,000 votes. CBS News President Heyward orders that CBS News retract the call for Bush.

By 4:05 AM: The other networks have rescinded the call for Bush.

4:10 AM: According to CBS, Bush's lead drops to 1,831 votes, which is roughly where it remains until the first recount.

4:30-4:45 AM:** Gore makes a second telephone call to Bush to retract his concession, saying that he is waiting for all the results from Florida.

*5:05 AM:*** A Florida election official announces a recount, with the two candidates separated by a few hundred votes.

According to the CBS report, "the call for Bush was based entirely on the tabulated county vote. There were several data errors that were responsible for that mistake. The most egregious of the data errors has been well documented. Vote reports from Volusia County."

Four thousand votes for Gore were omitted from the tabulation in Brevard County, and in Volusia, 4,000 votes were erroneously counted for Bush and 16,022 negative votes were recorded for Gore.

"The mistakes ... which originated with the counties, were critical," says the report. "They incorrectly increased Bush's lead in the tabulated vote from about 27,000 to more than 51,000. Had it not been for these errors, the CBS News call for Bush at 2:17:52 AM would not have been made."

If you strip away the partisan rancor over the 2000 election, you are left with the undeniable fact that a presidential candidate conceded the election to his opponent based on results from a second memory card (card #3) that mysteriously appears, subtracts 16,022 votes, then just as mysteriously disappears. If this isn't disturbing enough, consider these three points:

1) We don't know whether this was an isolated incident. It may have occurred elsewhere, but in smaller, less spectacular totals.

2) The errors were correctable because paper ballots existed and a 100 percent audit was done.

3) The fact that "negative votes" could be applied to a candidate's total demonstrates such a fundamentally flawed software model that it calls into question the competence and integrity of the programmers, the company and the certification process itself.

The Diebold Memos

During the middle of the night on Friday, September 5, 2003, a set of memos leaked into my FTP server. They originally came from a person with inside access to the Diebold server who used an employee I.D. number to obtain and copy them.[15] The memos were first leaked to David Allen on July 29, but, because of technical problems, he was unable to extract them from their compressed .tar file.

On Saturday, September 6, I downloaded this 15,000-document tarball, found a utility to open it and started reading. I read 7,000 memos and made 300 pages of notes, divided into five categories, and didn't come up for air until Monday, September 8. What I found was not good.

While the certified version of the voting software sat in escrow at the secretary of state's office, unauthorized versions were being put on the FTP site and, from there, downloaded and installed, overwriting the approved software. The memos documented this.

I therefore did three things. I made a copy of everything and put it into the hands of someone I trust. I burned the memos onto a CD and met face-to-face with a U.S. congressman,[16] who asked questions for 30 minutes, and then took the memos to Washington. And I selected 24 memos that describe the practice of substituting unexamined software for the approved version, and posted them on my Web site.[17]

While writing up my notes on the memos, I discovered a curious thing. I wanted to find out whether the software they were uploading (and using in elections) was certified or not. But for some reason, links to the official certification list had been pulled off both NASED and The Election Center's Web sites. I was able to locate an out-of-date version but could find nothing current.

The more I hunted, the odder it looked. If this whole system is based on certification, why make it so hard to find out which versions are certified? It ought to be a simple matter to compare the NASED certification number with the version number used by our local elections office.

Andy Stephenson, a researcher who worked with me on this project, called R. Doug Lewis of The Election Center to ask for the certification list. Lewis hung up on him. I called the Washington State Elections Division and was told someone would have to call me back. No one did. Linda Franz, of Citizens for Voting Integrity-Washington, found one document through an obscure link on the Johnson County, Kansas, Web site. After searching with an Internet tool that archives old Web pages, I found three more reports, which had been pulled off the Web.

Looking at every ITA-tested, NASED-authorized version number available leads to only one conclusion: Diebold has been putting unauthorized software into our voting systems.

When Georgia Secretary of State Cathy Cox says of ballot-tampering, "It would take a conspiracy beyond belief, of all these different poll workers ... I don't see how this could happen in the real world," she's dead wrong. It doesn't take a conspiracy beyond belief. If you can slip uncertified software into voting machines, it takes only *one person*, working alone at night.

* * * * *

The Diebold memos made their first public appearance on BlackBoxVoting.org in the form of 24 memos with a commentary about Diebold's use of uncertified software. Everyone yawned except Diebold, which issued a cease-and-desist.

You might be yawning now. Someone used version 1.18.14 instead of version 1.17.23. *Ho hum.*

Except for this: A programmer never changes a version number unless he changes the underlying computer code. If the versions are never submitted for certification, only the individual who programmed the change knows for sure what he put in there.

Certification is the foundation of the voting industry. Remove it, and the whole house of cards tumbles.

"Maybe they'll say it was just to fix bugs," one reporter suggested. Sure. And they'll say it was just to add features or to create a new report format. And that might all be true, but before you breathe a sigh of relief, let me give you a taste of just how out of control this problem has been:

"As far as we know, some guy from Russia could be controlling the outcome of elections in the United States," Lynn Landes wrote.

Lynn, meet Dmitry Papushin, some guy from Russia. He is one of the five Diebold programmers who have been putting programs on the FTP site. Take a look at his memos. What he's doing here is placing uncertified software versions on a Web site, and people are using them.

Underlines represent versions that were never certified, or the implementation of poor security procedures.

18 Jan 2000 memo from Dmitry Papushin: "GEMS 1-14-5 is ready.

January 25, 2000 memo from Steve Knecht: "Will all future 1.14x versions be compatible with 1.14.5 if we burn mem cards in San Luis Obispo now?"

15 January 2003 memo from Dmitry Papushin: "Ballot Station <u>4-3-14</u> for Windows CE and Windows NT are ready."

10 February 2003 memo from Cathy Smothers: "Can anyone send me the BS CE <u>4.3.14</u> .ins file? <u>I have a demo tomorrow</u> and <u>I need this to upgrade the TS units</u>."

From 1999 to 2003, Papushin uploaded more voting-system software onto the unprotected Diebold Web site than any other programmer. Papushin has been a keeper of the passwords and the king of single-sentence memos. He knows the voting-system programming intimately and has uploaded computer code that programs your smart card, captures your votes at the polling place and accumulates and reports them at the county.

His programming skills and his ability to distribute programs to techs and county officials make him a tempting target for bribery. We assume that Dmitry Papushin has integrity and ironclad ethics. But to deter the unscrupulous from making inappropriate solicitations to programmers like Papushin, we need to *enforce* regulations which require that only authorized software be used, and we need fraud-deterring audit procedures.

* * * * *

To examiners of the Diebold files, Ken Clark has become somewhat famous for his blunt writing and unique ethics. Clark's comments in the touch-screen source code are quite a hoot, though not inspiring of confidence in the touch-screen system:

"the BOOL beeped flag is a hack so we don't beep twice. This is really a result of the key handling being gorped. (Writeln.cpp,v)

" this is completely screwed up. the iIndex calculations are incorrectly based on nybbles for some unknown reason, and so the offsets are incorrect. This works only because the offsets are also incorrect when the card is read." (VoterCard.cpp,v)

"Reserve place in hell for person who renamed CRace and friends to CRaceKey." (BufferedSocket.cpp,v)

"Add and comment out code to work around bogus -1 in ballot level IDs." (BallotRstDlg.cpp,v)

"this is a sick hack to parse out a jurisdiction from a multi-line election title. The jurisdiction field should be eliminated altogether and this code removed. This whole section is fairly broken wrt GEMS. GEMS doesn't store the "election information" in any kind of multilingual sense, let alone rich text. For now just stuff the english into all languages." (BuildElecDlg.cpp,v)

Deep magic is not working? Tried input of 6 and got back 1" (CIssue.CPP,v)

"The scaling stuff is complete voodo.*[sic]* Trust me or rewrite it to make more sense." (TextCell.cpp,v)

"I justify the label by saying the existing code was crap structurally to begin with." (Votercard.cpp,v)

In a July 1999 memo, Ian Piper wrote, "What is GEMS written in?" Clark replied, "GEMS is written in my office."

So Clark programs the GEMS system that accumulates and reports votes from polling places. We have weak and sometimes unenforced procedures for comparing polling-place results with the county tabulations, so the GEMS program is a tempting target.

Clark repeatedly advises field technicians to skirt U.S. election law pertaining to using only certified software versions.

From: Cathi Smothers, June 05, 2000, to Ken Clark: How do I know which version of GEMS (i.e. 1.16.3, 1.16.4, etc.) to use?"

From: Ken Clark, 5 Jun 2000: "... Baring any certification issues, the latest stable release is what you want to upgrade accounts to ... Right now 1.16. latest is considered stable, 1.16.4 being the current release by my mail ... "Its fair to say the nature of this company and business make this process fairly informal, perhaps more so than I would like. Testing releases go out to customers when they shouldn't, and new features get added to stable branches when they shouldn't ... Sometimes a bug slips into a stable branch, in which case its better to ship a version you trust, or wait for it to get corrected ... "The DLL files shipped on the GEMS CD get updated from time-to-time as well ..."

From: Ken Clark, 6 Jul 1999: I hate more than anyone else in the company to bring up a certification issue with this, but a number of jurisdictions require a 'system test' before every election ... That is why the AccuVote displays *[sic]* the silly ***System Test Passed*** message on boot up instead of "memory test passed", which is all it actually tests. "No argument from me that it is pointless. You could probably get away with a batch file that prints "system test passed" for all I know."

From: Ken Clark, 7 Jan 2000: "*Any* testing we can do on 1.14 is a good idea. With the risk of sounding alarmist, 1.14 really needs more testing. Even though much of GEMS looks the same from the outside, the guts changed substantially between 1.11 and 1.14. That's why you see all kinds of things completely unrelated to shadow races broken in the early 1.14 releases."

From: Steve Knecht, 14 Jan 2000: "Is it the intention of development staff that California March election will be run on some version of 1.14 or will we end up in the 1.15 range ..."

(*Answer from Ken Clark, 14 Jan 2000*): "Needless to say, the changes were extensive. The paint is still wet ...

* * * * *

We know nothing at all about Whitman Lee, another Vancouver programmer who uploads software to the FTP site. His memos consist of fixing bugs and uploading replacement software, which he did three dozen times over a 24-month period.

From: Whitman Lee

"GEMS 1-5-3 is ready to download.
"GEMS has evolved so many times that it breaks some of the pre-election reports..."
"Here is the latest changes since 1.5.8."
"AVTS-3-4-1.zip is up. Here is this short "upgrade" instructions."
"The password for ATTemplate-3-4-1.zip is msd8sdh3isohr."
"GEMS-Reports-1-9-6.zip is ready for download."
"GEMS 1.11.2 is ready."
"The fix will be in GEMS-1-18-9."

* * * * *

Guy Lancaster's specialty is programming the optical-scan system. He has also arranged for uncertified software to enter our optical-scan machines. A lot of it, apparently.

From: Guy Lancaster, 27 Jan 1999: "For those romantics that fell in love with 1.94f, the latest flavor incorporates all the changes made since 1.94f<. This includes the changes in 1.94q, r, s, t*, and u. Pass your orders on to McKinney. * Note: The PC 1.94t release was preempted by 1.94u."

From: Guy Lancaster, 25 Feb 1999: "Our latest 1.94 releases have been rushed out to fix a bug that slipped out with 1.94u and 1.94f>. Namely, 1.94u and 1.94f> fail to detect unvoted ballots and therefore cannot return blank ballots ..."

From Ken Clark, July 2, 2002: "You have to be careful when talking about 1.94f firmware. There is a symbol after each f that corresponds to the actual release of the firmware. They very probably have a 194f that is in reality r, s, t etc."

From Don Bizmaier, Support services specialist, July 2, 2002: "I am not sure where they came from ... but Jeff Co [Jefferson County] KY uses an "S" chip in the Absentee and Mail in AVOS [Diebold optical scan machine] to ignore sequence nimbers *[sic]*."

* * * * *

Talbot "Tab" Iredale, senior V.P. for research and development, was hired when the company was still called North American Professional Technologies.[18] He became a stockholder in Global Election Systems, and he oversees the programming. You will find his work in the most sensitive sections of the touch-screen source code, and he also programs the Windows CE operating system.[19] According to Rob Behler, Iredale wrote the Georgia Windows CE patches.

From Ian S. Piper 12 Jul 2002 re: Windows CE changes: "Upgrading from WinCE 3.0 (June 7th edition) to WinCE 3.0 (July 5th edition.) When upgrading from the June 7th edition of WinCE 3.0 to the July 5th edition of WinCE 3.0 (we're ignoring the July 2nd and July 4th editions), the settings should remain in the internal Flash memory ... "

From Tari Runyan Tue, 2 Jul 2002: "Is it necessary to upgrade at this point - Early voting starts in 1 month and I am hesitant due to tight timelines ... "

(reply from Talbot Iredale 16 Aug 2002): "Yes, it is recommended to upgrad *[sic]* all units to this version."

From: Rodney D Turner , 31 Aug 2000: "The computer for LA has GEMS 1-16-9 and the AVTS units have 3-13-1-4. The computer for Alameda has GEMS 1-16-10 and GEMS 1-16-9 (there is a short-cut on the desktop for GEMS 1-16-9) the AVTS units have 3-13-1-4. "

From: Talbot Iredale, 31 Aug 2000 Re: Software for Los Angelas [sic], *CA* "Jeff and Rodney, LA and Alameda will need a revised version of GEMS and maybe BallotStation to support the import/export that they require. I am working on it now but I am certain there will be more changes."

From: Larry Dix, 31 Aug 2000 RE: Software for Los Angelas [sic], *CA* "Tab – Would you be willing to venture an outside guess as to when the revised GEMS version will be ready. This really becomes an issue since I need to coordinate staff to be onsite. Is this also the case for Alameda? Coordination of time and staff is everything on these 2 installs."

From: Ken Clark, 31 Aug 2000 Subject: RE: GEMS-1-17-1: "Is this a 'testing' release or not?"

From: Talbot Iredale, 31 Aug 2000 Subject: Re: GEMS-1-17-1: This is no more of a test release than 1.16.9 was though I would not be surprised if we have to make more changes to fully support LA and Alameda.

From: Talbot Iredale, 29 Oct 2002: "... We have found a serious bug in GEMS 1-18-14 ... We will be releasing a GEMS 1-18-15 that fixes this bug within the next 2 days. Please ensure that all accounts that are using GEMS 1-18-14 upgrade to GEMS 1-18-15* prior to the election."

Here are a couple odd memos pertaining to an uncertified version number popping up on the screen in Florida:

From: Greg Forsythe, 17 Feb 2000: "Just received a call from Beverly Hill, Alachua County [Florida] ... She is at the SA screen and the version is 1.92-15 ... This copy has 1.92-14. 1.92-14 is certified, 1.92-15 is not. SOLUTION REQUIRED!

From: Greg Forsythe, 17 Feb 2000: "... Solution might be to make the copy the official database showing the correct version."

From: Nel Finberg, 17 Feb 2000: "The problem has been fixed."

From: Nel Finberg, 17 Feb 2000: "... It would be a good idea to get rid of the original diskette in order to remove the perception of version conflicts."

From: Don Vopalensky, 12 Sep 2002: "Ken, Texas now requires ITA certification ... ITA certifications, state certifications, and time constraints play a big part in what needs to be done, and sometimes that means putting fixes or additions back into versions that are already in use ..."

Nel Finberg September 25, 2002: "What will be run in Texas will depend on the outcome of the Texas certification decision, won't it?"

From: Ken 25 Sep 2002: "Hard to say. It never has in the past."

Tari Runyan, July 15, 2002: "this bug affects Co [Colorado] - primary Aug 13 and Ga [Georgia] Primary Aug 20 are we proposing to upgrade again this close to an election?

From Ken - "That would be up to you."

Jeff Hallmark, October 08, 2002: RE: Tippecanoe, IN upgrade to 4-3 first then downgrade to 4-1-11, this is quite fast if one sets up 3 or 4 machines at a time. no backdoor humm..

Sue Page, October 16, 2002: - Maryland ... "We had some units that we downgraded from 4.1.11 to 4.1.6."

From Tyler to Ken Clark, 15 Feb 1999: "... But then again, with regards to the entire NASED certification process, I can never quite get a handle on the relationship between "ostensible" and "reality."... :-)"

Unknown programmers were putting unlooked-at code into our software. Probably, these programmers are honest, but we really have no idea. Regardless, it is idiotic to put seven million votes into the hands of a few unknown people without even doing a background check.

This problem isn't limited to Diebold, and it isn't just the vendors. County officials may or may not know the implications of using uncertified version numbers, but state officials absolutely know better. In the state of Washington, voting software must have a NASED number and must be signed off by the secretary of state.

Dozens of us went looking for the most recent NASED version numbers, and all of us came up empty-handed. Finally, after asking Washington State Elections Director David Elliott for these documents in front of members of the Washington legislature (I did this while giving public testimony, a breach of protocol which mortified the legislators and resulted in a reprimand),[21] I was able to obtain a supposedly complete set of NASED certification documents.

I say "supposedly" because someone took a pen and wrote a version number on it that wasn't there originally. In another case, a version number was overwritten in pen but its approval number was not overwritten, resulting in a mismatch.

I wondered why former Washington Secretary of State Ralph Munro, who is now chairman of VoteHere, signed off on GEMS version 1.11.2. (Or did he?) Why did current Secretary of State Sam Reed sign off on GEMS 1.18.18. (Or did he?) Who's minding the store here, guys?

Here is an e-mail from Dean Logan, former Washington state elections director, now director of King County Records, Elections and Licensing Services:

Tuesday, November 25, 2003 From Dean Logan to Andy Stephenson: "King County currently operates GEMS Software version 1.18.18. This version of the software was installed in August 2003 and was used for the September 16, 2003 Primary and the November 4, 2003 General Election. GEMS Version 1.18.18 was certified by the Washington Secretary of State on August 12, 2003 ... From 1999 through August 2003, King County operated GEMS

Software version <u>1.11.2</u> ... <u>No additional software patches or upgrades have</u>
<u>been installed or in use in King County</u>."

(Neither 1.18.18 nor 1.11.2 had a NASED number.)

Wed, 03 Dec 2003 From Bev Harris to David Elliott: "As I mentioned to
you after the meeting, I was astonished when Andy Stephenson, Democratic candidate for Secretary of State, discovered that King County, Washington, has been using uncertified software for four years ... In the case of
King County -- perhaps there is some old, obscure NASED document that
has never been published, which goes out of order numerically, and which
is for some reason missing from the discovery documents obtained for a
recent citizen lawsuit?

"You did tell me today that you have the complete set and that you will
provide it. I really appreciate your help. Because you sat on the NASED
committee for so many years and according to your testimony today, even
helped to write the standards, your expertise is quite valuable and therefore I would like to get your signature with the documents indicating that
what you provide does represent the 'complete set' of version numbers ..."

Dec 4, 2003 From David Elliott to Bev Harris: " ... I can not offer a 'complete set' of the NASED information although they serve as a continuous
log of the work done by the ITA's. The last should provide all that came
before it. I have contacted the FEC about whether there is an update to
the list past 6/5/03 and I was told that they are working on it."

Dec 4, 2003 From Bev Harris to David Elliott: "Thank you for responding
so promptly ... I did not get your response until too late to pick up the documents. But that's okay, because the answer is insufficient and perhaps we
can rectify that so that when I pick them up next Tuesday, we will have
what we need. Your response raises several questions:

("I have contacted the FEC about whether there is an update to the
list past 6/5/03 and I was told that they are working on it.")

"This is not an acceptable answer. In fact, I can't tell whether or not any
versions were certified after 6/5/03 or not. Are there any new versions after the June 2003 report, or not? ... I would assume that NASED would have
some system to inform the secretary of state when they certify new versions
... why do you have to call the FEC for it?

"I will arrange to come to Olympia by 4:30 p.m. on Tuesday, and at that
time I really do need ALL the NASED certified version numbers.

Dec. 8 2003 from David Elliott to Bev Harris: " ... I am providing you with
copies of the lists that I have received. ... Concerning the Diebold certifi-

cations: The optical scan reader was originally certified as the Global CF-1 in 1991. In 1992 software called Vote Tally System VTS version 1.81 was certified and the hardware was re-named the Accu-vote. The VTS software was rewritten and renamed GEMS and was re-certified in 1998. GEMS was re-examined again in 2001 as a part of the certification of the Accu-vote touch screen (DRE) finalized in September of 2002 as version 1.17.17. The most recent examination was completed in July and August of 2003 for GEMS version 1.18.18."

OK, now we get into some problems. There was no GEMS 1.18.18 NASED number on the documents Elliott provided, yet it was used in two King County elections. According to Dean Logan, the previous version was GEMS 1.11.2, and there were no upgrades or patches, but this cannot have been certified in 1998, as Elliott implies, because it wasn't released until 1999. [22] And if only 1.11.2 and 1.18.18 were used, and there were no upgrades or patches, why did Sophia Lee send a memo in 2001 referencing version "GEMS 1.17.16" in King County? [23]

King County has been using unauthorized software for six years. A whole bunch of citizens on the BlackBoxVoting.org forums went after all the state certifications, and mostly got stonewalled, but we did document the following problems:

Chelan County Washington is using GEMS version 1.17.21. Not certified.
King County Washington GEMS 1.11.2, 1.17.16, 1.18.18. Not certified.
Placer County used GEMS version 1.17.20. Not certified.
El Paso County Texas used GEMS version 1.17.21. Not certified.
Johnson County Kansas GEMS version 1.18.14. Not certified.
Alameda County California used GEMS version 1.18.13.9. Not certified.
Alameda County California also used GEMS version 1.18.14. Not certified.
Yavapai County Arizona optical scan version 2.0.11. Not certified.
Pima County Arizona optical scan version 2.0.11. Not certified.
City of Tucson Arizona optical scan version 1.94y. Not certified.
Johnson County Kansas optical scan version 2.00g. Not certified.
Yavapai County Arizona touch screen firmware 4.3.11. Not certified.
Los Angeles County California touch screen version 4.3.8. Not certified.
El Paso touch screen firmware version 4.3.9* Not certified at the time
Alameda County California touch screen firmware 4.3.11. Not certified.
Johnson County Kansas touch screen firmware 4.3.11. Not certified.

On December 16, 2003, the State of California held a certification hearing for the Diebold TSx system. An 18-inch-thick pile of copies containing the material you have just read was marched into the middle of the meeting, and California Secretary of State Kevin Shelley made an unusual personal appearance to express his displeasure. The results of an audit ordered by the California voting-systems panel were equally disturbing:

According to *WiredNews*, "At least five California counties were using versions of software or firmware that were different from what Diebold had indicated they were using. *All* counties were using uncertified software ... Marc Carrel, assistant secretary of state for policy and planning, said he was 'disgusted' by the situation and worried that it could call into question any close races that might have occurred in three counties that used federally unqualified software.

' ... And I'm frustrated ... that we're not going further today,' he said. 'There certainly needs to be something done to this vendor.' " [24]

* * * * *

While California was busy clearing up its unauthorized software, Washington state officials were denying that the problem existed.

Post-Intelligencer reporter Wyatt Buchanan got this answer when he asked for a response to the allegations made in this chapter:

"Elections officials said the two [Harris and Stephenson] *had never contacted them about their concerns."* [25]

Well no, I suppose not, unless you count six e-mails, a 20-minute conversation with assistant elections director Paul Miller, a confrontation with David Elliott in front of 12 witnesses outside Senate Room 1 in the Washington state capitol, and testimony before members of the Washington state legislature with Elliot present.

Elliott, the Washington state elections director, told Tacoma News Tribune reporter Aaron Corvin on December 17 that *"all software used in elections has been certified by the state."* [26]

OK. Stephenson and I will be picking up the signature pages for those certifications.

* * * * *

After issuing a cease-and-desist for publishing 24 memos documenting the use of unauthorized software, after a California audit revealed that 100 percent of Diebold's machines used uncertified programs and California threatened to revoke the company's right to do business in the state, after dozens of journalists including two documentary film producers and the AP wire covered this story, Diebold Election Systems President Bob Urosevich released a news statement:

"Diebold Election Systems, Inc. (DESI), is announcing a complete restructuring of the way the company handles qualification and certification processes for its software, hardware and firmware." [27]

I'm sure someone will slap me for saying this, but I'm reminded of the sociopath who discovers his conscience as soon as he goes to trial.

It wasn't just Diebold. On the Mike Webb radio show, Snohomish County (Washington) Auditor Bob Terwilliger admitted that one of his staff members wrote a program modification for his Sequoia touch-screen software. He said it was for the WinEDS central tabulating software (the Sequoia equivalent of GEMS; this software was also found on an unprotected Internet site during the fall of 2003).

What was this patch for? "Just to help run some reports." But it has to access the votes to do that. "It just uses the database." But the database consists of the votes. "I trust the person who made the changes." [28]

Let's suppose everyone in every jurisdiction is honest. That's not likely, but let's pretend. Here is an incomplete list of the bugs fixed on just one release of the Diebold software:

From: Whitman Lee, 23 Jan 2003
- Items are not being recorded in the Audit Log.
- Connect to Data Base security crack.
- Ballots printed from Ballot Viewer do not correctly reflect selections.
- Non-administrator users can assign themselves administrator privileges.
- Races marked "Not Counted" can be downloaded and appear in reports.
- Regional users can unset the election's status.
- No error message is displayed if 'Confirm password' and 'Password' fields don't match.
- Loading a file from backup results in the backup copy being deleted.
- Central Count drops a batch if a race on the ballot has headers.
- LA County Export: Election Id incorrect for Nov. 2002 election.
- Incorrect IP address displayed on the AccuVote-TS Server console.
- Resetting election on non-Host database gives "Internal Error".
- Summary Reports Cards Cast totals are incorrect

- Incorrectly enabled functions and settings when election status is "Set for Election."

It's bugs like these that get elections wrong. Would you rather have bugs in the software, or get them fixed by unknown people sticking uncertified modifications into your voting machines?

Here it is in a nutshell, folks: We have this flawed idea that we can certify and test our way into trustworthy voting. We can't. We need a model based on auditing, with certification as a side dish.

14
A Modest Proposal:
Everybody out of the pool

The next chapter is called "Practical Activism," and it's full of ideas to help us take back our vote. But what, exactly, are we fighting for?

In June 2003, I queried many in the voting-activism community about what, exactly, we should *do* with a voter-verified paper-ballot system when we get it. No one seemed quite sure. It's been a long, hard fight and I'm confident that we're going to get the paper ballot — but not soon enough, and it's not worth a thing if we don't audit.

Congressman Rush Holt from New Jersey proposed HR 2239 to mandate voter-verified paper ballots, get rid of risky remote-access tools and require a spot-check audit. His bill has been a giant step in the right direction but still doesn't address auditing.

The optical-scan machines in Volusia County, Florida, demonstrate that paper ballots don't necessarily provide security, and what you are about to read will show that paper ballots alone won't secure the system.

We are stuck with trusting those who have access.

In King County, Washington, an individual named Jeffrey Dean obtained a contract to program the voter-registration system. According to sources within the King County elections office, Dean also had a key to the computer room, the passcode to the GEMS computer and

24-hour access to the building. So here's a man with access to our personal information and to the programs that count 800,000 votes.

According to the Diebold memos, Jeffrey W. Dean apparently had access not only to King County, but also to the entire suite of optical-scan software used in 37 states and the security-sensitive Windows CE program for the touch screens. He had access to our votes, but what Jeffrey Dean is not allowed to have is access to handling any checks.

That is because his criminal sentence for twenty-three counts of felony theft in the first degree forbids him to handle other people's money, now that he has been released from prison. According to the findings of fact in case no. 89-1-04034-1:[2]

> "Defendant's thefts occurred over a 2 1/2 year period of time, there were multiple incidents, more than the standard range can account for, the actual monetary loss was substantially greater than typical for the offense, the crimes and their cover-up involved a high degree of sophistication and planning in the use and alteration of records in the computerized accounting system that defendant maintained for the victim, and the defendant used his position of trust and fiduciary responsibility as a computer systems and accounting consultant for the victim to facilitate the commission of the offenses."

An embezzler who specialized in sophisticated alteration of computer records was programming the King County voting system and is also mentioned specifically in the Diebold memos in connection with programming the new 1.96 version optical-scan software and the touch-screen Windows CE program. Let's look at some of the features Dean says he programmed for a "ballot on demand" optical scan application:

> *Jeffrey W. Dean, January 22, 2002 RE: serial numbers on ballots*: "The BOD [Ballot on Demand] application that we have been running in King County since 1998 does put serial numbers on the ballots (or stubs) along with a variety of optional data. The application also will optionally connect the ballot serial number to a voter."[3]

Diebold told The Associated Press that Dean left the company when they took over,[4] but in fact, Diebold retained him as a consultant:

From: Steve Moreland, 4 Feb 2002: "I am pleased to announce that effective today, John Elder will be assuming the role of General Manager of the Printed Products department of Diebold Election Systems, Inc. ... <u>Jeff Dean has elected to maintain his affiliation with the company in a consulting role</u>, reporting to Pat Green. <u>The Diebold Election Division management team greatly values Jeff's contribution to this business</u> and is <u>looking forward to his continued expertise in this market place.</u>

While in prison, Jeffrey Dean met and became friends with John Elder, who did five years for cocaine trafficking. At the time of this writing, Elder manages a Diebold division and oversees the printing of both ballots and punch cards for several states.

Punch-card manufacturers manage a high-risk security point because this is where the die cutting is done. By setting the cut so that some chads dislodge more easily than others, it is possible to manipulate a punch-card election. Diebold's printing division also bids on printing for other voting-machine vendors, such as Sequoia.

Jeffrey Dean was released from prison in August 1995, and Elder was released in November 1996. In their prison-release documents, both wrote that they had lined up employment at Postal Services of Washington, Inc. (PSI Group), the firm that sorts 500,000 mail-in absentee ballots for King County. [5]

King County contracts the mailing of its absentee ballots out to Diebold's print and mail division, which was run by Jeffrey Dean and is now run by John Elder. This division subcontracted with PSI Group to sort King County's incoming absentee ballots.

Sorting the incoming ballots is a high-risk security point for absentee ballots. We know how many absentee ballots we send out but don't know many are filled out and sent back in, especially if they pass through a middleman before being counted by elections officials. Elections officials may tell you they count the ballots before outsourcing for precinct sorting, but in major metro areas, up to 60,000 ballots arrive in a single day and elections offices are generally not staffed to handle this. It also makes no sense to count ballots by precinct and then send them out for sorting.

Jeffrey Dean, when released from prison, had $87 in his inmate account. He had been ordered to pay $385,227 in restitution for his embezzlements. Most of us would find it difficult to bankroll a busi-

202 | *Black Box Voting*

ness under those circumstances, yet somehow Dean (and his wife, Deborah M. Dean) managed to become the owners of Spectrum Print & Mail. According to securities documents for Global Election Systems, who hired Jeffrey Dean as a director and senior vice president in 2000 and 2001, Dean had been running Spectrum since 1995 — shortly after Dean was released from prison. In September 2000, Spectrum was purchased for $1.6 million by Global Election Systems.[6]

We've had a cocaine trafficker printing our ballots, an embezzler programming our voting system and our absentee ballots being funneled through a company that hires people straight out of prison. And when we try to find out what software is actually authorized, we get the buffalo shuffle.

I don't believe there is a certification program in existence that can protect us from inside access. We need criminal background checks, full financial disclosure for all state elections officials, and robust, fraud-deterring audits.

Everyone out of the pool. We have to disinfect it.

These public-policy issues can't be addressed with certification or even by mandating paper ballots. We need procedural protections. We just "got lucky" and discovered Diebold's files. What about the other companies? The truth is, we have no idea how big this problem is. Every time we ask questions, we get the wrong answers.

We need a short-term moratorium on counting votes by machine. I know it sounds radical. If, temporarily, we have to do the old-fashioned thing and count by hand, let's just roll up our sleeves and do it. We shouldn't require citizens to vote on systems that can't be trusted.

In an audit, when there is an anomaly with a spot check, you pull the whole subset of records for a more careful examination. We just spot-checked Diebold. I'd say we found an anomaly.

Now we need to pull the subset of voting-system vendors, give everyone a background check and send an auditor in to check their records. And perhaps their memos. We need to get an independent evaluation of the software on *all* of our voting machines, to find out what the heck is actually on them.

Public Policy

It's time to rethink our public policies for voting. We took away transparency, and look what happened: We got bit. Now we need to bring transparency back.

The Declaration of Independence does not say, "Governments are instituted among men, deriving their just powers from the consent of the computer programmers."

Unless ordinary citizens with no computer expertise can *see* with their own eyes that votes are being counted accurately, the audit system must be considered a failure. In a democracy like ours, you don't need to be a lawyer to sit on a jury. You shouldn't need to be a computer programmer to count a vote.

The "many eyes" method simply means that we let as many independent parties as possible view the vote-counting. I spoke with Christopher Bollyn, a reporter who has written several articles about the erosion in integrity of our voting system as it migrated to computerized counting. He described an election he witnessed in France:

When it comes time to count, as many citizens as can fit in the room are allowed to come in and watch the counting. Sworn election officials, some from each party in the election, in front of all the observers, count the ballots into piles of 100. Each set of ballots is placed in a bag. Then, one bag at a time, the election officials count the ballots, announcing each one. They tally up one bag and move to the next, until all are done.

It takes a relatively short time to count 1,000 votes, and by having many election precincts throughout the country, all of France can be counted in a matter of hours, in front of thousands of eyes.

In the U.S., we complain that our citizens don't think their vote matters. Here's a concept: Let people *see* their vote. Not a video representation of a vote hiding in a black box, but the *actual vote*. Count votes before they leave the neighborhood. Invite people in to watch the counting. And add a 21st-century twist: Install a Web camera, so citizens can watch the vote-counting live, on the Internet.

If we want people to care about voting, we mustn't take the people out of "we, the people."

Procedural Safeguards

To correct current procedural flaws, we need to bring in the right kinds of experts — auditors — and we need to keep the system simple. Here are some procedural safeguards we should consider:

• Verify the machine tally while still at the polling place. Run a report of the tally from the polling place before phoning, modeming or driving anything to the county. Post this report on the door of the precincts and make copies available to the press.

• Compare the polling-place tally with the matching totals assigned by the central county office. This makes it much harder to get away with changing votes after they leave the polling place, and manipulations of programs like GEMS will be caught.

• Provide clearly delineated accounting for the votes that appear separately from the precinct totals, like absentee votes and provisional votes. Polling-place tallies should always match what is posted at the polling place. Separate the other votes cleanly and record them in a way that is easily understandable for everyone.

• Hand audits must be a routine part of every election, not just used for recounts. Hand-audit any anomalies.

• Make "random" spot checks truly random by using a transparent and public method for random selection.

• Allow the press, and any citizen, to audit if they pay for it. If they discover that the election was miscounted, reimburse them. Find ways to do these audits inexpensively.

• Allow each party to select a handful of precincts to hand-audit. Discretionary audits shine more light into any precincts deemed suspicious.

• Require audits for insufficient randomness (e.g., three candidates get 18,181 votes; poll book shows voters arrived in alphabetical order).

• Require that the audit be expanded if discrepancies are spotted, *whether or not the identified discrepancy would overturn the election.*

• When voting machines miscount, require that fact to be disclosed, and if it is the fault of the vendor, require such failures to be disclosed to prospective buyers.

• *Consider a 100 percent audit of the paper ballots.* It may be easier and cheaper to do a 100 percent audit than to counter the political tricks that will arise when we introduce judgment (like what constitutes an "anomaly") into a robust spot-checking procedure.

The biggest objection to proper auditing is that it takes too much time. If we aren't willing to invest the time to safeguard the system, maybe we should rethink the idea of using voting machines altogether.

* * * * *

Words are important: "Paper ballot," never "receipt." A paper ballot is a legal record and substantial. A receipt is a small slip of paper we might stick in our pocket.

Three Proposals

I. The Mercuri Method

Who created the voter-verified balloting concept? Dr. Rebecca Mercuri did. She wrote of her design concept in a paper called "A Better Ballot Box,"[7] the first and probably the most widely accepted design for a hybrid electronic/paper ballot system, though of course it still needs the auditing procedures.

The Mercuri Method allows proprietary voting machines made by private manufacturers but requires that they modify touch-screen or DRE machines to generate paper ballots. The system should record votes electronically, then print a paper ballot and display it behind a plastic or glass panel, which prevents the voter from removing it from the polling place, or accidentally mangling it so that it can't be easily read. The voter reviews the ballot. If it does not represent her choices, she calls an election official, who voids the ballot, and she votes again. Once she approves the ballot, it drops into a ballot box for later tallying. This voter-verified paper ballot must be the definitive record of the vote.

The electronic count can be used to provide preliminary results, but the official result must come from the paper ballots.

II. An open source method, from David Allen

Suppose we want to open-source this and take ownership of the voting system back into public hands. Here is a proposal for such a system. Like Mercuri's plan, it does not address the auditing issue.

Allen's proposed system requires a paper ballot that uses anti-tampering features like those found in financial documents and requires that computerized data be stored on non-erasable media.

Allen recommends open-source development. Everyone should be invited to watch the system being built, in the open rather than in secret.

Allen suggests a real-time record of everything that happens on the voting machine. Each "keystroke" of the election is recorded. This can be done with a "write-once" CD-ROM drive.

"If we are going to use a 'black box' to vote on," says Allen, "then let's model it after the 'black box' found aboard airliners (even though they are actually orange, not black). If a plane crashes, everything the crew did can be reconstructed from the black box."

The computer should also print a ballot, which we inspect, and it is deposited into a secure ballot box. The third part of the system is the digital tally maintained on the voting machine's hard drive or memory card. All three should match.

So, won't we be creating tons more work by having to hand count ballots? Allen suggests that a bar code be printed along side each vote that a scanner can read, as long as the reader is generic and purchased from a source unrelated to the manufacturer of the voting machine. Ballots can thus be processed quickly at the precinct. Since the ballots are also readable by humans without requiring the aid of any device, it is easy to verify the accuracy of the scanner.

Do we really have to count *all* the paper ballots? Well, if we don't, we need a more complicated set of audit rules.

Open source development: This is a method whereby software is developed by a community of programmers in full view of the public. Once the code is developed, any company may use it and sell it to anyone they please. They just can't change the source code. They can bundle it with hardware, install it in precincts, teach poll workers to use it, and provide maintenance and support for the software and equipment. But, they must adhere to the inviolable commandment: Tamper not with the actual source code. It doesn't belong to you; it belongs to the taxpayer.

Some proposals for open-source electronic voting machines create code that is so simple that it can use inexpensive hardware and even recycle old computers.

III. All Paper Ballots, All Hand-Counted

Victoria Collier grew up discussing vote fraud around the dinner table. Her father, James Collier, and her uncle, Kenneth Collier, wrote *Votescam: The Stealing of America,*[8] published in 1992, the first hard-hitting book about high-tech vote fraud. In 1970, Ken Collier ran for Congress against Claude Pepper in Dade County, Florida, picking up about 30 percent of the vote. As the electronic voting-machine totals weighed in, Ken Collier and campaign manager James Collier noticed that they suddenly lost 15 percentage points. They didn't get another vote for the rest of the night.

According to the Collier brothers, "[when they] compared the official vote results with a print-out of the vote projections broadcast by the TV networks on the final election night, they found that Channel 4 had projected with near-perfect accuracy the results of 40 races with 250 candidates only 4 minutes after the polls closed. Channel 7 came even closer; at 9:31 p.m., they projected the final vote total for a race at 96,499 votes. When the Colliers checked the 'official' number ... it was also 96,499."

"In hockey, they call that a hat trick," the Colliers write. "In politics, we call it a fix."

"Listen, here's my idea," says Victoria Collier. "After the public touch-screen bonfire (we really need more community-minded events, don't you think?), we should march to our secretary of state's office and demand the restoration of a hand-counted paper-ballot system."

Collier recommends using properly designed, easy-to-use paper ballots and see-through boxes; and that the count be done by hand, in public, videotaped and aired live on television, with the results posted on the precinct wall. If we count all ballots at the polling place on Election Day, it will be much harder to alter ballots. She also recommends other security measures, to prevent ballot boxes from going missing on the way to the county elections office.

15
Practical Activism

"MoveOn should take this issue on."

"What about contacting the ACLU?"

"Have you thought about calling Bill Moyers?"

"Congress should launch an investigation."

All great ideas, but they are missing something. Taking back our vote is not something we can depend on others to do for us. This requires the top talent we have. Nothing less will do. This job needs *you*.

What are we fighting for? Simply this, and we must accept nothing less: We want voting systems to produce voter-verified paper ballots, and those ballots must be considered the legal record when used for recounts and audits. We must use robust fraud-deterring auditing methods, and we must place a much higher priority on catching and correcting software miscounts.

We need a temporary interim solution, so we can be confident that our votes are secure in the next elections. We also need a long term solution, a bill passed by Congress to solve the problems revealed in this book.

We need to develop public policy, auditing procedures, and tamper-proof voting machines based on input from experts in a variety of fields, and we must not allow our collective common sense to be overridden by profit motives, or the desire to save face because of past mistakes.

I've been told that simple solutions, like Australia's open-source system that cost only $150,000 to develop, could take all the profit out of making voting machines. Well, who thought it was a great idea to make a buck off a vote anyway?

Corporations make poor decisions all the time. Dot-coms go blam. Hardly anyone buys electric typewriters anymore. Try selling Thalidomide to a pregnant woman nowadays. I don't see anyone crying over those profits. Vendors who created unauditable systems with secret software will just have to dust themselves off and think up a new plan, because we are not going to compromise on our vote.

We need to block new legislation designed to protect and encourage flawed election systems, we need to identify public officials who allow such systems to grow or refuse to support sensible reforms, and we must re-educate those who are open to it. For the most intransigent, toss them out of office. And we need to spread the word as widely and quickly as we can.

A little conceptual work

Some of us have a stereotyped impression of activism. We think it means joining some group marching down Main Street or standing in front of a building, holding signs and chanting.

There may be opportunities for that, but that isn't what I'm asking you to do. The following information demonstrates how we can *all* get involved, even those of us who are not inclined to march down the freeway in the rain.

Swarms work better than centralized power. We can win more readily with a loosely organized set of allies, coming at the problem from different angles in unpredictable ways. You can't decapitate a swarm, and a series of stings tends to provoke reactions which in turn attract interest from new hives.

In the swarm method, those who show leadership and tenacity are encouraged to form their own followings. There are no requirements that groups share information about their doings with any central authority, nor should everyone use the same approach. Now and then we meet at the water cooler, but only if we feel like it.

We need not even get along or agree completely on what the solution should be, though that would be nice. Indeed, our opposition may try to wedge us apart, but we're quite capable of bickering and internal drama even without that. If one group of activists becomes irritated with another, as long as both keep coming after the issue without pause, the strategies of each group — because they are different — become all the more unpredictable to the opposition.

Ordinary citizens have already had a real impact, with almost no financial backing. Now we need to increase the number of people in the swarm and build more hives.

It is up to you to decide what your role will be in this movement. I offer the following suggestions to help you define your own role:

1. Take stock of what you like to do already. You'll be more effective if you invest your time doing things you enjoy.

2. Look at your skill set and apply your talents to this cause.

3. Create a group of friends, so that you can enjoy socializing as part of your activism.

The remainder of this chapter will illustrate how ordinary people like you have used their talents to make a difference. If you're not sure where to start, begin by visiting www.BlackBoxVoting.org.

* * * * *

One day, Washington Director of Elections David Elliott answered a phone call from a concerned citizen about a Washington State requirement for prior certification. In Washington, voting systems could be accepted only if they had first been certified and used elsewhere (in addition to NASED certification). The caller, Linda Franz, thought that requirement stifled state options for voting equipment. Elliot suggested she support pending legislation to delete those requirements.

I suppose he didn't expect her to look up the legislation and read all of it, because that set off alarms and a call to action.

After looking more closely, Franz found that the *only* positive aspect of the bill was dropping prior-use/certification requirements. The rest of the bill eliminated the requirement for a separate ballot, enhanced the legality of the electronic vote record and *gave the secretary of state free rein to accept voting-system changes, certified or not.* Franz, along with other concerned citizens such as computer consultant Marian Beddill (finance-committee chair for Whatcom County Democrats), stopped the bill — and its various incarnations — in its tracks.

Never underestimate the power of one or two determined people.

Linda Franz is not a very public person, and, though she is one of the driving forces on voting activism, she does things so quietly that few people outside the elections industry even know who she is. Why would a private individual such as Franz decide to take on voting legislation and the public officials who are promoting it?

"All I know is that I'm 50 years old, and I never expected to have to spend the second half of my life fighting for my son's right to vote," she says.

What are *your* talents and interests?

New York City's Jeff Matson has a knack for coming up with slogans and sound bites. He put out a call on the Internet for ideas on quick, appealing messages to help all of us spread the word.

What followed over the next 48 hours was a flurry of volunteer contributions for you to use on bumper stickers, pins, billboards, posters, flyers, T-shirts and ads.

This voter chose to highlight the failure of the Help America Vote Act (HAVA) to mandate proper accounting:

> **H**elp **A**merica **V**ote **A**ct?
> **H**ow **A**bout **V**oting **A**ccountability!

One voter suggested a play on words using the term "corrupted":

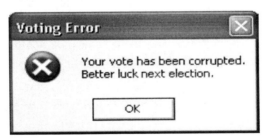

Matson got such an enthusiastic response to his request that we can cheer up the rest of this chapter with ideas triggered by his activism. You can use these concepts in your own efforts.

What other skills can you bring to the table?

Dogged determination — Keep the message up front and let your elected officials know you are not going away and that you expect them to defend your right to vote. Call them, write them, e-mail them, fax them and, by all means, visit them.

Number crunching — "The election went smoothly and no one reported any problems." You'll hear that on election night. Yet, in Chapter 2, you read about dozens of documented voting-machine miscounts, and hardly any of them were discovered while people were voting on the machines. Problems are found *after* the election — days later, when media interest has died down.

Help hunt out vote totals as they are coming in, catch anomalies, report them and join others in analyzing them. Hop online on election night and flag discrepancies, and post them in the forums at BlackBoxVoting.org, where you can compare notes with other voters.

A citizen volunteer who goes by the screen name "SirRhino" reported these numbers after returns came in for the 2003 California recall election:

"After printing the spreadsheet out, taping it to a wall and contemplating it for a while, there are three counties that give me pause, Alameda and Tulare, and possibly Humbolt. In Tulare, Jerome Kunzman (Ind) got 694 votes while he got only 56 in LA. (the county with by far the highest voter turnout). Jerome's second highest was in Fresno (366) and third highest in Humbolt (240)."

"SirRhino" wanted to take a look at why Kunzman got 14 times as many votes in a small county like Tulare as in Los Angeles, and he noted that Tulare, Fresno and Humbolt are Diebold counties.

Other volunteers joined in to examine the numbers, suggesting an explanation:

no paper?
no proof
[and you thought chads were bad?]

"Thanks for pointing out the Tulare ballot - don't know how the heck you found it, but it seems to answer the Palmieri/Kunzman issue. Wouldn't you know it – those blasted BUTTERFLY-type ballots are back." — "Harmony Guy"

From the 2003 Tulare County, California, recall ballot:

CHERYL BLY-CHESTER	Republican	PETER V. UEBERROTH	Republican	GINO MARTORANA	Republican
Businesswoman/Environmental Engineer		Businessman/Olympics Advisor		Restaurant Owner	
B.E. SMITH	Independent	BILL PRADY	Democrat	PAUL MARIANO	Democrat
Lecturer		Television Writer/Producer		Attorney	
DAVID RONALD SAMS	Republican	DARIN PRICE	Natural Law	ROBERT C. MANNHEIM	Democrat
Businessman/Producer/Writer		University Chemistry Instructor		Retired Businessperson	
JAMIE ROSEMARY SAFFORD	Republican	GREGORY J. PAWLIK	Republican	FRANK A. MACALUSO, JR.	Democrat
Business Owner		Realtor/Businessman		Physician/Medical Doctor	
LAWRENCE STEVEN STRAUSS	Democrat	LEONARD PADILLA	Independent	PAUL "CHIP" MAILANDER	Democrat
Lawyer/Businessperson/Student		Law School President		Golf Professional	
ARNOLD SCHWARZENEGGER	Republican	RONALD JASON PALMIERI	Democrat	DENNIS DUGGAN MCMAHON	Republican
Actor/Businessman		Gay Rights Attorney		Banker	
GEORGE B. SCHWARTZMAN	Independent	CHARLES "CHUCK" PINEDA JR.	Democrat	MIKE MCNEILLY	Republican
Businessman		State Hearing Officer		Artist	
MIKE SCHMIER	Democrat	HEATHER PETERS	Republican	MIKE P. MCCARTHY	Independent
Attorney		Mediator		Used Car Dealer	

Web design and Internet skills — If you can volunteer to create simple Web sites, you'll find many takers in the activism community.

Computer programming — If you have computer programming knowledge, your presence is needed at public testing and certification meetings. A 28-year-old computer programmer named Jeremiah Akin decided to show up at a public Logic and Accuracy (L&A) test in Riverside County, California. He was shocked when he was told to sign off on the test before it was completed. He wrote a 22-page report about various anomalies he spotted during testing of the Sequoia machines. Akin's story was featured in the online magazine *Salon.com*, exposing important problems with the certification process.

We also need computer scientists to develop and critique open-source voting-system software.

Writing — If you are a good writer, you can help other activists hone their message into concise, clear, credible handouts and assist candidates by providing material they can use in speeches.

Using the forums: If you have not used an Internet forum before, now is the time to learn. The BlackBoxVoting.org forum is "self-serve." You simply go to the Web page and log in, and you can ask for resources, request research, join projects, post your own documents and artwork for others to use. It's easy, and there are step-by-step instructions.

Several voting-issue forums are available. Among the sites that have forums for voting-issue activists:

www.BlackBoxVoting.org — Participatory activism
www.BlackBoxVoting.com — News & Comment
www.VerifiedVoting.org — Legislative activism
www.OpenVoting.org — Development of an open voting solution.
www.VoteWatch.us — Voting discussions and election reporting

Desktop Publishing — If you enjoy creating brochures, posters and handouts, volunteer your skills. Your work may very well end up at rallies, in libraries and at town meetings.

THINK chads were BAD?
(Now look what's happened)

Printing — Contributing at-cost printing is an important activism activity, to get newsletters and fliers into as many hands as possible.

Organizing — If you are a good organizer and like to get on the phone and work with the media, your help is needed both for events and to corral creative talents into applying their skills where they are most needed. Your help is also needed to moderate activism forums.

Public speaking — If ever there was an issue that begged for town meetings, this is it. You are a voter and therefore have a stake in telling people about the problems and what needs to be done. Feel free to draw from this book to develop your speeches, and you'll find much more information in the forum and the "Public Library" at BlackBoxVoting.org.

Sometimes we are blessed with a person who has organizing, writing and public-speaking skills all rolled into one, and when such a person also has tenacity and media skills, she can influence an entire state — even one as vast as California.

Kim Alexander, president of the California Voter Foundation, is such a person. With degrees in political science and philosophy, Alexander cut her teeth in activism while working with the powerful citizen lobby Common Cause. She then breathed life into the California Voter Foundation in 1994. For nearly a decade, she has been at the forefront of efforts to make our political system more accountable, with voting machines and other efforts.

Telephone work — If you are organized and unafraid of the telephone, your talents are badly needed. Andy Stephenson is one such person. On many occasions he helped me track down information that could only be obtained through telephone work.

Stephenson takes excellent notes, but more than that, he seems to be able to get people to do things for him. He called the secretary of state's office in Georgia and somehow persuaded it to fax him certification documents that had eluded Georgia activists even after two public-records requests. He called Bob Urosevich at Diebold Election

Systems to ask him if he was still the president, because they kept trotting out a person named Tom Swidarski as the president of Diebold Election Systems.
Stephenson learned that they had two
people wearing the mantle: Swidarski and
Urosevich. He says he received an aggres-

BBV

Black Box Voting =

Blind Faith Vote?

sive response to his queries from Urosevich: "If you don't back off,
you're gonna get a visit," Urosevich reportedly said.

(You might want to try less intimidating phone calls, like helping
local activists track down meeting times and records.)

Political and lobbying skills — If you have the ability to read
legislative law, which can be daunting to some, we need you. We
need citizens who can go into current and pending legislation, inter-
pret and make a concise translation.

Legislative activism requires people who refuse to let stubborn officials shake them loose. Linda Franz is such a person. She has a knack
for figuring out other people's alliances and positions, so she can quietly manuever around them. Franz admits she's still learning about the
legislative process from others; a lobbyist for other issues gave her
valuable help. If you are new to this, try to find someone to work with
who already knows the system.

Here are some of Franz's suggestions:

• When naming a group, make sure it encompasses a broad region,
like a state. Franz found that once citizens statewide learned there
was an organization working on the voting issue, they wanted to join.
Also, if you tie the name to a specific county, representatives from
other areas might not listen because they assume your group would
only represent that area.

• Don't forget ethics complaints. Some elections officials seem to
skate very close to the line when it comes to mingling with vendors. In

 OR

THE CHOICE should be YOURS !!!

some states, ethics allegation can be filed *after* the official's time in office, allowing redress after elections have become old news.

• You'll often hear Franz telling people to be careful how they use language because she has learned that clever lobbyists will weasel around any words they can.

Think YOUR vote counts?
- NO PAPER
- NO PROOF

"Voter-verifiable" ballot sounded good, until we learned that companies like VoteHere proposed to use printers at the polling place, not for printing a ballot that you can look at and authorize, but to print a receipt with a code on it, which you can take home and look up on the Internet to "verify" your vote.

One system proposes to print bar code on a paper ballot that is then read back to the voter via a bar code reader. Not acceptable. Can the average voter read bar code? How do you verify what was "read" vs. what the machine — and even the bar code — might actually say? This leads to an addition:

"Voter-verified paper ballot that the voter can read without an interface (except for certain disabled individuals who need such help), said ballot deposited in a secure ballot box at the polling place."

While you are watching your language, learn to say "ballot," not "receipt," because opponents have been passing laws to make the electronic record (not the paper ballot) become the legal representation of the vote. A ballot has legal standing. A receipt may not.

Affix the words "voter-verified" to the words "paper ballot," because if you don't, opponents will tell you the machines do produce a "paper trail." What they are talking about is the machine's ability to print individual pages from its internal data.

I

VOTED!

Or did I?

Franz also researched why Avante and AccuPoll (manufacturers that produce a touch screen with a paper ballot) were not being chosen for purchase in her state. Accupoll is close to meeting Washington State requirements, but she discovered that Avante, which *is* qualified, appears blocked from even beginning the Washington State certification process.

For some reason Washington didn't act on Avante's certification documents and issued statements that

DEMAND PAPER BALLOTS
(Voting should not be a touchy subject)

conflicted with the truth. Washington State Elections Director David Elliott told listeners on the Dave Ross radio show January 3, 2003, " ... and if anybody comes to market with something like that, we'll certify it for use in Washington State. No one has presented a system like that for certification yet." [2]

But Avante had applied for certification in December 2002 and has made repeated attempts since then. You, like Franz, can start pursuing questions like this. Find out what's going on with certification. Investigate. Don't take answers at face value.

A citizen who goes by the moniker "larry1" unearthed the request for sales proposal for Ohio and reports that Ohio will not allow any machine with a paper ballot that can be removed from the polling place. What is the purpose of such a law? We have been voting with paper ballots for 230 years, and this is the first I've heard of an uncontrollable urge on the part of voters to remove their ballots from the polling place instead of placing them in a ballot box. Such a law seems designed to protect and encourage flawed election systems.

Jim March is an entirely different kind of lobbyist. He decided in August 2003 to apply his bespectacled, 6-foot, 4-inch presence to voting issues. In "real life" he is a Republican/Libertarian gun lobbyist who lives near the Capitol in Sacramento, California. March thinks nothing of crossing the street (and party lines) to talk to Democrats, pulling out CDs he created which contain a certified version of GEMS software, with step-by-step instructions for how to slip by passwords and change the audit log. He brings this CD to reporters and public officials and demonstrates the software's flaws to them.

His style differs markedly from that of Franz; he does not focus on specific legislative language, but on influencing lawmakers' willingness to tackle the issue. He is flamboyant and makes some activists uncomfortable, but in twelve weeks, he managed to get two national news articles focused on voting-machine security problems. He pops up like poison ivy when there are certification hearings.

**PAPER BALLOTS
not
VAPOR BALLOTS**

Filming and videotape production — There's nothing like seeing an employee of the state election division literally turn tail and run when you show up with a camera. That's what happened to Greg Palast when he attempted to question Clay Roberts about the Florida felon purge.[3] Another videotaper caught New Orleans voting machines giving Susan Barnecker's votes to the wrong candidate.

A California activist who goes by the screen name "ParanoidPat" took to the streets in Alameda County on October 7, 2003, during the California recall election. He has been preparing a documentary about this issue. He's just an ordinary guy with a talent who is applying it to something meaningful. You can, too.

Flash Media and Shockwave productions — Michael Stinson, of TakeBackTheMedia.com, created a powerful presentation about voting-machine problems which has been making the rounds on the Internet. His presentation, set to "Revolution" by the Beatles, is politically charged and quite powerful.[4]

An entertaining presentation done with animation was created for TooStupidToBePresident.com, featuring Arnold Schwarzenegger quizzing Wally O'Dell, CEO of Diebold, about the Georgia patches and other matters. It is quite funny and makes a powerful point.[5]

You can participate in easy activism simply by e-mailing links to such efforts to all your friends and posting links on your Web site. If you have talent, create your own presentation.

Research — Faun Otter, concerned about the lack of any exit polling in the November 2002 general election, decided to research the campaign contributions made by Diebold executives — mind you, this was before the Diebold files were found on the Web, at a time when Diebold was receiving almost no scrutiny. He discovered that Diebold's campaign contributions were lopsided towards the Republican Party.

Who knows — perhaps the the next "scoop" that *Scoop Media* breaks will be your own.

Legal — If there is one group of citizens whose skills are badly needed, it is attorneys.

Should your vote be kept secret from **YOU?**

The American Civil Liberties Union was fighting for the wrong side of the issue. They were fighting *against* paper ballots. Let's not depend on someone else to fight this for us. If you are a lawyer, we need you. If you do legal research, we need you, too.

The Electronic Frontier Foundation filed a case, but it was limited to fighting Diebold copyright-violation claims. What we need are lawyers willing to work on three things:

1) Creating a template for a citizens' initiative. This can be distributed via the Internet to other states and citizens' groups.

2) Participating in legislative processes and helping write good legislation at the state and national level.

3) Filing public litigation.

One such suit, brought by Susan Marie Weber in California, takes the position that forcing voters to vote without a ballot (and therefore without auditability) is a violation of civil rights. The judge ruled against Weber; she appealed but lost. As of this writing she is preparing another appeal. This is an important suit, and had the original been filed at this point in time, the verdict might have been different. At the time Weber filed her suit very little information was available to help her prove her case.

Fraudulent claims: An RFP sales document is prepared when the machines are purchased. It contains the specifications the vendor must meet. We now know that they don't always come through on their promises. This opens a litigation avenue and will help counties recoup their investment from the manufacturer.

Use of uncertified, unsworn technicians to evaluate vote data: Nothing in the law actually allows temporary workers to help call an election. Some voting-machine techs are hired only for the day, and we know little or nothing about their

STAND
and be counted
DEMAND
your paper ballot

backgrounds. Candidates have standing to sue, and this may be a good issue when there has been a technical glitch.

Failure to follow regulations: Use of uncertified software, failure to certify key parts of the software, last-minute program modifications and use of unauthorized data-transmission methods such as cell phones all fit into this category.

In each case, decisions need to be made as to who the plaintiff will be (The voter? The candidate? The county? The state?), what harm can be claimed, what remedies will be requested and what venue (county? state? federal?) will receive the complaint.

It all starts with finding a few good men and women in the legal profession willing step up to the plate to help protect democracy.

Strategies

Use a variety of strategies, but remember that it all needs to end up on one doorstep: effective legislative change.

• Set up events and participate in meetups.

• Pay visits to public officials.

• Communicate with others via e-mail lists.

• Call and ask reporters to cover voting stories.

• Advertise — TV ads. Bumper stickers. Billboards.

• Put this book in people's hands. If you can't afford it, print a free copy off the Web.

• Enter politics yourself and fight for trustworthy voting.

• Become a vote watcher or poll worker during upcoming elections.

• Get involved with your community, especially if you have connections with the people most likely to be disenfranchised — ethnic groups, people with disabilities and senior citizens.

The whack-a-mole story

If you have been in an arcade, you've seen the game in which you take a big foam sledge and whack moles that pop out of holes, faster and faster until the moles (usually) win.

Brent Beleskey from Barrie, Ontario, Canada, is director and an investigative researcher for the International Voters Coalition (www.voterscoalition.com). Beleskey has taken it upon himself to fight the voting machine proliferation in Canada. Wait — isn't Canada famous for its calm, deliberate and speedy all-paper, hand-counted elections?

I vote.
The machine decides.
Not in any democracy!

Yes, but that hasn't stopped voting machine vendors from selling their machines, which are used in municipal elections. Beleskey has made it a mission to locate voting machines in Canada, which he told me he has found hiding in back rooms in various cities. Each time he finds one, he goes to bat against its use, fighting to get rid of it. No sooner does he whack one down than another pops up.

While you might call him eccentric — some do — it's also nice to know that someone is out there standing up for your right to vote.

Diebold's whack-a-mole adventure:

Diebold started whacking people who published embarrassing documents about how the voting machines work.

Whack.

The New Zealand server that posted program files from an unprotected FTP site got a Diebold cease-and-desist order.

Whack. Whack.

DemocraticUnderground.com got more than one.

Whack.

A forum participant who goes by the screen name "Zhade" received one for mirroring Jim March's rig-a-vote files.

Whack. (Oof!)

Jim March got one but kept the documents up and dared Diebold to come and get him, promising to enjoy the discovery process. They left him alone after that.

Whack. (Oops.) Whack. (Whoops, missed!)

I posted the 24 memos exposing the certification problem, and my ISP got one. Its attorney refused to comply, saying Diebold's attorneys didn't write it correctly. By the time they had prepared a better one, we'd shifted the memos elsewhere.

Whack!

I got another when someone posted a link to the memos on my site.

Whack.

An activist who goes by the name "Trogl" received one.

Whack everything!

"bpilgrim," a programmer who created a search engine that could find things in the Diebold memos, got one. Perhaps Diebold didn't like the suggested search terms: "boogie man," "fake" "hack" and "what good are rules." Diebold ordered him to destroy his search engine.

Whack. Whack. Whack. Whack. Whack. Whack. Whack.

IndyMedia, with Web sites all over the world, started posting links to the memos, and soon Diebold memos were popping up faster than mushrooms after a spring rain.

Whack — OUCH!

The Internet Service Provider (ISP) for *IndyMedia,* Online Policy Group, decided to fight the takedown orders. The Electronic Frontier Foundation agreed to fight the case.

WHACKWHACKWHACK!

Students at Swarthmore College began posting memos. But you don't whack college kids without drawing a little attention to yourself. Soon, students at eleven colleges were posting Diebold memos.

whackwhackwhackwhackwhackwhackwhack...

Students at 32 colleges posted the memos and *Indymedia* posted a running tally of cease-and-desists, along with the latest memo locations. *"I Got a Diebold Cease & Desist!"* bumper stickers popped up.

On November 2, 2003, *The New York Times* did a feature on all this whacking of memos.

I received a call from presidential candidate Dennis Kucinich's office. "Might we get some memos?" one of his staffers asked. "The congressman might want to post them on his Web site."

At least two "greatest hits" memo sets were prepared for the honorable Rep. Kucinich.

B O O M !!!

Kucinich delivered the knockout punch: He posted a selection of Diebold memos on his congressional Web site, with links to more, and issued a public challenge to Diebold to back off.

Diebold formally withdrew from the game.

* * * * *

Activism works. But we need your involvement: If *we* don't define our own voting system, someone else will do it for us. And in the next chapter, David Allen will introduce you to them.

WHERE'S MY BALLOT?!?

E-voting system flaws risk election fraud
New Scientist, UK - Jul 25, 2003

Election fraud risks attract wide notice
The Inquirer, UK - Jul 25, 2003

US researchers critical of electronic voting systems
The Age, Australia - Jul 24, 2003

Voting machine fails inspection
CNET News.com - Jul 24, 2003

Security Of E - Voting Systems Seriously Questioned
Information Week - Jul 24, 2003

High-Tech Votes Can Be Hacked, Scientists Say
Reuters, UK - Jul 24, 2003

Study finds computer voting system vulnerable to tampering
San Jose Mercury News, CA - Jul 24, 2003

E-voting flaws risk ballot fraud
MSNBC - Jul 24, 2003

Does it count accurately?
What do you base that 'yes' on?

16
Pay No Attention to
The Men Behind the Curtain

If you are inclined to let other people fix this problem for you, please remember that "other people" are already hard at work to change your voting system to suit their own agenda and profit margin. These other people may have a different view of democracy from yours.

What are their plans? Let's look behind the curtain at a secret meeting that took place at 11:30 a.m. August 22, 2003. Invitations were sent out to all the makers of computer voting machines and included the following agenda:

ITAA eVoting Industry Coalition DRAFT Plan, Activities, and Pricing

Purpose: Create confidence and trust in the elections industry and promote the adoption of technology-based solutions for the elections industry. Repair short-term damage done by negative reports and media coverage of electronic voting. Over the mid- to long-term, implement strategy that educates key constituencies about the benefits of public investments in electronic voting, voter registration and related applications.

The Information Technology Association of America (ITAA) is a lobbying firm that specializes in getting special treatment for technology companies.

In this proposal, the ITAA is trying to get hired to provide assistance to Diebold, Sequoia, ES&S and other voting-machine vendors to get the public to accept their products. Not to correct the flaws in their products, mind you, and not to do any type of "customer survey" to find out what we voters actually want. The idea is for these for-profit companies to define our democratic voting system and then invest in a PR campaign to show us that we like their system.

According to the ITAA, you should never use the word "lobby" because it has negative connotations in the mind of the public. Instead you should "educate key constituencies."

Audience: Public confidence in the integrity of the ballot box is absolutely critical to the democratic process. To build such confidence, the vendor community must address several constituencies:

1. Media
2. Elected officials at the federal, state and local level
3. Elections administrators, procurement officials and others involved in the purchase decision
4. Academia
5. General public
6. International counterparts
7. Systems integrators and related government contractors

Note that the general public, the people who actually use and pay for these systems, is fifth on the list of constituencies, and that they "address" us, not listen to us.

Success Benchmark: Achieve widespread acceptance among key constituencies that electronic voting is not just an alternative to other balloting systems, but is the 'gold standard' to which all should aspire.

They want to make insecure and unauditable voting systems a "gold standard." Notice that no one has yet funded a $200,000 lobbying effort on behalf of voter-verified paper ballots and proper auditing, but somehow hundreds of thousands of us got sold on that idea. Marketing the truth is not nearly as expensive as selling people something they don't want.

Next, the ITAA suggests models to indoctrinate the public into accepting the voting systems they chose for us.

Model 1 - Goals:

1. Help assure the integrity of IT [information technology] used in the electronic voting process

Sounds good, but this needs open-source software and a paper ballot, something most of the election industry rejects.

2. Generate positive public perception of the eVoting industry

Notice this is second on the list. Actually correcting the security problems is fifth.

3. Speak with a unified voice on industry standards

4. Develop liaison with key constituencies in order to build broader support for e-voting

5. Improve security of technology and development/ deployment processes

6. Improve public awareness of voting technology security

7. Reduce substantially the level and amount of criticism from computer scientists and other security experts about the fallibility of electronic voting systems.

Here's a better concept: Let's encourage computer scientists to continue to act like scientists so they can render an objective opinion.

8. Adopt an industry code of ethics

You mean there has been no code of ethics? This would explain a lot.

9. Generate collaborative research on non-competitive issues

I'm thinking this may involve research grant funding. We, the for-profit voting industry, hereby grant you, the once-independent scientist, a thick pile of money to underwrite your research. And we'd like the opportunity to make suggestions on what you study and how you study it and offer our expertise on the wording of your conclusions. See the pharmaceutical industry for examples.

Major Activities - Deliverables

1. Establish Blue Ribbon Task Force to evaluate voting technology development and implementation processes, propose process improvements, and establish code of ethics.

We, the men and women behind the curtain, should own the Blue Ribbon Task Force that tells public officials and taxpayers what to think. (There's nothing wrong with evaluations and a code of ethics. I'd just like to see these developed by voters, not vendors.)

2. Produce and publish collaborative research on noncompetitive issues - 2 annual white papers.

3. Assess public attitudes about electronic voting on a regular basis through public opinion surveys, focus groups and other research.

4. Hold seminar/briefings/webcasts on Blue Ribbon Task Force findings, code of ethics launch, white paper releases.

5. Create comprehensive media plan to articulate key messages, identify outreach strategy and tactics, synchronize timing of media outreach to election milestones and other significant events, and raise visibility of issues, activities and the ITAA Election Systems Task Force itself.

Bring the media over to our way of thinking.

To this end, it is interesting that Hart Intercivic, which helped organize this meeting, was one of the first beneficiaries of such a strategy. Let's take a moment to see "Deliverable #5" in action. Ellen Thiesen, a voting activist, noticed that a news story damaging to Hart Intercivic somehow got a midday rewrite.

The first story:

Voters encounter eSlate glitch[1]

"...Those who showed up at the Holiday Inn at 7787 Katy Freeway to vote found that the eSlate machines that were supposed to make voting so much easier and more accurate were on the fritz. Instead, election judges were passing out sheets of paper torn in half, along with sample ballots, and telling voters to write in their votes.

"David Puckett said he sat down on the floor and spent 25 minutes scribbling down his choices while other voters just took the time to write in their votes on the top races before dropping their homemade ballots into a pasteboard box. He said an election judge told him to write on the back of the paper if he ran out of room and then told him he might need to vote again this afternoon if the eSlate machines come back up. Then, Puckett said, the judges decided a second vote wasn't such a good idea.

"'They're making up rules as they go,' he said. 'It's unbelievable.'"

"Puckett's worried his vote won't count.

"'I will come back if I need to. I want my vote to count,' he said. 'It's my privilege. It's my duty. I want my people to win.' "

This version appeared a few hours later:

ESlate voting proves smooth, not flawless[2]

"...At the Holiday Inn Hotel at 7787 Katy Freeway, election workers decided to use paper ballots when they thought the eSlate voting machines were not working properly. About 75 makeshift ballots were cast — and signed.

"But the eSlates were not malfunctioning. Workers were entering incorrect information into the machines that assigned the wrong ballots to voters. David Puckett, who showed up shortly after 7 a.m., at first registered his vote on a piece of paper, but returned later to cast an eSlate ballot, concerned his initial vote might not be counted.

"'This isn't Houston's finest moment,' he said. 'You had to see it to believe it. Really, no one knew what to do.'

"Elections officials said they would ensure that only one vote per person would be counted."

* * * * *

Look, if the machines are too difficult for ordinary citizen pollworkers to operate, invent better ones or don't use them at all.

Back to the ITAA plan:

6. Develop liaison to national associations, government oversight bodies, customer trade associations
a. Attend national conferences, work to add agenda items to programming
b. Arrange guests at briefings, monthly meetings, receptions
c. Arrange meetings with key government executives, lawmakers, staff.

One question: While manufacturers of touch-screen voting invest wads of cash on influence-peddling, who speaks for the voter?

7. Provide customer interface opportunities
a. Arrange guests at briefings, monthly meetings
b. Develop a regular dinner, reception program.

You mean like vendor-sponsored party boats?[3] "Customer interface opportunities" has a nice ring to it — it certainly sounds better than "influence peddling" and "perks and cash contributions."

Fees in addition to annual dues: $100,000 - $125,000

For sale: One 227-year-old democracy. Asking price: $100,000 - $125,000.

Model 2 - Goals: Same as Model 1.

Plus: Perform a detailed evaluation of voting technology security standards and certification processes.

They will give themselves a check-up. But with $3.8 billion in Help America Vote Act (HAVA) money at stake, my bet is that they'll pronounce themselves healthy.

Major Activities - Deliverables: 1 - 7. Same as Model 1.

8. Retain consulting firm or think tank for review and evaluation of voting technology security standards and certification processes. Publish findings/ recommendations.

They want to have people they hire make recommendations about independent oversight procedures.

Meeting/Events

1. Hold monthly meetings in Washington D.C. or Dallas area

2. Hold bi-annual full membership meetings

Fees in addition to annual dues: $125,000 - $150,000

Model 3 - Goals: Same as Models 1 and 2.

Plus: Perform a detailed evaluation of voting technology security standards and certification processes.

Plus: Re-engineer voting technology security standards and certification processes, based on findings in report.

This is nice, but here is something that would be nicer: Instead of voting-machine vendors doing their own evaluation, how about an entirely independent evaluation by people who aren't vested interests and don't have $3.8 billion at stake.

Plus: Build media, public, and customer awareness of new security and certification processes.

Issue lots of press releases.

Major Activities - Deliverables: 1 - 7. Same as Models 1 and 2.

8. Retain consulting firm/think tank for review and evaluation of voting technology security standards and certification processes. Publish findings and recommendations.

Are they hoping no one will notice they are repeating #8 above?

9. Implement report findings/recommendations; reengineer security standards and certification processes.

10. Launch public relations campaign to build media, customer, and public awareness of new security and certification processes.

Well, actually, 8-10 are pretty much the same as what they do in Model 2, but they are charging more money for it.

Meeting/Events

1. Hold monthly meetings in Washington D.C. or Dallas area

2. Hold bi-annual full membership meetings

Fees in addition to annual dues: $200,000+

Schedule

With the Iowa caucuses (and therefore the start of the primary season) only five months away, time is exceedingly short to implement this plan. Americans must have full faith in the efficacy of the election systems infrastructure. Numerous factors, including the overarching need to conduct the 2004 election with no "hanging chad" controversies, suggest that work commence with a minimum of delay.

ITAA is ready, willing and able to work with firms in the election systems sector to build and, as necessary, restore, a high degree of confidence in the integrity of e-voting and related applications.

Notice they want to restore "confidence in the integrity of e-voting and related applications" as opposed to wanting to restore "integrity in e-voting and related applications."

ITAA provides an ideal forum to undertake this program, offering:

• a sophisticated government affairs and public relations apparatus

• over 20 years of industry engagement in public sector contracting;

• the premier trade association membership of contractors involved in the federal systems marketplace;

• an on-going state and local advocacy program; They have connections in high places. They have connections in low places.

• an existing Election Systems Task Force and internal staff resources well schooled in the underlying issues;

• and a track record of lobbying for federal funding to upgrade state and local electronic systems.

ITAA applauds the companies involved at the Election Center meeting for having the vision and determination to address the current doubts about election systems on an industry basis. Working together, ITAA believes that these companies have already taken the first step to meeting the common challenge.

It's going to make them millions of dollars; certainly that's worthy of applause. Perhaps a few billion if they play us suckers ... er, I mean if they "educate these key constituencies."

* * * * *

Shortly after this agenda was sent out, a secret meeting was held under voting-vendor-style "strict security," which means that only two reporters and *Black Box Voting* publisher David Allen managed to slip into the teleconference unnoticed. Allen, at least, introduced himself.

"David Allen, Plan Nine Publishing."

No one knew who he was, but no one asked, either.

The meeting appeared to have been set up with the help of R. Doug Lewis (executive director of The Election Center) and Hart Intercivic (a voting-machine company). Why someone in Lewis's position was setting up a lobbying meeting for voting-machine vendors is a matter of some curiosity.

From The Election Center's Web site: "The Election Center is a nonprofit organization dedicated to promoting, preserving, and improving democracy. *Its members are government employees* whose profession is to serve in voter registration and elections administration."

Perhaps colluding with for-profit companies and helping them hire a lobbying firm is in the spirit of this organization's charter — and since we aren't quite sure who set it up, how it gets all its funding or who exactly appointed R. Doug Lewis, his murky relationship with vendors and lobbyist might be exactly what they had in mind.

Lewis droned on about this being a long time coming and the need for the industry to "speak with one voice."

Harris Miller (ITAA) gave an introductory spiel about the firm and how it could help the industry "stave off short-term attacks" from academics and activists.

Apparently a meeting had been held in Florida the previous week to discuss how to broaden the base of support for e-voting.

A question was asked about how the ITAA can help the industry speak with one voice. Miller said this meant helping voting vendors establish their own certification standards and "coming to the defense of a company under attack." If anyone missed chapters 9 through 13, we presume this was triggered by Diebold's embarrassing blunders. He then added, jokingly (we hope), "unless you want use your knives on him as well."

Allen says he did not hear a peep from Diebold during the whole call. Miller also touched on the need to establish a "blue-ribbon" panel to help refute problems such as Diebold was having. One assumes this blue-ribbon panel will fill the same role for the black-box voting industry that the Tobacco Institute filled for the tobacco industry.

Because the conference was by telephone, it wasn't always possible to know who was speaking. One individual asked whether the lobby would be addressing Internet voting, which he described as "a train wreck waiting to happen." The ITAA said it was not on the agenda.

The ITAA said that it could help get academics and critics "on our side" (one assumes, then, since Lewis was involved in setting the meeting up, that he is on the side of the vendors). Miller did admit that some critics are unappeasable.

The ITAA felt the industry should help create its own credibility by setting high standards.

He said that working with the National Institute of Standards and Technology (NIST) is desirable; however, he said he assumed that if NIST mandated an oversite committee chaired by Dr. David Dill, "no one would want to play."

The ITAA suggested "re-engineering" the certification process to eliminate "side attacks vendors are subject to now" from people who "are not credible as well as people who are somewhat credible."

The Election Systems Task Force

One participant wanted to know if the "Election Systems Task Force" (who?) would be reconstituted or reformatted.

Though I can find out little about this group, the answer to this question was illuminating.

A voice, apparently belonging to R. Doug Lewis, said that they have been "more focused on the HAVA legislation but would be interested in meeting with this group." He went on to explain that the major companies involved in the Election Systems Task Force are Northrop Grumman, Lockheed Martin, Accenture and EDS (defense contractors and procurement agencies).

The goal of the Election Systems Task Force, he said, was very limited, because they just wanted to get the HAVA legislation enacted to create more business opportunities for themselves as integrators. Their agenda for HAVA, he said, was, "How do we get Congress to fund a move to electronic voting?"

As mentioned earlier, more than one guest attended the meeting. When I heard this astounding admission, I wanted more documentation. I will tell you this much: I listened to it myself, and this part of the conversation sounds even worse on tape. HAVA was pushed through to create business opportunities for defense contractors and procurement companies. *HAVA = Let's-make-a-buck-on-a-vote*.

In the segment I listened to, they mentioned that there were about twelve members of the Election Systems Task Force.

Antitrust concerns

Lewis suggested that the ITAA draft a legal brief to address possible antitrust ramifications so that members of the new group would know what they could and could not do. The ITAA said it would do so at the first meeting of the new group.

Returning to the topic of collusion a while later, Lewis suggested:

"One of the things that you ought to do is at least employ the ITAA to draft a legal memorandum that says under what conditions you guys can meet together ... and pay them for that ... and maybe even pay them for hosting this sitdown that you want to do to figure out your interests. Then make your determinations on whether you want to go forward with a specific proposal."

ITAA: "You don't even have to pay us for it ... and I appreciate Doug ... you are trying to look after my checkbook. I'm willing to come to a meeting wherever and have a couple of staff people come down and eat a couple of grand to do that. I won't do a hundred- page legal memo."

Another voice chimed in:

"Clearly one of the themes going around is related to collusion among industry sources, so any meeting of all the players is, by definition ... unfortunately taken by some people as not a constructive exercise, but one of negative exercise. So, it would probably be best, as Doug suggested, that it would be better that we pay you to do that."

Miller: "OK."

Another meeting participant: "That way, no one would perceive you weren't an independent body."

Miller: "OK."

Lewis appeared to recognize that this business of looking after the ITAA's checkbook might put him on shaky ethical territory:

"In that regard, other than helping you get set up and acquainted with each other and willing to start this process, while we are still in the quasi-regulatory phase ... although the Election Center has no judgments it can issue in any way, shape or form on this ... the Election Center is going to need to bow out of this also. We'll be glad to talk to you about anything you want to talk about and be a sounding board, but in terms of your organization and discussion of industry issues, we are probably best not being involved in that ... at least until we are no longer the place where we do work for NASED (National Association of State Elections Directors)."

Let's talk about protection

MicroVote asked what would happen if a non-member (in other words, a voting-machine manufacturer who didn't pony up his money) got into trouble over some issue such as security. Would the Blue Ribbon Task Force remain mute, or would it turn into "a loose Star Chamber, where you have commenting vendors commenting on another vendor's situation?"

Miller said that normally the members would not comment on a non-member's situation "unless the industry came to the conclusion that it was negatively impacting the entire industry." In which case, he said, they would reiterate their standards and the coalition's code of ethics and say that they can't comment on the other company.

Nudge: "Any group who gets in trouble would hopefully join us to get out of trouble," Miller suggested. Hint: If you don't, you might be the next Diebold.

Influencing certification

A representative of Accenture said that self-certification will be a "tough sell" to the public.

"We can't win the PR battle if ITAA tries to do an ITA's (independent testing authority's) job," he warned. "But I do think it is very important that the industry be more aggressive and more coordinated in the way that it gives input to the ITA process and the people who control the ITA process. They've solicited that input in the past, and I don't feel the industry has done a particularly good job of providing that input. And this is something I feel this industry can be a real conduit for."

Apparently, according to the men and women behind the curtain, our independent testing authorities should not be allowed to be *too* independent. Or, does providing "aggressive" input to the ITAs mean that they should have as little independence as possible?

The ITAA agreed that instead of involving themselves in an ITA-like certification process, they would bring in people "to re-engineer it."

Even the lobbying is a secret

The ITAA made a motion that its goals and "deliverables" be agreed to. One participant didn't have his special decoder ring and raised the objection that all goals had *not* been agreed to.

"I see no lobbying effort here, and secondly, I don't think we have, as a group, set down and defined what we want before we run off and subscribe to the ITAA process," said the voice. "We should sit down face-to-face before we spend $150,000 and determine what we want as a group."

Chet, from AccuPoll, weighed in: "Absolutely. Lobbying is an essential element for this industry."

Miller explained: "We were too subtle by half. Our No. 4 goal, 'develop liaisons with key constituencies,' is a nice word for lobbying. We just didn't want a document floating around saying the election industry is in trouble, so they decided to put together a lobbying campaign."

He went on to boast about his lobbying experience.

"My background is I worked on Capitol Hill for ten years and ran a lobbying firm for ten years, before I took over here in '95. A third of my staff has direct public-policy experience working on Capitol Hill. We are the most-quoted IT trade association in Washington. ... I can give you all the bona fides if you want them.

"I just don't like to put it in writing because if this thing winds up in the press somewhere, inadvertently, I don't want the story saying the e-voting industry is in trouble and decided to hire a lobbying firm to take care of their problem for them."

Except that within half an hour, "this thing" wound up in *Scoop Media*.[4]

R. Doug Lewis: "The truth of the matter is you're not on the same side of the issues when it comes to what you would lobby for. Some of you have a vested economic interest that it should get lobbied one way versus another."

I'm not quite sure where Lewis is going with this. It sounds like Chet, from AccuPoll — which produces a paper ballot and runs on open-source software — might not be a member of the club when it comes to "speaking with one voice."

Instead of Diebold's PR spokesman, journalists will have to ask their questions of the lobbying firm's PR person.

"Emmett" from Accenture learned that speaking with "one voice" to the media literally meant one voice:

"In terms of the task force responding to media inquiry, does the task force handle that role, where someone becomes a spokesman for the group?" he asked.

"If so, who does it?"

Miller: "The answer is ITAA. It usually goes out over my name, but we could add other companies if you wish. Let's assume we wanted to respond to some attack. ... Assume another academic came out and said something against one particular company and the task force wanted to respond. The task force would put out a statement, 'Harris Miller, on behalf of ITAA, says this is B.S.'... We would also invite other members of the task force to put in comments if they want. ... Normally the first person to put in a comment would be the chairman, and other companies would have a chance to comment ... and be included in the press release."

Emmett: "So that's the kind of protocol you have to deal with public debate."

Miller: "Similarly, when we get press calls and the press says, 'Joe Academic says your industry's full of crap and doesn't know what it is doing. What do you say, Harris?' The reporters always want to know what are the companies saying?

"And there can be two scenarios there: The companies may want to hide behind me, they don't want to say anything — frequently that happens in a trade association, you don't want to talk about the issues as individual companies. We have that issue right now with the Buy America Act, for example in Congress. No company wants to act like it's against Buy America — even though they're all against it. So I take all the heat for them.

"The other alternative is they say sure, my company wants to talk to them, my CEO, my PR director, whatever, I'll send them over. Our PR people know this. We never give out the name of a company member unless we know the company wants to talk."

Emmett: "All of that seems ... like currently useful for dealing with this kind of situation we've seen lately. It would be a big help."

A big help for voting-machine makers, perhaps, but this means reporters will have to address questions to a spokesman for the spokesmen. For those of us who are voters, this seems equivalent to taking democracy's pulse through two thick blankets.

Fixing the price on democracy

Tracy Graham of Sequoia Voting Systems had a question about the cost on "deliverables."

"Was that a per-member cost, or total cost?"

ITAA: "Total cost."

Another participant wanted to know how annual dues would be calculated and learned that they would range from $600 to $44,000, depending on the company's sales. Add that to the "deliverables," which were going to cost from $125,000 to more than $200,000.

Everyone pays dues, it was decided; project costs would be split amongst the members of the task force as they see fit.

Miller explained that the fees would depend on what is done. If a "blue ribbon" panel is needed, then fees must be allocated to compensate the panel members. "You would have to pay for some meeting time, for these blue ribbon people, you might have to pay them a fee ... a minimal fee to attend a meeting."

I guess having actual voters or regular citizens attend meetings would be out of the question.

Tracy Graham (Sequoia): "We must have a proactive strategy at this time to improve the overall perception in the industry, so we are absolutely supportive of this type of forum and action on behalf of the industry."

Jack Gerbel, of Unilect: "We agree as well, with what Tracy said. This is very necessary to do."

They proposed another conference call six days later, absent ITAA, to discuss whether to pay their dues and take their chances that the ITAA will come through on "correcting" the public perception of the problem.

Meeting adjourned.

* * * * *

December 9, 2003: Advanced Voting Solutions, Diebold Election Systems, Hart InterCivic, Sequoia Voting Systems, Election Systems & Software and UniLect announced that they had formed a trade group, called Election Technology Council, under the banner of the ITAA.[5]

Conclusion

Look, folks. Either we all get together to build the barn, or these people will build it for us and hire a marketing firm to tell us how much we like it.

I propose that we roll up our sleeves and get busy. It is my duty to tell you that as soon as we rebuild this one, we have to go over and help out some of the neighbors.

There are some who are using election-manipulation techniques to transfer a block of power to their friends. This is a business plan, or a form of organized crime, depending on how alarmed you are based on information you have put together yourself.

Manipulation of elections includes the following attack points:

• Strategic redistricting, ignoring normal timelines for reevaluation.

• Black Box Voter Registration: The HAVA bill wants us to do state-wide computerized voter registration, again with secret software produced by a handful of companies.

• Orchestrated vote suppression: Hiring "challengers" to confront voters in targeted areas; moving polling places at the last minute, "losing" the voter registration records for a percentage of targeted voters, booting up equipment late, or not having enough equipment in minority districts.

• Casting and counting the vote on manipulatable and insecure systems.

• Manipulating vote forecasting and calling races prematurely in the media, encouraging candidates to concede.

• Retaliatory recalls and "investigations" to unseat candidates who do not represent the choice desired by a few.

This book contains ammunition for the voting-machine issue. And if you think you are too small to be noticed, you've never had an ant crawling up your leg.

Now go out there and take back your vote.

Acknowledgements

Wow. This book was a long, hard, scary piece of work. It would not have been possible to create a body of work like this without help, and it is not possible to list you all in the space provided. Thanks to Lynn Landes, and Linda Franz, and Rebecca Mercuri. And to the Colliers, all of 'em, and Ronnie Dugger, and Peter Neumann, and Doug Jones, the pioneering voices of concern. To publisher David Allen, who said of the private corporations that were throwing their weight around, "I've always wanted to be on an 'Enemies List.' " And to editor Lex Alexander, a voice of encouragement when David Allen and I were shouting at one another. "It's understandable that you're feeling a little tense," said Lex. "We're just expecting you to save American democracy. No pressure." To Roxanne Jekot, who guided me through the basics and was a dear friend. And to DemocraticUnderground.com, perhaps my greatest source of inspiration and courage during the research and investigation phase. To Daniel Hopsicker, and Dan Spillane, and Jim Condit, and Brent Beleskey, and Mark Crispin Miller. To David Dill and Kim Alexander, and Greg Dinger and Denis Wright, and ParanoidPat, who never fails to make me laugh. To Alastair Thompson and Skinner, and Jeff Matson and gristy and punpirate. To Al Marzian and coalminer's daughter, bpilgrim and Faun Otter and Marian Beddill, and that quiet force in the background, Jack Maples. To Slashdot's Roblimo, and pioneering Susan Marie Weber, and two of the gutsiest guys I know, Charlie Matulka and Rob Behler. To Dan Wallach, Avi Rubin, Yoshi Kohno and Adam Stubblefield, for having the courage to go public and apply solid credentials to the problem. To Angka, SoCalDem, abcdan, Cap, HarmonyGuy, Papau, Phoebe, Trogl and Zhade; Eloriel, and HeddaFoil. Thanks to Greg Palast, who offered his expert advice when I found the Diebold FTP files, and to William Rivers Pitt, who shared ideas and his own research, and Thom Hartman, who knows the perils of privatization better than anyone. To the honorables Dennis Kucinich, Jim McDermott, Rush Holt, John Conyers and Barbara Boxer. To Robin, who stepped in with a shoulder to lean on when I most needed it, and Big John Gideon, the force on the forum. To the irrepressible Jim March, with his cleverness and great personal courage. To Andy Stephenson, a kick-ass researcher and a steadfast friend. I promised myself I'd quit when the page ran out.

About the Authors

Bev Harris began writing on the subject of electronic voting machines in October 2002. Her investigative journalism has since been cited in *The New York Times* (three times), and on CBS, Fox News, ABC News, *Mother Jones,* the Associated Press, and CNN. In writing *Black Box Voting*, Harris spent over two thousand hours researching voting machines, and interviewed hundreds of witnesses including many election officials and even voting machine programmers who work directly for the firms that build these machines.

In a single year, Bev has brought the entire question of electronic voting machines from the backwater of esoteric technical journals to the forefront of national discussion.

When not causing Diebold and the rest of the electronic voting machine complex gastrointestinal distress, Bev runs the public relations firm Talion.com

David Allen is a freelance writer, publisher and computer systems engineer. His writing has appeared in local and national publications such as *Internet Underground, .Net, Eye, Triad Style, ESP,* as well as his political blog *Thoughtcrimes.*

For over 18 years David has installed, repaired, adminstered and taught about computers and computer networks, with eight years devoted to software and hardware for community banks. He holds credentials as a Microsoft Certfied Systems Engineer, Compaq Accredited System Engineer, A+ Technician, and Certified Software Manager.

David owns and runs Plan Nine Publishing.

Appendix A: Compendium of problems, continued from Chapter 2

(Footnotes for this section located at the end of "Footnotes: Chapter 2")

September 1986, Dallas, Texas: The number of voters changed on various report printouts, but votes for individual candidates remained the same. The problem was attributed to a computer-programming error. Note the date on this report: Officials have been expressing concerns about computerized vote-counting for nearly two decades.

"With paper ballots, I can make the numbers add up ..." said Assistant Texas Attorney General Bob Lemens. "We are running into much tougher problems here."

Texas Attorney General Jim Mattox said the computerized vote-counting clearly has the potential for fraud.

"I can't send a reasonably good programmer to look at this system and determine that it is properly tabulating the ballots," Mattox said. [72]

November 1988, Hillsborough, Broward and Dade counties, Florida: A dropoff was observed in Senate votes from the previous general election, but only in counties that used computerized vote-counting machines. Counties without computerized vote-counting showed a 1 percent dropoff, while counties with computerized voting showed a dropoff of 8 percent.

"Something stands out there like a sore thumb," said Michael Hamby, executive director of the Florida Democratic Party. [73]

November 1989, Lima, Ohio: Representatives of Sequoia Pacific, makers of the voting machine software for Lima, failed to appear as requested, and election results were delayed until someone could work out the programming error and recount the votes. Nobody was quite sure how many races were affected, but the mayoral race and the school board races were in question for nearly a week after the election. [74]

November 1990, King County, Washington: Worse than the butterfly ballot, some Democratic candidates watched votes alight, then flutter away. Democrat Al Williams saw 90 votes wander off his tally between election night and the following day, though no new counting had been done. At the same time, his opponent, Republican Tom Tangen, gained 32 votes. At one point several hundred ballots added to returns didn't result in any increase in the number of votes. But elsewhere, the number of votes added exceeded the number of additional ballots counted. A Republican candidate achieved an amazing surge in his absentee percentage for no apparent reason. The miscounts were sporadic and thus hard to spot, and the errors disproportionately favored just one party. King County's election manager recommended a countywide recount. [75]

1994, New Orleans, Louisiana: Voting machine tests performed and videotaped by candidate Susan Barnecker demonstrated that votes she cast for herself were electronically recorded for her opponent. This test was repeated several times with the same result. (The video footage of this incident can be seen in Dan Hopsicker's documentary video *The Big Fix 2000*, Mad Cow Productions). [76]

November 1996, Bergen County, New Jersey: Democrats told Bergen County Clerk Kathleen Donovan to come up with a better explanation for mysterious swings in vote totals. Donovan blamed voting computers for conflicting tallies that rose and fell by 8,000 or 9,000 votes. The swings perplexed candidates of both parties. For example, the Republican incumbent, Anthony Cassano, had won by about 7,000 votes as of the day after the election, but his lead evaporated later. One candidate actually lost 1,600 votes during the counting.

"How could something like that possibly happen?" asked Michael Guarino, Cassano's Democratic challenger. "Something is screwed up here." [77]

November 1996, Thurston County, Washington: An inexplicably large number of people went to the polls but did not vote in the hot House contest. A whopping 11.5 percent of Thurston County voters ignored the congressional race — nearly twice as many no-votes as other races in Thurston County and twice as many no-votes as other counties recorded.

"We have absolute confidence our machine is counting appropriately," said Bob Van Schoorl, Thurston County's chief deputy auditor.

J.R. Baker, of Democratic challenger Brian Baird's campaign, was not satisfied. "They have not gone through any special testing to see if their machines are adequately counting the votes. Perhaps they need to do sample hand counts of precincts and compare them with the machine." [78]

November 1996, Guadalupe County, Texas: Officials discovered a voting machine counted more votes in the presidential election than the number of ballots cast. Guadalupe County Elections Administrator J.R. Perez said the problem was with new software for the county's Business Records Corp. Eagle vote counting system. Perez said a problem was identified with the software before the election, and he thought it had been fixed.

"I had no reason to believe the system was not tabulating right," Perez said. [79]

Tucson, Arizona:

1984 - 826 legitimate ballots were discarded in Oro Valley because of a computer error. The error wasn't discovered until after the deadline for counting them.

1996 - A software programming error mixed up the votes cast for two Republican supervisor candidates.

1997 - More than 8,300 votes in the City Council race were initially left uncounted because of defective punch-card ballots, which were provided by the voting machine company.

1997 - The city had to hand-count 79,000 votes because of a manufacturing defect in the ballots, provided by the voting machine company.

1998 - 9,675 votes were missed in the tabulation. After canvassing, officials realized that no votes had been recorded for 24 precincts even though voter rolls indicated thousands had voted at those polling places. Global Elections Systems (now called Diebold Election Systems) tried to figure out why the computer had failed to record the votes. [80]

November 1998, Franklin County, Ohio: One candidate was incorrectly credited with 14,967 votes; another received 6,889 in error. Deborah Pryce and John R. Kasich gained 13,427 votes and 9,784 votes, respectively, after election officials hand-checked vote totals in 371 machines that were affected by a software programming error. A spokesman for Danaher Corp., which supplied electronic voting machines to the county, told the board that such a problem had never before happened in Franklin County. No one caught the error while downloading the data into voting machine memory cartridges. [81]

November 1998, Washoe County, Nevada: A breathtaking number of snafus in the Washoe County registrar's office caused candidates in Reno to liken the election to the movie *Groundhog Day*, in which the lead character relives the same day over and over again. Count votes. Computer failure. Go to court. Recount the votes. Software error. Back to court. Start over counting, and so on. [82]

December 1998, Canada: What was billed as a historic first for the Canadian Wheat Board turned into an embarrassment as a programming error threw the election results into question. The firm hired to count the ballots found a flaw in the computer program that tabulated results for the agency's first-ever board of directors. [83]

September 1998, Kansas City, Kansas: Republican John Bacon, a staunch conservative, celebrated a resounding victory for the 3rd District Kansas Board of Education seat, defeating moderate Republican Dan Neuenswander by 3,018 votes. Two weeks later Neuenswander learned that the margin of loss had been just 24 votes. No one offered any explanation for the discrepancy. [84]

August 1998, Memphis, Tennessee: In the governor's race, a software programming error in Shelby County began crediting votes to the wrong candidates. Computer cartridges containing 295 individual precinct results were taken to a central location because the scanner couldn't read them. The system that was shut down had posted the incorrect results to newsrooms across the city. At least one television station broadcast the bogus results. [85]

November 1998, Chicago, Illinois: One hundred eight of 403 precincts were not counted. A pin from the cable connecting the ballot reader to the counting computer had gotten bent after three-fourths of the precincts had been counted correctly. No one could explain how a pin inside a cable had become bent during the middle of the count. Democrats requested a full recount; a judge disallowed it. [86]

November 1998, Honolulu, Hawaii: A state senate investigation was conducted into the 1998 malfunction of voting machines in seven precincts at once. ES&S acknowledged the error and paid more than $250,000 for the recount, in which the biggest expense was hand counting, according to Vice President Todd Urosevich. ES&S financial officer Richard Jablonski said ES&S would have saved a lot of money if it had been permitted to do only a machine recount, giving voice to a financial incentive for vendors to get rid of paper ballots. [87]

November 1999, Norfolk, Virginia: Machines showed totals of zero but votes had been cast. Edward O'Neal, Norfolk Electoral Board vice chairman, said, "Somehow, they lost their ability to count the votes." [88]

November 2000, Arapahoe County, Colorado: Officials agreed to reconfigure the vote-reading machines for a recount because they had been set wrong and therefore did not read all of the votes. Because Democrats wanted the additional recounts, they had to pay the bill, which came to about $11,000. [89]

November 2000, Denver County, Colorado: Four voting machines malfunctioned. Voting officials mistakenly assumed those machines were not used, but there were 300 votes on them. [90]

Crozet, Virginia (anecdotal report from a voter): "When I pushed the button beside 'No' the machine registered my vote as a 'Yes.' I tried this a couple of more times and got the same result. Finally, I poked my head outside the curtain and asked the 'attendant' what I should do. Whenever I made my choice, the opposite choice lit up. He suggested then that I should intentionally push the wrong button." [91]

November 2000, Volusia County, Florida: A clerk in one precinct could not reach election headquarters to report that the computer had shut down, so the clerk turned the computer off, then turned it back on, accidentally erasing 320 votes. This was discovered only when workers counted all ballots by hand. Election supervisors across Florida say the phone clog happens during most presidential elections, but few people notice. [92]

November 2000, Davidson County, North Carolina: A computer error allowed election software to count about 5,000 early and absentee ballots twice. A reporter brought the discrepancy to light during the county election board's official canvass. The incorrect vote totals appeared only on the official report sent to the state Board of Elections in Raleigh. [93]

November 2000, San Francisco, California: In polling place 2214, machines counted 416 ballots, but there were only 362 signatures in the roster and the secretary of state found only 357 paper ballots. [94]

February 2000, Manatee, Florida: A power surge was reported to be the cause of incorrect computerized vote tallies. A hand count was performed. And because the hand count showed that a candidate lost by just two votes, another hand count was done. All results, including two hand counts, were completed within 48 hours. [95]

November 2000, Albuquerque, New Mexico: A software programming error in New Mexico led officials to withhold about 60,000 ballots from their vote count. According to an AP wire service report: "Their (voting) machines have a problem in the database," elections bureau director Denise Lamb said, "and they can't count any of the straight-party ballots." [96]

November 2001, Buffalo, New York: The poll book showed 96 Republicans signed in to vote at the polling place at Ohio Elementary School, but when the machine was checked, it tallied 121 votes for mayor: 74 for David Burgio and 47 for Mary Kabasakalian. [97]

April 2002, Johnson County, Kansas: Johnson County's new Diebold touchscreen machines, proclaimed a success on election night, did not work as well as originally believed. Incorrect vote totals were discovered in six races, three of them contested, leaving county election officials scrambling to make sure the unofficial results were accurate. Johnson County Election Commissioner Connie Schmidt said that internal checks revealed that the system had under- and over-reported hundreds of votes. Schmidt said the voting machines worked fine, they just tabulated wrong.

"The machines performed terrifically," said Robert J. Urosevich, president of Diebold Election Systems. "The anomaly showed up on the reporting part."

The problem, however, was so perplexing that Schmidt asked the Board of Canvassers to order a hand recount to make sure the results were accurate. Unfortunately, the touch-screen machines did away with the ballots, so the only way to do a hand recount was to have the machine print simulations of ballots from its internal data. Diebold tried to recreate the error in hopes of correcting it.

"I wish I had an answer," Urosevich said. In some cases, vote totals changed dramatically. [98]

November 2002, Palm Beach, Florida: A Florida woman, a former news reporter, discovered that votes were being tabulated in 644 Palm Beach precincts, but only 643 precincts had any eligible voters. An earlier court case in Florida had found the same discrepancy, and the reason for it was never satisfactorily explained. [99]

November 2002, New Jersey: A reporter in New Jersey observed 104 precincts with votes in an area that has only 102 precincts. "Ghost precincts," no matter what the official explanation, do not provide the transparent accounting needed to protect voting integrity. [99]

March 2002, Palm Beach County, Florida: Touch-screen machines sometimes froze up when voters selected which language to use. Phil Foster from Sequoia Voting Systems attributed the problem to a software programming error. Elections Supervisor Theresa LePore also said she heard that some people touched one candidate's circle on the screen, only to see an X appear by another candidate's name. [100]

November 2002, Dallas, Texas: When 18 machines were pulled out of action in Dallas because they registered Republican when voters pushed Democrat, Judge Karen Johnson, a Republican, quashed an effort to investigate the accuracy of the tally. [101]

March 2002, Medley, Florida: Voting machines gave the town council election to the wrong candidate. The problem was attributed to a programming error by a voting machine technician. County Elections Supervisor David Leahy said he was concerned because the computer did not raise any red flags; humans had to spot the error. [102]

November 2002, Monterey, California: California machines couldn't add. The problem in Monterey, California, was that the department's mainframe computers refused to add the results of early absentee votes and those cast on touch-screen computers prior to Election Day.

"We didn't have any problems whatsoever during our pre-election tests," said the elections official. [103]

November 2002, South Carolina: A software programming error caused more than 21,000 votes in the close race for S.C. commissioner of agriculture to be uncounted, an error margin of 55 percent. Only a paper ballot hand count was able to sort it out. [104]

November 2002, Taos, New Mexico: Just 25 votes separated the candidates in one race; another race had a 79-vote margin. After noticing that the computer was counting votes under the wrong names, Taos County Clerk Jeannette Rael contacted the programmer of the optical-scan voting machine and was told that the problem was a software programming error. [105]

November 2002, Pennsylvania: In Pennsylvania, a voter reported that he had followed his conscience and voted Libertarian. When he reviewed the results for his precinct, though, the Libertarian candidate received zero votes. There are two ways to look at this: unimportant, just a vote; or a 100 percent error. Either way, this man did not get to vote for whom he wanted. [106]

November 2002, New York: Voting machine tallies were impounded in New York. Software programming errors hampered and confused the vote tally on election night and most of the next day, causing elections officials to pull the plug on the vote-reporting Web site. Commissioners ordered that the voting tallies be impounded, and they were guarded overnight by a Monroe County deputy sheriff. [107]

November 2002, North Carolina: Elections officials tried to find 300 voters so they could vote again. In Wake County, North Carolina, one out of four new touch-screen voting machines failed in early voting, losing 294 votes. Election workers looked for the 294 voters to ask them to vote again. (A voter-verified paper ballot would have solved this problem.) [108]

November 2002, Florida: Gubernatorial candidate Bill McBride was a tough guy to vote for: One voter said that he tried 10 times, and every time he pressed McBride, the Jeb Bush choice lit up. He could only get his vote to light up the McBride choice when he pressed a dead area of the screen. No paper ballot was available, so no one really knows who got any of the votes, regardless of which candidate lit up. Similar problems were reported in various permutations, for various candidates, by several Florida voters, and an identical problem was noted in Texas. [109]

November 2002, St. Bernard Parish, Louisiana: All the king's horses and all the king's men couldn't put the tally together again: With a 34-vote margin separating the two candidates for justice of the peace in St. Bernard Parish, the machine ate 35 absentee votes and left everyone guessing about the outcome of the race. The ballots became inaccessible when the system locked up; even the technician couldn't get at them. [110]

November 2002, Georgia: In one Georgia county, ballots in at least three precincts listed the wrong county commission races. Officials shut down the polls to fix the problem but didn't know how many wrong ballots were cast or how to correct errant votes. In another, a county commission race was omitted from a ballot. Cards voters needed to access machines malfunctioned. Machines froze up, and dozens had been misprogrammed. [111]

November 2002, Nebraska: Charlie Matulka, the Democratic candidate for U.S. Senate in Nebraska, arrived at the polls to vote for himself. When he looked at the

Black Box Voting

optical-scan ballot he had been given, he discovered it had already been filled out for his opponent, Chuck Hagel, giving Nebraska the most newfangled voting of all — not just electronic voting, but *automatic* voting! [112]

January 2003, Everett, Washington: If there was any doubt that Republicans were right to ask for a recount of some Snohomish County absentee ballots from November's general election, it was erased by one sobering number: 21.5 percent of the ballots cast in 28 selected precincts were not counted. The Snohomish County Auditor's Office recounted 116,837 absentee ballots after county officials discovered that the optical-scan ballot-counting machines had miscounted.

The problem was attributed to a faulty "read head" on each of two optical scanners; the heads failed to read ballots with blue ink. The machines had passed the test on blue ink before the election. The Sequoia representative could not recall that the "read head problem" had ever happened before.

When asked by a citizen how many machines of the same make and model number Sequoia has in the United States, she said, "About 1,500." When asked how many years they'd been in use, she said about six years.

"Why, then," asked a citizen, "would this unheard-of problem happen at exactly the same time in exactly the same place on two different machines at once?"

The Sequoia rep said she had no idea. [113]

* * * * *

This compendium is by no means complete. Worse, these are examples that were noticed and covered in the press. For the 100 examples listed here and in Chapter 2, there are undoubtedly a great many more that were not written up in the newspaper or were never noticed at all.

FOOTNOTES

Chapter 2

1 – *Mobile Register,* 28 January 2003; "Voting Snafu Answers Elusive"

2 – Factiva.com is a search engine frequently used by reporters for background. In 2002, it was known as DJInteractive.com.

3 – *The News & Observer* , 9 November 2002; "'Winners' may be losers"

4 – *Omaha World-Herald,* 6 November 2002; "A late night in Sarpy; glitches delay results"

5 – *Chicago Tribune,* 4 April 2003; "Returns are in: Software goofed Lake County tally misled ... "

6 – *Newsbytes News Network,* 24 April 1998; "Feature — Glitches Of The Week"

7 – *Chicago Tribune,* 4 April 2003; "Returns are in: Software goofed ... "

8 – Associated Press, reported in the *Wichita Eagle,* 22 August 2002; "Mayo won by a landslide ...Election reversed ... "

9 – *The Las Vegas Review-Journal,* 30 November 1994; "Voter fraud allegations continue"

10 – *Houston Chronicle,* 8 November 2002; "Ballot glitches reverse two election results"

11 – *The Atlanta Journal - The Atlanta Constitution,* 3 September 1998; "Elections Board Case: Candidate's lawyer knows the feeling"

12 – *Newsbytes News Network,* 5 August 1997; "Feature — Glitches of the Week

13 – *Newsbytes News Network,* 22 April 1999; "Feature — Glitches of the Week"

14 – *Newsbytes News Network,* 9 December 1997; "Feature — Glitches of the Week"

15 – *The Salt Lake Tribune,* 25 June 1998; "Commission Primary Recount ... "

16 – *The Omaha World-Herald* , 15 June 1990; "Vote Confusion Blamed on Human Error"

17 – Company press release: PR Newswire, 12 September 2002; "Diebold Touch-Screen Voting Terminals Perform Well in Primary Elections"

18 – *The Omaha World-Herald,* 21 April 1992; "Omaha Firm Taps North Platte Native"

19 – *The Wall Street Journal,* 17 November 2000; "Fuzzy Numbers: Election Snafus Went Far Beyond ... "

20 – *Indianapolis Star,* 9 November 2003; "Vote count marred by computer woes"

21 – Associated Press, in the *Dallas Morning News,* 13 April 1996; "Vote tally miscounted in runoff ... "

22 – *The Arizona Daily Star,* 8 December 1994; "826 votes vanish in Oro Valley precinct ... "

23 – *All Africa,* 11 November 2002; "US Polls Plagued With Glitches"... 'While the American government has been too quick to attack most Zimbabwean elections won by the ruling Zanu-PF party, its own polls continue to be marred ...'; Also reported in *The Washington Times,* 6 November 2002; "Glitches cited at some polls ... "

24 – *The Baton Rouge Advocate,* 5 February 2002; Bill McCuen, guilty plea to felony charges of bribery, tax evasion and accepting kickbacks.

25 – *Honolulu Star Bulletin,* 3 February 1999; "Voting checks failed to detect fault twice; A flawed ballot counter passed a manual check and a mechanical test"

26 – *The Dallas Morning News,* 11 November 1998; "Election system company apologizes, offers partial refund Fixes proposed for problems that led to

undercounts" (related articles Nov. 5 and 28)

27 – *Honolulu Star Bulletin,* 6/7/2000; "Firm admits errors in counting votes for Hawaii, Venezuela"

28 – *The Arizona Daily Star,* 11 November 1998; "Computer fails to record 9,675 Pima County votes"

29 – CNN: Breaking News, 8 November 2000; "Election 2000: Strange Events Plague Florida Polls"

30 – *The Post-Standard,* 5 December 2002; "More Florida Blunders; Precious Votes Should Be Counted"

31 – *Chicago Tribune,* 6 November 1993; "Kane Election Results Just Didn't Compute"

32 – *Albuquerque Journal,* 19 November 2002; "County Certifies Vote Tally"

33 – Notes on "Workshop" on Voting Machine Security for Santa Clara County Supervisors, 11 February 2003; see http://verify.stanford.edu/dill/EVOTE/sc-2-11-2003.html

34 – *The Everett Herald,* 20 January 2003; "County to Discuss Ballot-Counting Foul-up"

35 – *The Seattle Times,* 22 November 1990; "Thousand of Lost Votes Turn Up in Recount"

36 – *The Tampa Tribune,* 2 May 1997; "Grand jury probes contested election"

37 – *Newsbytes News Network,* 4 June 1999; "Glitches of the Week"

38 – *The Knoxville News-Sentinel,* 8 November 1996; "A betrayal of voters; Disaster over early votes on unification demands action"

39 – *The Herald,* Rock Hill, SC , 25 October 2001; "The city election foul-up"

40 – *The Bradenton Herald,* 17 September 2002; "Sometimes the old ways are best"

41 – *The Atlanta Journal; The Atlanta Constitution,* 23 July 1998; "Election '98 - Cobb glitch delayed tabulations statewide"

42 – NPR: *Morning Edition,* 6 November 2002; "Analysis: Senate races in Minnesota and South Dakota"

43 – *Orlando Sentinel,* 7 October 2001; "Election Goal: Low Profile, Changes Aim to Keep Day Fiasco-Free"

44 – *Daniel B. Spillane vs. VoteHere Inc.,* filed in King County, Washington; case no. 03-2-18799-8SFA

45 – *Seattle Times,* 19 November 2003; "Fired engineer reaches deal with election-software company"

46 – *The Las Vegas Review-Journal,* 19 July 1998; "The Clark County vote: How secure is it?"

47 – *Houston Chronicle,* 16 March 2002; "Candidate zeroes in on computer glitch"

48 – *The Commercial Appeal,* 7 August 1998; "Vote Totals ... "

49 – *Newsbytes News Network,* 20 March 1998; "Feature — Glitches of the Week"

50 – *The Daily Oklahoman,* 6 November 1996; "Big Computer Glitch Causes Election Hitch"

51 – *The Baltimore Sun,* 4 November 1999, "Manufacturer of voting system assumes blame for Baltimore's Election Day glitch; Failure to test software resulted in breakdown, delays in vote"

52 – Caltech/MIT Voting Technology Project, July 2001; www.vote.caltech.edu/

53 – Unpublished manuscript and interview with Dr. Susan Battley, May 2003, "Success Traps."

54 – *Deseret News*, 9 November 2002; "Texans tally triple match in exceptional election"

55 – *The Virginian-Pilot and The Ledger-Star*, 25 August 1997; "Warner Doggedly Pursues Divisive Election Inquiry"

56 – *The Las Vegas Review-Journal*, 19 July 1998; "The Clark County vote: How secure is it?"

57 – *Miami Herald*, 10 November 2002; and call-in report from a Miami accountant

58 – *The Tampa Tribune*, 6 November 1998; "Computer crash leads to countywide recount of votes"

59 – *The Commercial Appeal*, 5 March 2000; "Computer Glitch Hampers Voting ... "

60 – Minutes of City of Glenwood Springs Special City Council Meeting, 9 November 2000

61 – *Pittsburgh Post-Gazette*, 4 May 2001, "Hearing Gets Landslide of Voting Problems"

62 – *The Record*, 23 February 2000; "Expert Finds No Sabotage in Election, Reverses Stance ... "

63 – *The Baton Rouge Advocate*, 7 November 2002; "Voting machine glitches worrisome ... "

64 – *The Washington Times*, 6 November 2002; "Glitches cited at some polls ... "

65 – *Newsday*, 6 November 2003; "Voting glitches"

66 – *Newsday*, 6 November 2003; "Voting glitches"

67 – *The Baton Rouge Advocate*, 7 November 2002; Voting machine glitches worrisome ... "

68 – *Telegraph-Forum*, 6 November 2002; "Glitch sends vote count to Richland"

69 – Associated Press, 6 November 2002; "Equipment causes voting problems in several counties"

70 – *Atlanta Journal-Constitution*, 8 November 2002; "2002 Election: 2,180 Fulton ballots located after tally 67 memory cards misplaced ... "

71 – 7 November 2002; Interview with Paul Rosberg, candidate for Nebraska governor

(From Appendix A: Continuation of compendium from Chapter 2)

72 – *The Dallas Morning News*, 24 September 1986; "Dallas Officials Deny Election Fraud Claim"

73 – *Atlanta Journal; Atlanta Constitution*, 11 November 1988; "Thin Lead Allows Mack to Proclaim Victory in Senate Race"

74 – *The Plain Dealer*, 10 November 1989; "Tally mix-up still under investigation"

75 – *Seattle Post-Intelligencer*, 20 November 1990; "Recount of All Election Returns Recommended"

76 – *The Las Vegas Review-Journal*, 19 July 1998; "The Clark County vote: How secure is it?" and *The Big Fix, 2000*, Video by Dan Hopsicker, Mad Cow Productions

77 – *The Record*, 16 November 1996; "Bergen County Paper Ballots Finally Counted ... "

78 – *Seattle Post-Intelligencer*, 16 November 1996; "Democrats Seek Recount in 3rd District — Thurston County in Question."

79 – *San Antonio Express-News*, 8 November 1996; "Computer glitch skews Guadalupe vote results"

80 – *The Arizona Daily Star*, 20 November 2001; "Year-old Votes Discovered in City Precinct Box"

81 – *The Columbus Dispatch*, 8 December 1998; "Tallies from November Election Change ... "

82 – *The Las Vegas Review-Journal*, 12 November 1998; "Washoe's nightmare"

83 – *Winnipeg Free Press*, 9 December 1998; "Glitch forces recounts in CWB vote"

84 – *The Kansas City Star*, 19 August 1998; "Ballot tally change 3,000-vote error ... "

85 – *The Commercial Appeal*, 7 August 1998; "Computer Glitch Delays Final Vote Total ... "

86 – *Chicago Daily Herald*, 6 November 1998; "Computer glitch leads to vote error"

87 – *Honolulu Star Bulletin,* 10 March1 1999; "Vote Recount to Cost $250,000" http://starbulletin.com/1999/03/10/news/story9.html

88 – *The Virginian-Pilot and The Ledger-Star*, 3 November 1999; "Tallying-machine malfunction leads to Norfolk recount"

89 – *Denver Post*, 29 November 2000; "Recount confirms Polis won seat ... "

90 – *Denver Post*, 28 November 2000; "Recount adds 300 'lost' votes"

91 – *The George Loper Home Page*, letter to the editor, 30 November 2000; "Voting Irregularities in Crozet, Virginia." http://loper.org/~george/archives/2000/Nov/30.html

92 – *St. Petersburg Times*, 17 November 2000; "Busy signals taunt clerks at precincts"

93 – *Greensboro News & Record*, 15 November 2000; "Davidson Computer Glitch Doubled Votes ... "

94 – *The San Francisco Chronicle*, 11 February 2002; "2000 election finds work was sloppy"

95 – *Sarasota Herald-Tribune*, 10 February 2000; "Election recount makes no change"

96 – AP Online, 8 November 2000; "Ballots Withheld in New Mexico"

97 – *Buffalo News*, 18 October 2001; "Voting Snafu Won't Change Mayoral Primary"

98 – *The Kansas City Star*, 5 April 2002; "Election errors unnerve Johnson County official"

99 – Call-in reports; November 2002 election; See also: Dr. Rebecca Mercuri's work on voting machines, where she has similar reports: www.notablesoftware.com

100 – *The Palm Beach Post*, 14 March 2002; "Human goofs, not machines, drag vote tally into next day"

101 – *The Fort Worth Star-Telegram*, 30 October 2002; "Democrats to appeal voting case ruling"

102 – KRTBN Knight-Ridder Tribune Business News: *Miami Herald*, 4 April 2002; "Despite New Voting System, Human Error Mars Medley, Fla., Council Election"

103 – *Monterey Herald,* November 2002

104 – *The Herald,* Rock Hill, SC , 7 November 2002; "Machine glitch keeps votes from being counted"

105 – *Albuquerque Journal*, 7 November 2002; "Taos To Recount Absentee Ballots"

106 – 1 November 2002; Citizen report on the VoteWatch forum: http://pub103.ezboard.com/fsoldiervoicefrm44.showMessage?topicID=1.topic

107 – *Democrat & Chronicle* (Rochester, NY) , 7 November 2002; "John squeaks out victory"

108 – *The News & Observer* Raleigh, NC, 31 October 2002; "Machines lose 294 early votes"

109 – Votewatch citizen reports;
   http://www.votewatch.us/election_2002_findings.htm
110 – *The Times-Picayune*, 7 November 2002; "Machine snag leaves race up in the
   air; Trapped absentee ballots delays news of JP winner until today"
111 – AP Online, 5 November 2002; "Glitches Hit High-Tech Voting Systems"
112 – 6 November 2002; interview with Charlie Matulka, Democratic candidate for
   U.S. Senate in Nebraska
113 – Citizen meeting in Snohomish County, 23 January 2003

Chapter 3

1 – Excerpted from article at *Common Dreams*, 16 September 2002, "Elections in
   America: Assume Crooks Are in Control," by Lynn Landes
2 – *CNN AllPolitics*, 5 November 1996; "Hagel scores big upset for Republicans"
3 – *The Washington Post*, 13 January 1997; "Brothers in Arms ... "
4 – *Hastings Tribune*, 6 November 1996, "Hagel savors upset win"
   http://www.cnweb.com/ tribune/old/nov96/nov6/nov6_hagel.html
5 – *The Omaha World-Herald*, 21 April 1992; "Omaha Firm Taps North Platte
   Native"
6 – *The Omaha World-Herald:* 3 June 1994; "Welsh Named Top Executive ... " Hagel
   took over as interim CEO from Bob Urosevich in November 1993. William F.
   Welsh III took the CEO position from Hagel in June 1994. Hagel remained as
   chairman.
7 – "Fact Sheet" faxed from Chuck Hagel's office. Hagel resigned his chairmanship
   of American Information Systems on March 15, 1995, and announced his
   candidacy for the U.S. Senate on March 31, 1995.
8 – *Business Week*, 10 July 2000; "Chuck Hagel ... landslide upset"
9 – United States Senate Public Financial Disclosure for New Employee and Candidate Reports: Chuck Hagel, 1995.
10 – Salon.com, 20 February 2003; "Hacking Democracy"
11 – *The Hotline*, 3 January 2003; "White House: Hagel cares about the U.S. and yes,
   all mankind."
12 – *The Hill*, 29 January 2003; "Hagel's ethics issues pose disclosure issue"
13 – The AP, 31 January, 2003; "Hagel not ruling out run for White House"

Chapter 4

1 – Testimony before the U.S. House of Representatives Committee on Science, May
   22, 2001; "Problems with Voting Systems and the Applicable Standards," by
   Douglas W. Jones, University of Iowa Associate Professor and Former Chair of
   the Iowa Board of Examiners for Voting Machines and Electronic Voting
   Systems. http://www.house.gov/science/full/may22/jones.htm
2 – *The Wall Street Journal*, 17 November 2000; "Fuzzy Numbers ... Who Was
   Collecting Ballots In Oregon?"
3 – *The San Francisco Chronicle*, 19 February 2002; "S.F. voting system in shambles,
   mistrusted / Errors, mismanagement, instability"
4 – *San Francisco Election Fraud: June 1997 Stadium Bond Election*, http://
   brasscheck.com/stadium/; also *The San Francisco Chronicle*, 19 February 1997;
   "Supervisors Pass Ball to S.F. Voters ... "

5 – Great thanks to the researchers at DemocraticUnderground.com for helping me source this widely reported story. Sources for LBJ vote-rigging story: *Worldnet Daily:* "Vote Early, Vote Often," by Kay Daly; http://www.worldnetdaily.com/news/article.asp?ARTICLE_ID=16460 and, from the Kansas Taxpayers Network, "The Chad Farce," by By Karl Peterjohn; http://home.southwind.net/~ktn/karl104.html; and the LBJ biography *Means of Ascent*, by Robert Caro. The connection with John Connally can be found at http://www.swt.edu/~lfl4/conspire/lbj.html and in his bio, http://www.tsha.utexas.edu/ handbook/online/articles/view/CC/fcosf.html.

6 – Thanks to researchers Fredda Weinberg and Hedda Foil from DemocraticUnderground.com for uncovering the links between Connally and the Johnson vote fraud, and finding documents on the connection of R. Doug Lewis to Connally. University of Virginia Center for Government Studies, "Presidential Selection: A Guide to Reform": Doug Lewis bio, managed affairs for John Connally: appendix. http://www.centerforpolitics.org/reform/

7 – *Los Angeles Times*, 12 November 2001; "Election 2000: A recount ... "

Chapter 5

1 – *Creative Loafing*, 2 April 2003; "High-Tech Train Wreck?"
2 – *CBC News*, 5 January 2003; "Computer vandal delays leadership vote."
3 – *The Guide to Identity Theft Prevention,* author: Johnny May
4 – Report from a pollworker, Marin County, California; reported by Greg Dinger of www.VerifiedVoting.org
5 – AP / Miami Herald, Saturday, March 15, 2003

Chapter 6

1 – See Chapter 16, "The Men Behind the Curtain"
2 – Associated Press Newswires, 3 February 2000; "Thurston County official kicks off campaign to succeed Munro"
3 – *Printing World*, 20 November 2003; "Sequoia scandal"
4 – The Tallahassee Democrat, 6 October 2002; "Former official profits from election reform Sandra Mortham was lobbyist for touch-screen machine maker"
5 – *Los Angeles Times*, 31 October 2002; "Conflict-of-Interest Probe of Ex-Elections Staffer Sought; The official helped certify voting machines, then joined a firm that sells the ... "
6 – Newsbytes News Network, 13 November 2003; "Cashing In on E-Voting?"
7 – *The Columbus Dispatch*, 1 September 2003; "Lobbyists going all out to get ballot contracts"
8 – *Palm Beach Daily Business Review*, 30 September 2003; "Contract Law"
9 – www.VerifiedVoting.org "Resolution on Electronic Voting"
10 – *Wired News*, 1 Feb 2003; "Silicon Valley to vote on tech"
11 – Interview of Dr. Britain Williams by the author, 12 February 2003
12 – Dave Ross Show, 3 January 2003, David Elliott, guest.
13 – Diebold memos, 14 January 2002; "Nearterm AVTS 4.x roadmap" Ken Clark wrote: "The California change should also require a major version number bump to GEMS (because of the protocol change). We can't reasonably expect all of California to upgrade to 1.18 this late in the game though, so we'll slip the change into GEMS 1.17.21 and declare this a bug rather than a new feature.

What good are rules unless you can bend them now and again."

14 – Source code files for Diebold Election Systems, cvs.tar, Accutouch directory, VoterCard.cpp,v

15 – www.NASED.org, August 2003; "General Overview for Getting a Voting System Qualified"

16 – University of Virginia Center for Governmental Studies National Symposium, professional credentials of R. Doug Lewis.

Chapter 7

1 – InfoPlease.com: History and Government, U.S. Elections, Election Statistics: "National Voter Turnout in Federal Elections: 1960–2000" *Source:* Federal Election Commission. Data drawn from Congressional Research Service reports, Election Data Services Inc., and state election offices. http://www.infoplease.com/ipa/A0781453.htmls

2 – WNYC radio interview: with Jeet Heer, graduate student at York University in history and frequent contributor to *The Boston Globe* on American culture, explaining the influence of the intellectual icon Leo Strauss. May 22, 2003

3 – *International Herald Tribune*, 15 May 2003; "The long reach of Leo Strauss Neoconservatives." According to Pfaff, Deputy Defense Secretary Paul Wolfowitz, and Abram Shulsky of the Pentagon's Office of Special Plans took their doctorates under Strauss. Another neoconservative, William Kristol, studied under Strauss protogé Allan Bloom. Jeet Heer disputes this, saying that while Wolfowitz may have taken classes with Strauss, he took his main influence from Allan Bloom.

Chapter 8

1 – *The St. Petersburg Times* (Russia), 23 September 2003; "Chris Floyd's Global Eye"

2 – *The Wall Street Journal*, 27 December 1985; "Cronus Director Lowers Stake to 5.4% From 12%"

3 – Dow Jones News Service - Ticker, 26 July 1984; "Cronus Indus announces several acquisitions"

4 – The Wall Street Journal, 2 November 1984; "Cronus Unit Acquisition"

5 – Dow Jones News Service, 8 November 1984; "Cronus Industries unit acquires two firms in Oklahoma"

6 – Dow Jones News Service - Ticker, 22 February 1985; "Cronus Industries unit buys Roberts & Son Inc."

7 – Dow Jones News Service - Ticker, 28 March 1985; "Cronus Indus unit acquires Frank Thornber Co."

8 – Dow Jones News Service - Ticker, 27 March 1985; "Cronus Indus unit acquires Dayton Legal Blank Co."

9 – PR Newswire, 16 December 1985; "Cronus Industries Inc. Acquires Computer Election Systems Inc."

10 – Dow Jones News Service - Ticker, 8 January 1986; "Cronus Indus unit acquires Integrated Micro Systems"

11 – Dow Jones News Service - Ticker, 5 March 1986 "Cronus Indus unit combines with Computer Concepts"

12 – Dow Jones News Service - Ticker, 5 March 1986 "Cronus Indus unit acquires two businesses"

13 – *The Omaha World-Herald*, 28 February 1984; "Election Year Boosts Fortunes of Omaha Firm"

14 – *San Francisco Examiner*, 4 August 1999; "Conservative group gears up for 2000 vote in California"

15 – *The Omaha World-Herald*, 3 June 1994; "Welsh Named Top Executive, Board Member"

16 – *The Omaha World-Herald*, 10 April 1996; "McCarthy Transfers Acceptance Shares"

17 – *Barron's*, 17 June 1996; "The Other Man From Omaha"

18 – *The Omaha World-Herald*, 12 June 1984, "84,000-Acre Kiewit Ranch Fails to Attract Any Buyers"

19 – *The Omaha World-Herald*, 15 July 2001; "Business People Lyman-Richey Names Officers"

20 – *Newsday*, 25 March 1986; "Convicted Firm Got City Pacts"

21 – Political Transcripts by Federal Document Clearing House, 18 July 1996

22 – *The Sunday Oklahoman*, 3 July 1983; "Public Agencies, Probed Firms Doing Business"

23 – *Sunday Times* (London), 17 November 1996; "Rec bidder under fire"

24 – *The Baton Rouge Advocate*, 16 August 2001; "Ala. businessman pleads guilty to role in election-machine scam"

25 – *The Press-Enterprise*, 19 August 2001; "Louisiana charges are unrelated to work with Riverside County voting machines"

26 – *The Baton Rouge Advocate*, 20 August 1999; "Fowler indicted in scheme, Audit led to malfeasance, laundering counts"

27 – *Saturday State Times/Morning Advocate*, 15 February 2003; "Appeals court affirms decision to toss case Immunity deal was in place, judge says"

28 – Business Wire, 27 October 2003; "Kathryn Ferguson, Former California and Texas Election Official, Joins Hart InterCivic to Head Company's Voter Registration Group"

29 – *Denver Post*, 30 December; "1998 Election chief takes job with department contractor"

30 – *Los Angeles Times*, 15 November 2003; "The State; Elections Worker Is Transferred; A state employee involved with screening new voting machines is moved after it is revealed that ... "

31 – Datamonitor Company Profiles, 23 May 2003; "De La Rue PLC - Products & Services Analysis"; and Business & Media, 21 September 2003, "Business - Business Comment"; and The Observer Ruelette, 14 July 2003; "Observer Column"

32 – Reuters News, 28 May 1997; "UK government outraged by lottery salary rises"

33 – Hoover's Company Capsules, 4 September 2001; "De La Rue PLC"

34 – Reuters News, 27 July 2003; "De La Rue investors gunning for Gough"; and *Print Week*, 17 July 2003; "Investigation at De La Rue arm"

35 – *Citywire*, 11 July 2003; "Australia's richest family buys De La Rue"; and *The Sunday Times*, 16 March 2003; "Aussie billionaire goes for De La Rue banknotes"; and The Sydney Morning Herald, 8 April 2002; "The $300,000 Lord Who Lobbed Westfield Into Tony Blair's Court"

36 – *Australian Financial Review*, 26 October 2002; "Perspective - Westfield - The cut-throat corporate"

37 – Business Wire, 4 August 2003; "Sequoia Voting Systems and VoteHere to Provide Additional Electronic Ballot Verification Options"

38 – *The Seattle Times*, 22 November 2000; "Computer balloting gets a boost Bellevue start-up gains new financing"

39 – Master's thesis, 26 April 2001, University of Virginia, by Philip Varner: "Vote Early, Vote Often and VoteHere: A security analysis of VoteHere."

40 – Business Wire, 3 October 2000; "Compaq Teams With VoteHere.net To Deliver Online Voting Pilots For Fall Presidential Elections"

41 – *Newsday*, 27 February 2003; "Saudi Link to LI Start-Up / Unnamed investors take over voting Web site"

42 – *Austin American-Statesman*, 28 February 2001; "Times of change at Hart; Founder reflects on end of an era for Austin institution"

43 – Knight Ridder Tribune Business News, 28 February 2001; "Austin, Texas, Graphics Company to Close after 89 Years in Business"

44 – Hoover's Company Profiles, 11 March 2002; Triton Energy Limited.

45 – *InformationWeek*, 2 October 2000; "Cost Of Compliance"

46 – *Austin Business Journal*, 8 November 2001; "Investors cast $7.5M vote for Hart InterCivic."

47 – CN group web site http://www.thecapitalnetwork.com/advisory.php# and www.OpenSecrets.org

48 – *Global Energy Business*, 1 August 2001; "CAES: Ready for prime time" 34 Vol. 3, No. 4"

49 – www.polarisinstitute.org/corp_profiles/public_service_gats_pdfs/maximus.pdf

50 – *The San Francisco Chronicle*, 6 August 2002: " ... Though Republican candidate for governor Bill Simon insists he knew nothing of his former investment partner's criminal background, an investigation ordered by Simon's accounting firm revealed four years ago that the man was a convicted drug dealer. ... Even a quick Internet search would have shown that Paul Edward Hindelang's 1982 conviction for smuggling 500,000 pounds of marijuana into the country had been splashed over the front pages of Florida newspapers. ... Simon and Sons ... and their partners, as well as his attorneys and accounting firm, spent nearly $1 million in so-called due diligence research on Hindelang and others involved."

51 – Common Cause report: "President Bush's Top Fundraisers"; source, Bush-Cheney '04 Inc. as of June 30, 2003.

52 – *Akron Beacon Journal*, 1 July 2003; "Cheney cashes in for GOP at fund-raiser Fairlawn event brings in $600,000; critics try to get message out"

53 – *The New York Times*, 9 November 2003; "Machine Politics In the Digital Age"

54 – *The Plain Dealer*, 16 September 2003; "Diebold executive to keep lower profile O'Dell says he regrets mixing politics with firm"

55 – Canada Dept. of Corporations, *Financial Post* database: Moly Mite Resources Inc. (B.C. 1982 amalg.) Name changed to Macrotrends Ventures Inc. April 4, 1986; Macrotrends Ventures Inc. amalgamated with Racer Resources Ltd. to form Macrotrends International Venture Inc. effective Aug. 17, 1988; Macrotrends International Ventures Inc. name changed to Global Election Systems Inc. following amalg. With North American Professional Technologies B.C. Ltd effective Nov. 22, 1991; Global Election Systems Ind Plan of Arrangement with US-based Diebold, Incorporated and Diebold Acquisition Ltd. Effective Jan. 31, 2002.

56 – Guy Lancaster resume, meeting with Guy Lancaster, Annual corporate information in the Canadian Survey of Industrials, which begins listing design of the ES-2000 in 1988.

57 – *Vancouver Sun*, May 11 1991; "The Money Pit? Taxpayer's money marked for loans to western firms can disappear on VSE."

58 – *Barron's*, May 1989; "Saga of an Unrepentant Tout — Meet Norton Cooper — and Why Investors Are Sorry They Did"

59 – *Vancouver Sun*, 3 September 1993; "Two blasts from the past find new connection in Farm Energy company"

60 – *Vancouver Sun*, 30 March 1994; "Unauthorized fees upset investors in fund."

61 – *Vancouver Sun*, 20 May 2000; "Ex-Vignoble boss committed to trial: Businessman who borrowed money for his bail from disgraced Eron Mortgage Corp. facing fraud charges."

Chapter 9

1 – "If You Want To Win An Election, Just Control The Voting Machines," by Thom Hartmann: http://www.commondreams.org/views03/0131-01.htm. Thom Hartmann is the author of *Unequal Protection: The Rise of Corporate Dominance and the Theft of Human Rights* (www.unequalprotection.com)

2 – PUBLIC RECORD ACT REQUEST: Responding Agency: Alameda County Registrar of Voters, filed by Jim March on 29 July 2003. http://www.equalccw.com/voteprar.html

3 – PUBLIC RECORD ACT REPLY: Responding Agency: Alameda County Registrar of Voters, filed 8 August 2003. http://www.equalccw.com/alamedafollowup.pdf

4 – *The Palm Beach Post:* 17 September 2002; "Reno consults electronic voting foe"

5 – Unpublished interview of three experts on electronic voting, by William Rivers Pitt, author of *The Greatest Sedition is Silence.* Excerpted on Democratic Underground, 1 August 2003.

6 – *The Risks Digest,* Vol. 22: Issue 25. Monday 23 September 2002: Memo from Chris Riggall, press secretary for Cathy Cox, Georgia Secretary of State.

7 – Georgia Secretary of State Press Office; Media Backgrounder: *Multilevel Equipment Testing Program Designed to Assure Accuracy & Reliability of Touch Screen Voting System*

8 – Diebold AccuTouch Technical Data Package TSx, final certification; *Appendix D: Quality Control Manual* and *Appendix E: Testing Procedures*, submitted to Wyle Laboratories for certification in January 2003.

9 – RFP Sec 3.28, "Schedule for Deployment,"[#] submitted by Diebold Election Systems to the state of Georgia in March 2002.

10 – Math for Georgia testing: 22,000 machines x 10 minutes = 220,000 minutes; 220,000 minutes x 3 times = 660,000 minutes; Divide by 60 minutes = 11,000 hours; Divide by 40-hour work week = 275 work weeks, or 68 months; 68 months divided by 12 = 5.7 years; Amount of time available for acceptance testing: 4 months; Now add people: 68 months divided by 4 = 17 people working 40 hours per week for 4 months doing nothing but rigorous testing.

11 – Interview of Michael Barnes, assistant director of elections for the state of Georgia, by the author, 11 February 2002; Full, unabridged interview can be found in the library at www.blackboxvoting.org

12 – Interview of Dr. Britain Williams by the author, 12 February 2002; Full, unabridged interview can be found in the library at www.blackboxvoting.org

13 – Sources: Diebold memos about the Windows CE modifications; interview with a Diebold programmer in Vancouver on 6 December 2003; Interview with Rob Behler, a technician in Georgia who was instructed to install Iredale's Windows CE patches, internal memos from Iredale; Windows CE source code found on the Diebold FTP site tagged to Iredale's personal computer.

14 – County voting statistics and Diebold sales document submitted to Santa Clara County, California, in February 2003

15 – AccuPoll voting system: http://www.accupoll.com/Products/Top10/index.html; "Non-proprietary hardware and open source software significantly reduce both initial acquisition and ongoing maintenance costs."

16 – Diebold internal E-mail, 4 April 1999. From Ian Piper to Talbot Iredale.

17 – *The Register*, February 2003, republished 2 August 2003; "Computer ballot outfit perverts Senate race, theorist says" by Thomas C. Greene. http://www.theregister.co.uk/content/55/29247.html and (read also) http://www.theregister.co.uk/content/35/29262.html.

18– *The Guide to Identity Theft Prevention,* by Johnny May, CPP. Statistics on identity theft are available from the Federal Trade Commission Identity Theft Data Clearinghouse: "Figures and Trends on Identity Theft in Texas" http://www.consumer.gov/idtheft/statemap/texas.pdf (2001) and http://www.consumer.gov/sentinel/pubs/Top10Fraud_2002.pdf (2002).

19 – *Cleveland Plain Dealer*, May 2002 interview with Wally O'Dell sent out as a company press release in September 2003.

20 – Interview with Guy Lancaster, 4 February 2003; According to Lancaster's Web site, he was in charge of the site for Global Election Systems; Lancaster has a small computer consulting firm and was under contract to Global Election Systems. When Diebold bought Global in January 2002, they transferred responsibilities for the site to a full-time Diebold employee but kept Lancaster on under a new contract.

21 – *The Washington Post,* 28 March 2003; "New Voting Systems Assailed; Computer Experts Cite Fraud Potential "

22 – Interview with Joe Richardson, Diebold spokesman, by the author, February 2003.

Chapter 10

1 – Thomas Jefferson to Archibald Stuart. 1799

2 – Thomas Jefferson to Thomas Cooper, 29 November 1802

3 – *The Best Democracy Money Can Buy*, by Greg Palast (Pluto Press)

4 – Thomas Jefferson to George Washington, 1792

5 – Phone conversation between Bev Harris and Jim Galloway, March 2003

6 – *Scoop Media*, 10 February 2003; "System Integrity Flaw Found at Diebold Election Systems" http://www.scoop.co.nz/mason/stories/HL0302/S00052.htm

7 – *Scoop Media*, 13 February 2003; "Georgia's Last Minute 2002 Election Machine Fix" http://www.scoop.co.nz/mason/stories/HL0302/S00095.htm

8 – *Scoop Media*, 8 July 2003; "Sludge Report #154: Bigger than Watergate"
    http://www.scoop.co.nz/mason/stories/HL0307/S00064.htm
9 – *Baltimore City Paper*, 11 December 2002; "Computerized Balloting is Taking
    Over Elections In Maryland — But Can We Trust the Results?"
10 – *Salon.com*, 5 November 2002, "Voting into the void: New touch-screen voting
    machines may look spiffy, but some experts say they can't be trusted"; 20
    February 2003, "Hacking Democracy"; 23 September 2003, "An open invitation
    to election fraud"
11 – Associated Press, 25 February 2003, "Silicon Valley Wary of Voting Machine"
12 – *Wired News*, 7 August 2003, "New security woes for e-vote firm"
13 – *The Plain Dealer*, 28 August 2003, "Voting machine controversy Head of firm
    seeking Ohio contract committed to Bush victory "
14 – *The Beacon Journal,* 15 August 2003, "E-Voting Becomes Touchy Topic" by
    Erika D. Smith
15 – *The New Yorker*, 7 November 1988, "Annals of Democracy: Counting Votes" by
    Ronnie Dugger
16 – Rules of Office of the Secretary of State Election Division Chapter 590-8-1,
    Certification of Voting Systems
17 – Diebold internal document: "Certification Requirement Summary" Governing
    entity: Georgia
18 – Open Records Request, 25 March 2003, Response to Open Records Request
    from Denis Wright by Clifford Tatum, Assistant Director of Legal Affairs,
    Georgia Election Divison
19 – "Security in the Georgia Voting System," 23 April 2003, by Britain J. Williams,
    Ph.D.
20 – Interview of Michael Barnes by the author, 11 February 2003 and "Security in
    the Georgia Voting System," 23 April 2003, by Britain J. Williams, Ph.D.
21 – *Salon.com*, 20 February 2003, "Hacking Democracy," by Farhad Manjoo
22 – Interview of Diebold spokesman Joe Richardson by the author, 26 February
    2003

Chapter 11

1 – "Security in the Georgia Voting System," 23 April 2003, by Britain J. Williams,
    Ph.D.
2 – *WiredNews.com*, 13 October 2003; "Did E-Vote Firm Patch Election?"
3 – *Georgia Vine* Vol. III, Issue 18, 25 September 2003.

Chapter 12

1 – Digital Millenium Copyright Act of 1998
    http://www.loc.gov/copyright/legislation/dmca.pdf
2 – "Security in the Georgia Voting System," 23 April 2003, by Brit Williams
3 – Georgia RFP Sales Proposal for Diebold Election Systems: Phase I, Tech
    Proposal.
4 – Analysis of an Electronic Voting System, Johns Hopkins Information Security
    Institute Technical Report TR-2003-19, 23 July 2003. http://avirubin.com/vote/
5 – *Scoop Media*, 8 July 2003; "Sludge Report #154: Bigger than Watergate"
    http://www.scoop.co.nz/mason/stories/HL0307/S00064.htm

6 – *The New York Time,s* 24 July 2003; "Computer Voting Is Open to Easy Fraud, Experts Say"

7 – *WiredNews.com* 4 August 2003; "More Calls to Vet Voting Machines"

8 – *The Plain Dealer,* 14 August 2003; "Voting machines under review in Columbus"

9 – *EcoTalk.org* 18 August 2003; "Voting Machine Fiasco: SAIC, VoteHere and Diebold" http://www.ecotalk.org/VoteHereSAIC.htm

10 – "Risk Assessment Report Diebold AccuVote-TS Voting System and Processes" 2 September 2003; Science Applications International Corp.

11 – Ohio Secretary of State Web site, 2 December 2003; "Blackwell Seeks Improvements and Additional Security Assurances from Electronic Voting Machine Vendors" http://www.sos.state.oh.us/sos/news/release/12-02-03.htm

Chapter 13

1 – *The Tribune*, 4 September 2003, "Security of SLO County's voting system called into question"

2 – Interview with Julie Rodewald by the author, 4 September 2003

3 – Posts to Democratic Underground and BBVreport forums by Greg Dinger, 8 October 2003.

4 – *New York Daily News,* 14 November 2000; "TV exec's kin-do attitude"

5 – Report: "CBS News Coverage of Election Night 2000: Investigation, Analysis, Recommendations prepared for CBS News"

6 – Fox News, 29 November 2000; "Special Report with Brit Hume"

7 – Diebold Memos: 17 January 2001 from Lana Hires; "I need some answers!"

8 – Diebold Memos: January 2001 from John McLaurin

9 – Diebold Memos: 18 January 2001 from Talbot Iredale; "Here is all the information I have about the 'negative' counts"

10 – "CBS News Coverage of Election Night 2000"

11 – "The Best Democracy Money Can Buy," Greg Palast

12 – "CBS News Coverage of Election Night 2000"

13 – Agence France Presse, 8 November 2000; "Chronology of US election night confusion"

14 – *Dow Jones Business News*, 7 November 2000*; "Bush Claims Cautious Victory, But Gore Narrows Lead as Recount Continues" (Note: Date listed in Factiva news database was November 7, but it would seem that this would have to be November 8.)

15 – Associated Press, 27 October 2003; "Diebold warns on electronic voting papers"

16 – Meeting with Rep. Jim McDermott (D-WA), 12 September 2003

17 – BlackBoxVoting.org, 12 November 2003; "Internal Memos: Diebold Doing End-Runs Around Certification"

18 – Annual Report for Global Election Systems, 2000

19 – Interview with Rob Behler; also, on the Diebold FTP site were two directories containing the Windows CE source code. These directories contained within them an identifier for Talbot R. Iredale's server, "sinbad/tri."

20 – NASED documents provided by Washington Elections Director David Elliott

21 – Washington State Legislature Technology Committee hearing, 3 December 2003

22 – Diebold memos, Whitman Lee Wed, 7 July 1999: "GEMS 1.11.2 is ready ... " GEMS 1.11.2 was also found on the Diebold FTP site, dated 1999, release notes confirm July 1999 release date.

23 – Diebold memos: 4 March 2002 from Sophia Lee; "Cards Cast Incorrect"

24 – *WiredNews*, 17 December 2003; "E-Voting Undermined by Sloppiness"

25 – *Seattle Post-Intelligencer*, 17 December 2003; "Secretary of state seeks paper trail for e-votes"

26 – *The News Tribune*, 17 December 2003; "High-tech voting weighed"

27 – PRNewswire, 18 December 2003 "Diebold Election Systems, Inc. is announcing a complete restructuring of the way the company handles qualification"

28 – Mike Webb radio show, 1 December, 2003

Chapter 14

1 – Securities filing for Global Election Systems, Canada: 2001

2 – Washington State Department of Corrections records for Jeffrey W. Dean

3 – Source: Diebold memos

4 – Associated Press, 16 December 2003; "Critics: Convicted felons worked for electronic voting companies"

5 – Washington State Department of Corrections records, Jeffrey W. Dean and John L. Elder

6 – Securities filing for Global Election Systems, Canada: 2001

7 – October 2002; IEEE Spectrum — "A Better Ballot Box: New electronic voting systems pose risks as well as solutions" by Rebecca Mercuri http://www.notablesoftware.com/Papers/1002evot.pdf

8 – *Votescam: The Stealing of America*, by James and Kenneth Collier; Victoria House Press, 1993

Chapter 15

1 – 20 February 2003, Salon.com: "Hacking Democracy" by Farhad Manjoo.http://www.salon.com/tech/feature/2003/02/20/voting_machines/index2.html

2 – 3 January 2003, The Dave Ross Show, KIRO radio

3 – *Counting on Democracy*. Powerful investigative reporting into the Florida election fiasco by Greg Palast. Globalvision. http://www.gregpalast.com

4 – *Voterevolution*, by Micheal Stinson. TakeBackTheMedia.com http://www.takebackthemedia.com/voterevolution.html

5 – *Term-Eliminator 3 – Total Davis Recall: Rise of the Digital Voting Machines*. http://www.toostupidtobepresident.com/shockwave/votingmachines.htm

Chapter 16

1 – 4 November 2003 9:56 a.m., *Houston Chronicle*: "Voters encounter eSlate glitch" By John Williams and S.K. Bardwell

2 – 5 November 2003, 10:19 a.m., *Houston Chronicle*: "ESlate voting proves smooth, not flawless" By Eric Berger

3 – 11 December 2000, *Los Angeles Times*: "A Place in Politics for Salesmen and Wares". Excerpt: "Four hundred convention guests [election officials] dined aboard a Hornblower yacht cruising San Francisco Bay, partly financed by $10,000 from the Sequoia Pacific vote supply firm ... "

4 – 23 August 2003, *Scoop Media*: "SAIC Connected To E-Voting Whitewash" www.scoop.co.nz/mason/stories/HL0308/S00173.htm

5 – 23 CNET News.com, 9 December 2003; The Election Technology Council